RIDING THE FIRE

ALSO BY DON LEDGER

NON FICTION

DARK OBJECT

SWISSAIR DOWN

FICTION

BLOOD SHOCK

RIDING THE FIRE

A BIOGRAPHY
OF
BUSINESSMAN, PILOT & ADVENTURER

DAVID DONALD MCCULLOCH

DON LEDGER

Comments and queries can be made via www.donledger.com
ISBN-13:9781979183239
ISBN-10:1979183236

I

Forward

I'm honored to know Dave McCulloch as an accomplished aviator as well as an astute businessman. He is an active pilot traveling in his own airplanes around the world to this day.

I've had the pleasure of knowing Dave since 2005 when he purchased a home in our community, an airpark here in Florida. He was the first one to fly a military jet trainer into our airpark. He subsequently allowed me to fly the jet with him and inspired me to get checked out in it. He later purchased a 1965 Learjet Model 23. He became type rated in that airplane and I had the pleasure of obtaining my SIC rating in that airplane and flying with him. I am just one of many people he has influenced and helped in aviation and business while always encouraging anyone interested in flying or starting a venture that they can do it.

Dave would say "Never break a spirit". He has many, many accomplishments which are well documented. He is a member of the Earth Rounders. Their members are people whom in their own personal small private airplanes have circumnavigated the World. As of April 2015 his is one of 355 flights. Consider there are 7.4 Billion people on Earth.

In 1986 he set a World Speed Record, Westbound, around the world in a Cessna 414. That record is still standing to this day. He has flown around the North Pole several times.

Aircraft that I know he owned and flew included a Cessna 150, Cessna 414, Citation 500, Paris Jet, Hansa Jet, and a Mig 17. He currently owns and flies the Learjet 23, a Piper Dakota and an Aerostar.

In the business world – in the late 80s - Dave was involved with the first Twin Tire option for automobiles. Basically it was one rim with 2 tires mounted on it. They were proclaimed to have much better handling in wet conditions and added safety if one went flat.

II

You could literally keep driving for miles and miles.

He started a successful water business before it was in vogue to buy bottled water. This became a huge franchise. During this time period he met a great group of people called the Hutterites .

I have been fortunate enough to have traveled with Dave to visit the colony in Manitoba as well as South Dakota. To say these people are warm, loving, intelligent and hard workers would be an understatement. He started another business partnering with the Hutterites in a furnace company. Dave eventually turned that business over and now is involved with a high end pie company with the Hutterites. It has been an exciting venture to follow. No doubt this pie company will be a household word.

I'm excited to get my hands on this book and read about the fascinating life of Dave McCulloch before I met him. There is so much that I don't know about him but what I do know about him and the time I have spent with him has been exciting. It seems that he will help anyone along his path of life to make them a better person.

I can say Dave has given me better insight of what is important in life. It's not all about money but more about "Making Memories". He told me early on, "Joe, I've made a lot of money and spent most of it, buying memories. In the end that might just be one thing we can take with us!" I like it!!!!

Dr. Joe Campbell
North Fort Myers, Florida

III

Life isn't about waiting
for the storms to pass...
it's learning to fly in the rain.

David Donald Mc Culloch

IV

Chapter One

W hen he was nine years old David McCulloch was shot in the neck. He and his friend, Donald, were horsing around in a small barn behind the house. The rifle went off. The .22 calibre 'short' bullet entered on the left side of his neck and nicked the carotid artery.

The blood spurted from his neck with each beat of his heart. "Don't tell my mother." he told his friend. He feared her gentle anger more than death. They were not supposed to be playing with the gun. Apparently he did not consider that once he had bled out he would have nothing to fear from his mother or anyone else.

But the blood continued to squirt out of his neck. His friend panicked; and rightly so for as it turned out young David would have bled to death. Donald found David's father who ran to the little barn scooped his son up and sat him on his knee. He put a finger over the hole and a doctor was sent for. There were few phones, no ambulances and no police in this sector of rural Nova Scotia. A neighbour's phone was used to call for a doctor.

They sat like that for four hours waiting for the country doctor to arrive.

They held him down while the doctor probed for the bullet and extracted it with forceps and stitched up the hole.

"Will I die?" He remembers asking.

"No you won't die, boy...but you were darn lucky."

He had been a centimetre from being killed; a fraction of an inch from spending eternity in a pine box in the local United Church's graveyard. He never did catch hell for playing with the . 22. He figured his parents thought he had learned his own hard-won lesson since he had nearly killed himself. He recalls his neck being stiff for a long time after, but no other ill effects. He bears the scar on his neck to this day.

Dave McCulloch spent the rest of his life living close to the edge; the poor boy from New Scotland who made it big - perhaps large - in the world of business and in aviation. He would spend the rest of his life
looking over the horizon; seeking something better, something exciting, different; something that would stir his mind and heart.

And it wasn't the first time he had nearly killed himself. The family has often told him that when he was nearly two years old - it was around the time that Germany invaded Poland on September 1st 1939 - and still in his highchair that he pushed it over backward. He smashed his head on the floor. He knocked himself senseless and was unconscious for over a half an hour. No doctor was called, probably due to their remote location in 1939 or 1940; most likely there was no doctor within 50 miles of their home.. They waited it out. Finally he came to. There seemed to be no ill effects from that accident but as science knows now usually there is some effect to any brain trauma. Was there a possibility that Dave McCulloch's future was shaped by the accidents of his youth?

These misfortunes continued. The end of the fore-finger of his left hand was cut off when his older brother closed a door while his finger was on one of its hinges. In this case a doctor was called who examined the appendage and wanted to amputate below the first knuckle. His mother objected. In fact she was so fierce in her objection the doctor relented and sewed the end of his finger back on. "It looks a little odd, but it works fine today." McCulloch mused.

It sounds almost cliché but maybe there is something to it. How often have we read about or heard and watched celebrities from all walks of life reminisce about their early years? Their hardships, their upbringing in poor families, their struggle to get out of the ghetto or away from oppressive regimes and then their climb in later life to wealth, fame and influence. Could there be something to this formulae; to be born poor - born to a segment of society that sees little hope in the future other than a life of grinding poverty, just getting by or taking the easy road via a life of crime; or face the possibility of losing one's life in order to escape to a better place? If so then David Donald McCulloch is one of those who unwittingly applied this unwritten formula for success. His growth from a youth with little education by today's standards to a world travelling entrepreneur and award winning pilot who flies his own Lear Jet – his sixth jet airplane - and who has flown these and other airplanes around the globe to eighty five countries - for business and pleasure - once again tends to prove that from humble beginnings come great men and women. This biography will show how hard work, guts, a positive attitude, an adventurous spirit and the belief in one's ability to succeed can bear fruit.

David Donald McCulloch was born on January 24, 1938 in a one and a half story house on North Noel Road – then a dirt road in East Hants County, Nova Scotia. The road runs north to south with the northern end coming right to the shore of the

Minas Basin. The Minas Basin is some four to five miles (eight kilometres) from the easternmost section of the Bay of Fundy which is famous for the highest tides in the world. McCulloch was the third child of six beginning with the eldest sister, one brother older and three younger sisters.

The family lived on a small twenty acre plot boasting a cow, a pig and a few chickens. There was no phone, no electricity or running water. His mother was a school teacher and his father a woodworker. His mother was of Irish decent, her ancestors having come to Nova Scotia some two hundred year before while his father was of Scottish decent and harking back to the same era. After their defeat in the Battle of Culloden and subsequent crushing of their Scottish spirit through the use of laws forbidding Gaelic as a language, traditional dress and even the use of the bagpipes, some Highlanders went to the Carolinas in the United States. Even then they were required to take an Oath not to fight against the British.

So it was axiomatic that when the American Revolution broke out, they found themselves fighting with the British. Regiments, such as the 82nd and 84th Regiments, came to Windsor, Nova Scotia to train. After the war they were disbanded in Nova Scotia, and the soldiers given land grants in Hants, Halifax, Cumberland and Pictou Counties.

The McCullochs were one of three clans to receive land grants in Hants County, Nova Scotia. One of nature's little curiosities is a geological fact. Seventy-five million years ago when the one great vast continent of Pangaea began breaking up a small section attached to Morocco drifted westward and became part of North America. This section came together in what is called Economy Rift and pushed up hills on another sector that immigrated across the great ocean from what is now Scotland. Seventy-five million years later the Scots came over and claimed it back. This blob of land comprised of the two sectors sticks out in the Atlantic Ocean and is now Nova Scotia. It just goes to show how determined the Scots can be.

His father worked hard labouring in the woods as a woodsman and often took jobs as a carpenter. His mother was a school teacher who taught at the local school. They were not wealthy by any means. McCulloch's parents told him they were not poor because they had a cow, a pig and some chickens. "We had a garden, a cellar full of food and wood and we felt sorry for the poor people." Young David had no proof to the contrary since he had no contact with others from outside of his small community and that is often the case with the very young-at least back then-wealth was where you found it; usually that wealth of childhood experiences and adventures.

Even when he was less than a decade old McCulloch and his friends would walk the five miles to the village of Noel which was on the Minas Basin's south shore. They would swim there and explore the caves along the shore when the water receded a mile or more from the shore. "It was a different time back then. We were unsupervised; we were supposed to stay near home... nobody worried about you. As long as you showed up at night time, everything was okay."

They were surrounded by forest and the ancient lore of the Mic Mac (Mi'kmaq) Indians as they were called during that time. Hunting was not only a pass time but a necessity.

The forests abounded with deer, moose, rabbits, beavers, trout and a host of other animals rich for their furs. The rivers and lakes were full of trout and bass and the less favoured perch. The province was rich in coal, fish and lumber products. McCulloch himself was hunting by the time he was ten years old using the same .22 rifle that nearly killed him and a single barrel twelve gauge shotgun.

His Father had a Ross .303 rifle-surplus from the war-but that was off-limits. His Father – like every other family who lived in the country in those days, hunted deer; even moose the whole year around. It was considered a staple source of food.

McCulloch admits that he wasn't always supposed to be using the .22 or the shotgun but he shot or trapped rabbits and squirrels that he skinned and sold. He dug worms and fished for trout in the local rivers.

When he was five years old he attended North Noel Road School which had as many as forty students in the class. Both higher and lower grades were taught in the same room-the typical one room schoolhouse; eighty students in one room. His mother taught at the same school so during some of his years at the school his own mother was his teacher. One can imagine the conflicts at home when it came time to do homework. If it was noticed during the evening that he wasn't doing his homework he could not fall back on the excuse that he didn't have homework assignments that evening. Homework was done by the light of a kerosene lantern; the house was heated by hardwood.

"We had two wood stoves in our house. There was no stove upstairs, just a hole in the floor above the stove downstairs. One winter's evening, my oldest sister, Joyce, saw flames coming right up through that hole. She woke Father and he got us out and then put out the fire using water buckets. There was no running water in the house before I was ten years old".

McCulloch considered himself a poor student but relates that years later several of his old schoolmates remembered him as being one of the brightest in class and that they relied on him for tutoring.

"I don't recall that being the case, but it was over sixty years ago."

McCulloch loved Geography. "It was my favorite subject in school." Probably a hint of what was to come when he became an adult. "Reading about Marco Polo was an inspiration. What an exciting life he led. And he only got the one trip." He planned more than one. "I was always anxious to get out there, see the world."

McCulloch recalls that he got beaten up a lot because he was always small and of slim build in his youth. He wasn't a boxer - a physical fighter as such - and he never really had much to defend himself with, just his sense of humour, his intelligence and an unquenchable spirit. But he never ran from a fight either. "These were obstacles to be overcome." An objective observer of McCulloch's youth would likely have seen the signs of his later life reflected in a small boy with hopes and dreams who never gave up until he achieved them. He lived to see the day when those kids who gave him such a hard time failed to achieve anything meaningful; died early in life, having never left the small confines of the county of their birth.

The winters were harsh in Nova Scotia in those days. The snow often fell in feet rather that centimetres or inches. "The drifts ran to five or six feet (two meters) and it was damn cold. We walked to school. My mother walked it too." She was the teacher after all. But unlike present day, school never stopped so you were required to attend regardless of the weather; and school was over a mile away. Uphill both ways as McCulloch recalls. The North Noel Road School was heated with hardwood burning in a homemade barrel stove constructed from a 45 gallon (50 gallon US) oil drum.

There was no family car until McCulloch was almost twelve years old.

"My Aunt Ruby left the back country as a girl. She was self-educated. All the same she became the superintendent of a Seattle hospital in the early 1900s. She retired in 1938 and returned home with a new Chrysler convertible. She would receive cash in the mail every month. She'd tell me great stories of what went on in the world and hired me to cut wood and feed her thirteen cats."

It was an eye opener for McCulloch. He began to understand that there was a big world out there; that not everyone lived as they did.

When he was 13 years old he got a job cutting wood for his grandfather. "He paid me three dollars a cord." A cord was cut and split wood that measured four feet by four feet by eight feet (1.2 M x 1.2M x 2.4M). It was a lot of work. McCulloch hired some of his friends and paid them two dollars a cord to do the work. It was his first experience at leveraging labour. He had others do the work and still collected a dollar for himself. He realized even then that you could only do so much of the labour yourself. That same cord or wood these days would probably bring in between $180.00 and $250.00 in today's market.

"It was at that early age that a light went on in my head."

"He always had some little business going," his older sister Joyce recalls. "Cutting wood, gathering bottles or selling furs that he had cured...he'd sell anything. He was always busy."

Joyce remembered that she and her brother Gordon would take two year old David along when they went into the woods to play games. Joyce is six years older than David; Gordon five years older.

"I remember getting the switch across my bottom – Gordon did too - for taking Dave to a little pond in the woods in beyond our property. Our parents were beside themselves with worry because they didn't know where their baby was. They both were at work and we were responsible for looking after Dave. They found us at the pond. Dave was full of mud and playing happily at the edge of the pond."

Just another day back in 1940. "These days it would have made it into the newspapers and on TV. Nobody knew...there was no communication."

McCulloch doesn't recall ever hearing about the terrible war going on a couple of thousand miles to the east in Western Europe; never heard the war in Europe or about Japan. "If I did, I don't recall it." There was no radio to hear news of the terrible conflict overseas because there was no electricity although battery operated radios were available. Again there was no money for such a luxury. "My Grandfather would press his ear against his battery radio to listen, but I didn't understand what was going on."

By today's standards the family was poor, money wise. "I don't recall that being an issue." McCulloch mused. "Our parents were good parents; we never went hungry. We were clothed and warm. We had a roof over our heads. We visited our relatives and neighbours, played cards and made ice cream. As children we made our own adventures. That's what was important to us kids. Not money or social status."

On some level though, McCulloch must have realized that there was more to be had from the world than what was available to him back in the 1940s. Perhaps it was the stories told by his Aunt Ruby who made a career in the United States in Washington state a place about as far west of Nova Scotia as one can get and still be in continental North America.

For whatever the reasons McCulloch decided to explore beyond the adventurous locale of his youth. He had quit school; ending his formal education at grade nine and went west to Toronto with his brother Gordon to take a course in diesel mechanics.

McCulloch decided to begin exploring the world, something he is still doing to this day.

He was 15 years old.

Chapter Two

Taking the long way home

In 1954 when McCulloch was fifteen years old he travelled by car to Toronto. He and his older brother Gordon hitched a ride with another man who charged them for the trip. The road to Toronto from Nova Scotia was more dirt and gravel than pavement in 1954. It took many days to get there.

When they arrived in Toronto he and Gordon took an automotive diesel mechanics course. Dave worked at Loblaw's stocking groceries on the weekend while his brother got a job with a contractor installing dry-wall. Gordon got David on as well so they could rent a room outside of Toronto near the airport. The course completed they returned to Nova Scotia where Gordon became a mechanic while David applied for jobs in Halifax, the Provincial Capital. He was supposed to have begun High School in the fall however he applied to the Royal Canadian Mounted Police Marine Services but in hind sight thanks his lucky stars he was turned down for a position because he was shorter than the five foot eight inch minimum. He considered the Royal Canadian Navy because there was the promise of seeing the world. And the girls were supposed to love sailors. That was an attraction.

"When I got back to Halifax I put my name in at a steamship line looking for a job that would get me out of Nova Scotia and a chance to see some of the world." The company in question- Imperial Oil (ESSO) - had its own fleet of sea-going tankers.

Imperial Oil's refinery was across Halifax Harbour in Woodside, just south of Dartmouth. It is still there to this day, a major refinery in Atlantic Canada

"One night I got paged at a movie theatre." His name was scrolled across the bottom of the screen requesting that he go to the box-office.

"First time to hit the big screen." He quipped.

He was requested to report to the Imperial Oil dock where their tanker *Imperial Toronto* was tied up.

Like many of Imperial Oil's tankers - and those owned by other oil companies - these vessels were built during World War Two. They were called T-2 tankers. Their design was based on two ships built in 1938-39 by Bethlehem Steel for the Socony-Vacuum Oil Company. The ships were constructed as merchant marine vessels which could be converted over for US Navy military use in case of war. Nearly 500 were constructed by the end of the Second World War. They were 501 feet 6 inches (152.86 meters) in length with a beam of 68 feet (21 meters) displacing 21,000 tons. They cruised along at about 16 knots (30.4 kilometers per hour).

McCulloch was hired on as a mess boy. "I was now one of a crew of about forty or forty-five.

"The next thing I know, I am gone; out to sea on my way to Colombia, South America. Good-bye high school. Hello to the rough and tough life of a merchant mariner. I am 16 weighing 130 pounds." It was October, 1954.

Chapter Three

McCulloch spent the next four years plying the waters of the world in the engine room of an Imperial Oil tanker. He looks back on his days at sea with amusement and a degree of wonder when he considers some of the adventures he experienced while still a very young man. "I was only 16 when I went to sea. You wouldn't see that happening these days." One of the first things he learned was that, "Being a mess boy meant that you waited on tables and that the ships officers lived better than a mess boy.

"Lesson; rich people live better than poor people. Duly noted and filed away."

Colombia was an eye-opener for McCulloch. The *Imperial Toronto* docked in Cartagena on the north coast of Columbia. Cartagena was a city in a state of flux from 1945 to 1965. Following World War Two and the onset of the Cold War and Soviet aggression, immigrants from Europe-France, Italy, Lithuania and other Balkan states made their way to Colombia. Some remained there while others passed through the city on their way to other cities in Colombia. The country itself was in the throes of La Violencia (The Violence) during those years as it has been for much of its history. The people, the military and the governments and dictatorships were at each other's throats, each vying for power, each with its own agenda. Back in the 1950s however the drug trade would not be an option and drug lords were a thing of the future. During this time period democracy and communism of a sort were warring with one another for supremacy; trade unions fought for rights and a decent wage.

None of this made much of an impression on young McCulloch however. He was sixteen years old. His education was that of a young sailor...from the Maritimes. He liked booze and he liked women; just what a sailor was supposed to be.

"I wasn't a virgin when I was sixteen but my strict upbringing and social morality made sex a forbidden fruit. You never got to actually see the body of the female. Not in 1953 or 1954. Not in Nova Scotia, not when you were a teenager."

He quickly got a crash course on how sailors got their reputations. After weeks on-board the tanker the crew was restless, thirsty, rowdy, randy and looking for girls. The first stop was always the nearest bar. There the restlessness could be assuaged for a brief period. One's thirst could be attended to at monetary rates unheard of back home - not that young McCulloch would have ready access to alcohol at home; it was tightly controlled in Nova Scotia and expensive compared to prices in the Caribbean. What cost dollars in Nova Scotia amounted to pennies in Colombia.

Once the cheap booze was consumed in large quantities, rowdiness - fuelled by testosterone - and the release from confinement in a steel vessel which had been many days or weeks at sea would then erupt in bar fights that would make the writers of a John Wayne movie pale.

"What used to happen back then was we'd all go ashore, find the first friggin' bar and get drunk and chase girls.

"One of my first impressions of the people of Colombia was that they all had bad breath. I thought, 'My God, these girls are really nice, but their breath is really bad.' But it was easily overlooked however because of the booze and the girls that I encountered." Later McCulloch learned that a spice called garlic was used in the cooking process in Colombia, a herb he had never heard of or tasted before that time. Not in Nova Scotia. "We had never heard of it in Hants County." It was responsible for what he had deemed, bad breath.

The young sailor could easily afford the two dollars it cost for one of these girls and they were plentiful. And so were the steaks from the street vendors at thirty-five cents each.

"All of a sudden I am around brown people speaking a foreign language. Both mother *and* daughter are working for the Yankee dollar. We were paid in American dollars back then. I am suddenly a 16 year old man." At least he had his experiences with the large population of Toronto to fall back on. It's population was about twice that of Nova Scotia which boasted about 665,000 people in 1954. Cartagena's close fitted community of 130,000 numbered three times that of Halifax. It was hot and it was humid.

"I was on my own. I had no friends on that first trip. It was grow-up-fast time....and I did."

He got drunk, he fought, he got laid and grew up in a matter of a few days. The world wasn't what he had imagined; and he was just getting started.

Sometimes when they arrived at a bar all hell would break loose. "I remember...some of these guys were really tough-they were a hard bunch. Big guys...been at sea their whole lives. They had money in their pockets, they'd go ashore and one of them would say, 'Let's clean this fuckin' bar out.' They'd start a fight, wreck the place, throw the furniture out the door into the street."

Pressed for the point of this violence McCulloch said. "Who knows...we were just a bunch of drunken sailors from Canada."

To some degree, when he could get off whatever tanker he'd been assigned to - usually the *Imperial Toronto* – the world opened up before him. He sailed to places he never knew existed.

His ship was docked in Rio de Janeiro on one occasion. It was during their Mardi Gras. He was in a bar celebrating; perhaps it was the Mardi Gras, he can't remember after all of these years. At some point the floor of the bar filled with water. He ran to the door and saw a man fighting a river of water as it swept him by the front of the place. The street was a river. A flash flood had overflowed river banks and quickly flooded the floor of the bar as well. At some point they were up to their waists in water and were then literally swimming for their lives to get out of the place. "After all of the cheap booze and girls I'd had I was in heaven and remembered thinking. 'The hell with it, I'll wait for Noah to come along and pick me up'." Unfortunately he never showed. "Somehow I made it out of there."

On another occasion their ship the *Imperial Toronto* had offloaded crude in Rio de Janeiro. The crew was allowed to go ashore. McCulloch found a bar, girls and the usual scenario ensued. He had tracked down a source of cheap wine and then forgot about the time. "I remember that night. I was out partying of course, I'd been drinking. Something held me up -probably a girl - I used to think with my pecker in those days. I got back to the dock and the ship was gone." The *Imperial Toronto* was nowhere to be found. His ship had left without him.

Even though the youth was still half drunk he realized the predicament that he was in.

In those days there were no resources in developing 'third-world- countries' like Brazil for sailors stranded on foreign soil. "You had no visa or credit cards; and you are not supposed to be there." There were no phones. You were on a 24 hour shore pass and you didn't dare go to the police because you would be arrested and thrown in some terrible jail to rot until your ship came back to port again.

"There were horror stories about stranded sailors taking to the jungles, living off the land and the kindness of strangers, waiting out the many months until their ship came back again or perhaps another ship from the same company." Others either waited in jail or were located by their ship's company who would then sometimes pay to have the sailor shipped to the ship's new location. Those who waited it out in the jungle would suddenly show up at the dock when their ship came in and get back aboard and tell stories about how horrible it had been.

These stories were now recalled by McCulloch when he arrived at his ship's berth and The *Imperial Toronto* was gone.

"Being on a wharf at two o'clock in the morning with money in your pocket, was not a safe place to be. Not then, not even now."

Realizing the uncomfortable and possibly terrible predicament he could be in, McCulloch asked around and eventually found someone on the fog-shrouded dock cloaked in the warm night air who informed him that the *Imperial Toronto* had indeed left its moorings but was now anchored somewhere out on the bay waiting for the tide. Relief flooded through the 17 year old. But he wasn't out of the woods yet. "He pointed out to the bay. I couldn't see anything because of the fog but you could make out some lights."

There were at least a couple of dozen ships lying at anchor out on the bay that were showing lights. Most of them were obscured by the fog hanging on the water. No one including himself knew which ship was his vessel. Somehow he had to get out there and find the right ship.

McCulloch offered to pay a couple of the locals to take him out on the harbour in one of their canoes to look for his ship.

"I'm the only white man in a sea of black and brown humanity, most of whom don't trust us; some even despised us white foreigners. The two men I hired could just as easily have taken me out there on the harbour and pushed me overboard and nothing more would have been heard of me. The police certainly wouldn't have done anything about it."

In those days Canada did little if anything for its nationals who have gotten themselves in trouble and the situation is still the same to this day. Canada abandons its citizens for the sake of expediency unless they are embarrassed into action by exposure and the media. But it was considerably worse back in the years after World War Two.

"So now we are out on the harbour, at night and in the fog. I had no choice but to go from ship to ship looking for my own. You could not really tell one ship from another.

After some time McCulloch and his paddlers finally stumbled onto his ship. Even by today's standards these ships were big. Over five hundred feet long and now empty of fuel; she was riding high in the water. The lowest portion of her sides amidships was at least fifty or sixty feet above the water. To those sitting in the little canoe alongside of the hull the *Imperial Toronto* appeared massive. He had no flashlight or a loud hailer or anything with which to draw attention to him.

"Eventually after yelling to anyone who might be on the deck I did get someone's attention. I holler out that it's McCulloch and I'm down here. Throw me a rope." The word was out that he had missed the ship because he had not been there for the count.

"With my bottles of wine tied around my waist and still half-in-the-bag, I climbed up the side of the ship. It was rolling in a mild swell; the ladder kept coming away from the hull then slamming back into it again. I knew if I banged my head and knocked myself out, or lost my grip that I was not likely to be rescued. The two men who brought me out had left already."

After a perilous climb he made it to the rail and was pulled aboard. The Captain was informed that now McCulloch was once more aboard. How the hell did that happen? Well, he'd been brought out in a rum boat from shore. The Captain was also informed about the wine the errant sailor had brought on board and that was confiscated.

Liquor was not allowed on the ship, but on one occasion our captain relented.

The *Imperial Toronto* had docked in St. Thomas, an island just east of San Juan in the US Virgin Islands. The captain of that trip was known as a drunk by the crew. He told the crew they could load up on booze, a couple of cases each. Liquor was so cheap that a couple of cases would have been a pittance compared to retail prices at the "Government Stores" back in Canada. The crew didn't ask twice; they loaded up and brought cases of rum aboard. Maritimers and Newfoundlanders like their rum. (One year many years ago the Minister in charge of the Nova Scotia Liquor Commission advised the Legislature that more rum had been sold in Nova Scotia the previous year than in the rest of Canada for the same period-DL)

"They brought truckloads down to the ship. Everyone got drunk."

We were forced to anchor off Panama for four or five days. The pilots came aboard and saw the condition of the Capitan and crew and would not let the ship proceed. They made us fly a flag that informed other ships that we were a hazard to navigation. The Captain was pulled off the ship and sent back to Canada and replaced by another Captain."

Once in Baton Rouge, Louisiana – McCulloch thinks it was late 1955 or early 1956 - he nearly got thrown off of a bus because he sat in the back when he got on. The driver pulled the bus over and approached him and told him either to get up to the front or he would throw him off.

Astonished he complied and would find out later that the back of the bus was where the Negros sat while the whites sat up in the front. It was McCulloch's first brush with rabid racism. He noticed then what the world knows now; that there were black and white drinking fountains and black and white public washrooms. The law concerning this segregation was strictly enforced.

"I usually sat in the back of any bus I got on, so it was natural for me to do so." He knew of America's history with slavery but little else. "What happened was culture shock for me."

In 1955, McCulloch was 17 years old. He had saved some money and now he wanted an automobile. It would be his first car but not of course his last. The car in question was a used 1948 Ford sedan with a price tag of $400.00. Problem was that McCulloch only had $200.00 in his bank account.

McCulloch's mother was a big influence in his life. She offered good advice when needed and he sought out her council many times in later years. On this occasion however he needed his mother to co-sign a loan for him so that he could finance the balance of $200.00. She readily agreed. Her son was a good risk, a hard worker; his word was his bond - even back then.

They went to the bank and made application for the loan but then they ran into a snag. The bank manager advised McCulloch's mother not to take on this responsibility but should force her son to save the rest of the money then buy the Ford. McCulloch hated the man instantly. The bank manager had the big three weapons needed to keep the little guy down as far as he was concerned; power, position and wealth. And he was getting between McCulloch and what he wanted most right now, that '48 Ford and all of the freedom it engendered. No more reliance on others to get him around. No more barriers to going where he wanted. And of course one of the biggest reasons was he could use it to pick up girls.

It was a tense moment with McCulloch ready to vent his anger and probably blowing any possibility of his getting the loan and the car; and his mother sitting in front of the powerful banker and being told how she should conduct her financial matters.

McCulloch's mother was a strong women, not easily bowled over by the male domination of the sixties, a period when that superiority would begin to erode.

"My mother had big balls," McCulloch says respectfully, "she told the banker that she had more than enough money in her account to cover the loan and that the decision to sign or not was hers, not the manager's. She stood up to him. That was something women didn't do in those days."

They got the loan. McCulloch realized then that the bank manager didn't always have to have the upper hand.

McCulloch got his used Ford. It was the first of over a hundred automobiles that he would own up to the time of writing (some 50 years). He became obsessed with cars and was an excessive spender. He was forming an outlook on life even then that one should live for the moment not for some hazy future that you might not live long enough to see. He might be waiting tables on the superior ranks in the Imperial Oil tankers but he was beginning to think then that he didn't always have to be at the bottom of the ladder looking up at other people's rear ends.

Position, power and wealth. These three words were worth remembering.

In 1957 Imperial Oil sent McCulloch and other crewmembers to Japan to pick up the newly constructed Supertanker the *Imperial St. Lawrence*. They were flown from Halifax to Calgary on a North Star. It was McCulloch's first flight. From Calgary they flew to Vancouver in a Viscount and Constellation from Vancouver to Nagasaki, Japan via Alaska.

Japan was producing its first Supertanker at the shipyard in a city that only 13 years before had been destroyed by the second Atomic Bomb to be dropped on Japan. This was Nagasaki.

McCulloch knew very little about the Second World War and even less about Japan. But he was curious to see the areas that had been barricaded from visitors where the ground and what rubble remained was still radio-active. Wherever he went- whether alone or with friends-they ran into sections of the city where no one was allowed to pass. He saw little evidence of the residents that had been permanently maimed by the nuclear blast.

One thing McCulloch noticed was that fully 60 percent of the workers building their ship were females. So many Japanese males had died during the war that females were needed like latter day Rosie–the–Riveters to keep the economy going.

McCulloch soon found out that by renting rooms in which to stay while in Japan for the two months it took to get the ship completed he was denying himself an experience that he remembers to this day. He was told that he should use the Geisha houses that were still legal in Japan at the time. There he could eat, sleep, drink, be bathed and be pampered in a way only the Geishas knew how.

Four years after he had signed on with Imperial Oil, McCulloch had worked his way from a mess boy to the lowest rank; an engineer 4th class. "My diesel training course had gotten me to junior officer rank."

"It was a Christmas day and for some reason I began to think about my future and I could see my life stretching forty years ahead of me. I remember telling the Chief Engineer who had a first class ticket and who had been going to sea for thirty-five or forty years that I didn't want to do this for the rest of my life.

"With that thought in my mind I went to the captain and told him that I wanted off the ship at the next port we docked in." As it turned out that would have been in Portland, Maine. In actuality the protocol was that as a junior officer, McCulloch would have had to make this request to his immediate superior on his deck - the next level Engineer's grade above him - to whom he would have made his request to leave the ship. That engineer in turn (they were all males back then) would make representations for McCulloch to the next higher up and so on until it got to the Captain.

McCulloch thought 'the hell with that'. "I went marching right to the Captain. I told him I'd made up my mind and that I wanted off the ship."

McCulloch wasn't supposed to have been up in Officer's Country, not in those days - not when you were a lowly Engineer-Forth Class and certainly not without an appointment. The Captain told him he'd get off the ship when he said so and not before. He told McCulloch to get aft to his station or he'd have him arrested.

The Captain was accustomed to being listened to and obeyed without question. Everyone on the ship was in fear of him. He ruled at sea. Maritime Law made it that way.

But McCulloch was anxious to get off the ship and move on into another career – it was the beginning of a character trait that would drive him for the rest of his life. So he tried another tactic.

When the ship-the *Imperial St. Lawrence* docked in Portland, Maine McCulloch claimed he was not feeling well. He was sent to a doctor ashore. The doctor, however, could not find anything wrong with the now twenty-year old Engineer 4th Class, and he was sent back to his ship.

It appeared that he was doomed to return aboard the ship and possibly have to endure a lengthy stay at sea until the *Imperial St.*

Lawrence finally returned to a Canadian port. There was the possibility that he might be confined to ship in foreign ports where he might jump ship. Another possibility was harsher treatment and restricted duties aboard ship as well. McCulloch's obstinacy might have opened up a real can of worms for him.

That's when fate intervened. Fate can sometimes be a handy ally. In this case Fate was an immigration officer that just happened to be on the dock when McCulloch returned from the doctor.

Dock security while not what it would be these days in an American port; particularly at a possibly volatile oil transfer facility – or most ports on the planet for that matter – was tighter than it would be in the third world countries of the Caribbean. U.S. Customs was present and on this occasion so was the immigration officer.

McCulloch is not exactly sure after fifty-five years how he managed to attract the attention of the US Immigration officer but for some reason he took notice of McCulloch's reluctance to return to his ship. The official asked the 20 year old sailor what the problem was and upon hearing that the lad wanted to leave the ship and that the Captain had told him that he had no choice but to re-board the ship, the agent took exception to this state of affairs.

Perhaps it was because it was Christmas or the agent had history in his own family which no doubt had immigrated to the United States at some point to the Land of the Free and the Home of the Brave – with Free being the operative word here - that is not known but whatever the reason he decided to take up McCulloch's cause at this juncture. He and several other officers and a couple of police officers went aboard with the young man. They went to the Captain and told him he was taking McCulloch into his custody and furthermore the *Imperial St. Lawrence* was under arrest and could not leave the oil-transfer dock until the matter was settled. Even in those days this represented thousands of dollars an hour being charged to the ship while it tied up that berthing space and other tankers waited in the roads with holds full of transferable oil.

The situation was becoming costly for Imperial Oil (Esso and later Exon). The cash was removed from the Captain's safe and McCulloch placed on a train with two police officers and escorted to the nearest Canadian border and returned to Canada free of the ship-and his job. He was back in Canada, he had no job It was 1959. McCulloch decided to become a salesman.

He became a Fuller Brush Man.

David Donald McCulloch 18 months

David (left) and (Gordon) and the barn where David was shot.

Top left: Joyce, Gordon, David, Bottom left: Marilyn, Joanne and Alice. David wears an RCAF tie despite never having seen an airplane.

David McCulloch goes to sea.

McCulloch in engine room of Imperial Toronto

ESSO Tanker Imperial Toronto

McCulloch's first car, a Ford sedan purchased in 1954, sports Alberta plates in the 70s.

McCulloch (21) a Fuller Brush Man turned vacuum cleaner and sewing machine salesman signs papers on his wedding day – Oct. 1959.

Chapter Four

McCulloch was teamed up with a more experienced salesman when he began selling Fuller Brushes. Like most beginning salesmen he had shyness, an ingrown reluctance to bother people who were in their own homes. He would get tongue-tied with the housewife who usually answered the door when he knocked during the body of the day. He had to overcome the reluctance to intrude or interrupt a person's routine while he attempted to sell them something they could very well purchase themselves at a hardware store should they require the product.

The get-in-the-door ploy was to give the prospect a free Fuller Brush with no strings attached to break the ice and then hope for the promise of more of that person's time. He worked that line of sales for a couple of months then felt there was more money in selling vacuum cleaners and sewing machines.

He made a modest living in the Halifax Dartmouth area and was doing well enough that he decided to ask the girl he had been dating – Carol Thomas - to marry him. They were married in October of 1959. Three children quickly followed; Jeffery, Dawn and Stephanie. "The three children came one right after the other before we figured out what was causing it."

On one fateful day McCulloch happened to be driving on old highway No. 2, a curvy, hilly, old two-lane highway that connected Dartmouth to Truro, Nova Scotia which in turn would take travellers from Halifax to the rest of Canada or to Cape Breton.

During World War Two the only civilian airfield on the Halifax peninsula, Halifax Municipal Airport (dubbed 'pocket handkerchief field' by many pilots) had been taken over as a munitions depot with its periphery claimed by the department of National Defence (DND) to erect pre-fab housing to handle the influx of military personnel that had flowed into the Warden of the North, the largest convoy assembly harbour on the western side of the Atlantic. The former Halifax Aero Club was a victim of this loss and to survive had to turn their wheeled aircraft operation into a float plane operation. They set up their new club, the Halifax Flying Club on Lake Williams on the west side of the No.2 highway some nine miles from downtown Dartmouth.

McCulloch had driven by the club on different occasions and noted the aircraft tied up to the docks. By the year 1959 the Provincial Government's Department of Lands and Forests had set up an operation at this water aerodrome as well. Frequently one could see a DH-2C de Havilland Beaver tied up to the dock as well. But on August 21 of 1960 rather than admire and then pass by the place something made him pull off the pavement and into the gravel parking lot and on an impulse he asked to take a flight. "I had dreamed about flying an airplane for many years now." Two of his flying heroes were Howard Hughes and Charles Lindbergh. Hughes had flown around the world in the same year that McCulloch had been born. He liked their adventurous lifestyles; liked the fact that Hughes was a rich business man who took chances, who didn't want to live the way others lived.

"I was a poor boy from Nova Scotia. I wanted that kind of life." He wanted to live until the day he died.

McCulloch isn't sure what made that day special, the day he made the move is a mystery. Fate took a hand as it often does with many pilots. Whatever the reason, that day's decision would profoundly affect his future.

During the next few weeks he took four hours of instruction on a float equipped Piper J-3 Cub with the registration CF-IUI. In September he ran out of money. His modest income would not support a family, a dwelling, a car and flying lessons; not at $8.00 an hour to rent a plane with an instructor. His license to fly would come in fits and starts as will be seen.

McCulloch continued selling sewing machines into the early part of 1960 when again fate took a hand. One of his own salesmen, Len Hooper, mentioned that he had bumped into another salesman from another company. He told McCulloch that this guy seemed to be making great commissions selling business machines.

McCulloch was introduced to Ed Vlahos an Egyptian from Montreal. Vlahos impressed McCulloch with his big new automobile and his smooth and fast talking manner. He told McCulloch that he sold for Paymaster Corporation whose head office was in Toronto. He sold check machines to businesses. The commissions were good McCulloch learned. He envied the professional salesman, hung on his every word and wished to be like the man.

The salesman told McCulloch that he thought him too young to be selling business machines to businessmen. But McCulloch impressed Vlahos with the fact that he had read a book Think and Grow Rich; that he was earnest about becoming wealthy through sales. Vlahos told McCulloch that if he met him in St. Stephens, New Brunswick a week later he would train him to sell for Paymaster Business Machines.

McCulloch sold all of his samples and used the money to get there and for his expenses. Vlahos trained him as promised then took him to see a couple of local bank managers and the police chief in St. Stephen. The reason for this was to allay the fears of any prospects in the area that might be inclined to think that Vlahos and McCulloch were a couple of check forgers because part of their sales pitch was to show just how easily they could forge the prospects signature. If the prospect got nervous and phoned the police or their bank managers they would then assure them the pair was above board. Often they knew that they were actually showing small town police forces tricks of the trade even they were not aware of but would flatter them by making statements such as "…we know you are already aware of this type of crime and how the criminals go about it but the small businesses don't." Naturally the police would agree rather than admit ignorance.

There was another reason as well. Vlahos did not go to the bank managers with hat in hand. He was a good salesman with a well above average income and he clearly exuded this when he talked with the bankers. He was in a subliminal fashion letting them know he was wealthier than they and he was not to be considered some poor second cousin. He was communicating with them in a language they would understand; wealth.

This was not lost on McCulloch who had developed a mistrust of bank managers when he went to purchase his first car. What Vlahos was doing was wiping out the bank managers advantage of wealth which gave him power and position. McCulloch was learning that, "You will never have problems with bank managers when they think you have more money than them. Perception is everything."

A few hours into their first sales pitch Vlahos sold Ganongs Chocolates some of their machines. Ganongs was then and still is one of the largest chocolate manufacturers in North America.

The following week McCulloch drove to Newcastle, New

Brunswick and was turned loose on the small businesses there. On his own the new Paymaster salesman made just over $500.00 in commissions in the first week.

McCulloch was very happy; he had found a business worthy of his considerable energies.

Back in Nova Scotia he quickly became one of Paymaster's leading salesmen. He was making as much as $500.00 a week which was exceptional money for the times. Credit cards were coming into use and were considered a prestigious way to pay for services. McCulloch wasted no time in shifting to this modern form of currency. He used Diner's Club and American Express Platinum cards to impress his clients. It was a practice he would continue for many years and accumulated over seven hundred expired cards which are now part of his personal collection along with automobile and airplane memorabilia.

McCulloch left no stones unturned when it came to exercising sales in his territory.* He, of course, targeted businesses in the larger centers of the Atlantic Provinces but he went the extra mile as well. He visited small villages in Nova Scotia, PEI and New Brunswick. He sold business machines in these places when no one else thought to even try. He travelled to Grand Manan Island in the Bay of Fundy off the coast of New Brunswick in an old twin engine Piper Apache he had chartered. He loaded it with business machines and sold to the local shops and fishermen there as well. He was received with surprise and with enthusiasm. He filed away the fact that flying in as a salesman with the product on board the airplane gave him a certain mystique not available to the average salesman.

Flying in to an area to sell product in a plane gave him what is called posture power which was as powerful a tool then as it is today

McCulloch often hired fishing boats in Newfoundland to take him to out ports where roads did not go to sell business machines. He went where other salesmen did not tread; which in fact they rarely considered. Not so with McCulloch. A new frontier was a sales opportunity and not to be ignored. This would become one of his strengths; an ability to see a sales possibility where others never even considered there might be an opportunity.

"Why," they might ask, "would anyone buy a cheque machine in a place where no one used cheques?" McCulloch's answer to that was, "well maybe they were never given the chance."

A case in point. He recalls a trip he made to Isle aux Mort (Island of the Dead) in Newfoundland. The only way out was by boat so once again he hired one. Again, no one even thought to give the place a try. When he arrived at one of the businesses, a small local market, he proceeded to sell the owner a cheque machine. When McCulloch asked for a cheque to cover the cost the owner gestured to his wife behind another counter. "We got no cheques here, Son. He'll pay you." He being his wife. The woman reached down under a counter and bought up a Carnation Milk carton about two feet square and eighteen inches high. She dipped into the carton - which McCulloch was surprised to see was jammed full of paper money and paid him in cash. The salesman realized that he had sold a cheque machine to a business that did not use cheques; or, apparently, a safe either. It was a system he would use later in his career; go (like Captain Kirk) where no others have gone before.

For McCulloch his travels to these isolated locations were just an extension of his love affair with seeing new places and meeting new people. More often than not he was received in these places with smiles and open pleasure at his arrival rather than suspicion and rancor. He was a welcome deviation from the daily routine and constant isolation. Salesmen were a rarity if they even visited these communities at all.

McCulloch was made a sales manager for the Atlantic Region for Paymaster Corp. in 1965 and transferred to Saint John, New Brunswick. This was his first small move westward. Eventually he trained and had twelve salesmen working under him. McCulloch received overrides from their sales. This was a percentage of their percentage. Once again he learned the lesson of leverage.

"If you want something to multiply and grow, give it away. Make money by helping others make money. This is a theme I have practiced throughout my life."

By sharing parts of his sales territory with other agents he extended his working day. "As a single salesman I could only be in one place at a time. Handing off some of my territory to other salesmen while receiving a percentage of their sales in the long run brought in personal revenue far exceeding what I could achieve on my own; even if they weren't producing at the same level as me."

Once again the flying bug bit. "In 1968 I took 4 more hours flight training in Saint John NB and went solo in a Piper PA28 Cherokee 140, registered to the Saint John Flying Club as CF-WEL. It is a testament to the strength of design and materials that this aircraft still flies today some 47 years later. It is registered to a pilot in Ontario. McCulloch had a sentimental attachment to the aircraft and has tried to re-purchase the aircraft on a couple occasions.

McCulloch could now fly an airplane without an instructor on board but he was not yet licensed to fly a non-licensed passenger. He still had ground school to complete and more hours of practical flying before he would write his exams and pass a flight test with an examiner from the (then) Department of Transport. The dream of experiencing the adventures of those such as Howard Hughes and Charles Lindbergh gnawed at him still. It was a goal that he was determined to achieve. That would come sooner than he expected.

If McCulloch was not already a living legend among salesmen in Atlantic Canada he was fast becoming one. His prowess in sales was not overlooked at the head sales office in Toronto either. His ability to ferret out sales opportunities not before recognized was one of his strengths. But there was his ability to run a sales team in the Atlantic region as well. He had to learn the difficult ways of management; balance the weighty problem of being the boss while still maintaining a working friendship that could foster the loyalty of his team.

The machismo exhibited by aggressive salesmen – and in those days they were all men – has been adequately portrayed in many books and movies. It could be a cut-throat profession fostering jealousy and envy among the team; even hatred. It would be McCulloch's job to keep his team on an even keel, producing sales while curtailing open hostility other than that rivalry between salesmen required to keep sales climbing.

McCulloch's years of travelling around the world on oil tankers with some of the toughest men in any profession while dealing with the dangers of foreign ports, the country's police and assorted thieves and hookers had put him in good stead. He knew how to handle men; not by force but by tact and diplomacy.

McCulloch is not a big man. He dealt with bullies while in school and got pushed around when he went to sea. But he learned how to deal with situations by the use of common sense – or for at least as long as that would keep him from being beaten up. Sometimes it was enough. He developed a steel backbone that he possesses to this day. You might not see it but you sense it.

McCulloch's life was moving along in a predictable manner. He was making good money, he had two cars, a Ford

Thunderbird which continued his obsession with big and powerful automobiles-and a Volkswagen for his wife, a nice house and a family. The future looked bright. Then Paymaster's head office in Toronto made him an offer that he could hardly believe. They asked him to take over as the sales manager for western Canada; a territory that stretched from the eastern Manitoba border to the Pacific Ocean, including British Columbia and the far north to the Arctic Ocean.

In typical McCulloch fashion he weighed the pros and cons of such a huge move and thirty seconds later said yes.

It was 1968. In ten years McCulloch had gone from 4th Class Engineer on an oil tanker to a top selling salesman for Paymaster Corporation in Atlantic Canada. He had completely changed his life around. He had forsaken the safe route of ensuring himself a job with a good pension with Imperial Oil if he stayed with the job for another 40 years for that of a job where if he didn't produce he failed; if he starved his family starved...it was as simple as that. He would lose everything, his cars, his home and possibly his self respect. Those are powerful enough incentives, but McCulloch also had a point of fire burning inside of him that would drive him ever further along, to new horizons and to greater heights. He had a dream but he wasn't even sure what that was back in those early days and he probably would have scoffed at the idea of becoming a man dealing with millions of dollars and companies listed on stock exchanges while flying fighters and business jets; burning across the heavens in the high blue; riding the fire.

McCulloch might have been taking a hell of a chance this second time because he was uprooting everyone and taking them westward; counting on himself and a new gamble for wealth and riches.

McCulloch and family arrive in Calgary in their Thunderbird

Chapter Five

"If you want something to multiply and grow give it away. Make money by helping others make money." Dave McCulloch

With everything financed to the hilt including the two cars, McCulloch sold his house, packed his family in the Ford Thunderbird and the Volkswagen. He asked his brother Gordon – already a successful truck salesman in Saint John – to come with him; offering him a job as a salesman at Paymaster. Gordon had seen how well his brother was doing and he too up-rooted his family. They kicked the dust and fish scales from their shoes and drove westward. Canadians themselves have a hard time imagining the size of their country. Europeans never do until they move here. Americans can appreciate its size if they remember it is even there but one thing is certain; Canada is huge and western Canada is nearly twice the size of Western Europe. You can put two Australias in the square miles covered by western Canada and the northern territories. Pilots appreciate the size. Flights from Victoria BC to the eastern border of Manitoba can take four or five hours to cross over travelling in an airliner at .86 Mach (approximately 600 mph - 955 kph). Once clear of the Rocky Mountains and heading east the prairies unfold below. They are in sight hour after hour. It's then that one realizes the scope of this land mass.

Western Canada is vast.

Into this huge territory McCulloch arrived in June of '68 and took up station in Calgary. He had a lot of work to do. He would have to familiarize himself with the territory, check out the staff and see who was and who wasn't producing, devise a plan of action to increase sales and most of all combat the resentment that would have arisen over some goddamn hip-wader wearing, rum drinking, Cod-fish smelling Easterner from Nova Scotia taking over the largest region of Paymaster's Canadian Territory. "I mean, what the fuck did he know...right?"

They were about to learn.

Paymaster supplied no funds for McCulloch's move, nor did they allow him any set-up money to survive on while he got his feet under him. He did receive some over-rides from the salesmen already working the western territory which he recalls netted him about $180.00 that first month which was worked out at $3.00 per unit sold. That wasn't very much considering that he had inherited a sales force of 50. It was a miserable showing and simply would not do. He would increase the overrides to about $1,000.00 a month. And into the bargain he increased the number of sales his staff was achieving. They were making more money and so was McCulloch.

He trained his brother Gordon who had settled in Winnipeg. He began to train some of the people he had; he gave them the benefit of the doubt at first. He found he would have to hire some other sales people. He was now a firm believer in helping other people make money so that he too could make money. If they were making money, then they were happy.

He was generous with his time and his territory. Positive salesmen were hired and negative people were fired. He was making money as the new sales force was built.

McCulloch was now thirty years old, but as far as his business career was unfolding, he was still in his infancy.

Dave Yates would become a lifelong friend of McCulloch's. In 1968 he was out of a job. He had been working for a flooring company but it had gone out of business. To make matters worse the company had reneged on his last pay cheque. He needed a job in a hurry. He was looking through the want ads in the newspaper when he came across one that required a salesman. He had considerable sales experience so he decided to apply. He got an invitation for an interview at one of the best hotels in Edmonton. This would be his first encounter with McCulloch who was holding interviews in his room.

Once again McCulloch was employing posture power. He was paying for the room and wanted a good room in one of the best hotels so that potential prospects would be impressed. It must have worked because Yates remembers the hotel and the room. He arrived to find that he was not the only one that had applied which was somewhat disheartening. There were several other men waiting for interviews for the same job. Yates was given to understand that there was only one position open. This was not true but McCulloch was not about to reveal this to potential salesmen. Better to let them think they only had one shot at the job. They were given the impression that they were lucky to be chosen for this one position. He had his reason which Yates would realize years later.

Voices-past and present.

"Mr. McCulloch gave the impression that he was only looking to hire one salesperson, we were all told to go home and think about it (what he had been offered) and when the decision about who would be hired was made we would be contacted.

"I got the job! Later I found out that anybody who would accept the commission only job was hired also. So began my career selling Paymaster Chequewriters.

"I thought I was a pretty good salesperson as I had sold Fuller Brush door to door while going to school, then vacuum cleaners then carpet.

"Dave McCulloch taught salespeople how to sell chequewriters by taking them out with him and showing them how to sell. During one of my first training sessions Dave and I went into a small business.

"When Dave introduced himself the business owner said 'Not another one of you guys. I only write one or two cheques per month and I already have two chequewriters.' The business owner proceeded to lift two different competitors' chequewriters up onto the counter.

"Dave took off his hat, laid it on the counter and about fifteen minutes later the business owner was making out a deposit cheque with his new Paymaster Chequewriter.

"When the business owner asked if Dave would at least take the other two competitor chequewriters in trade Dave asked 'Do you ever go fishing in deep, swift water?' When the business owner said he indeed did go fishing Dave said, 'Then use those chequewriters for weight.' Both Dave and the business owner had a chuckle over this suggestion and we left. "When I asked Dave what made him bother even trying to sell to a fellow that only wrote a couple of cheques a month and already owned two chequewriters he answered, 'Obviously he is a buyer. He already bought two competitor models.'

"I realized that Dave McCulloch thinks differently than most people, he proved he was a superior salesperson and over time a superior pilot and businessman. I learned a lot about not only selling, flying and doing *business but about different ways of thinking from Dave. I found Dave had a passion for many things but high on the list was selling, flying and doing business. Over the years we sold, flew, did business together and became good friends." Dave Yates*

It was only a couple of months after McCulloch arrived in Calgary that he was drawn to the airport; partially because he was feeling the tug of flight and because a germ of an idea was forming in his head.

While he was there a salesman showed him a 1965 Cessna 150, a two-seater aircraft with a 100 horsepower engine. The price was $5,500.00. McCulloch really liked the little high-wing plane. But at this juncture he was in a cash poor position.

"I'll take your Ford Thunderbird on trade and I'll get you financing for the balance." The salesman offered. Deal.

McCulloch bid his T-bird goodbye and said hello to his first airplane, a Cessna 150, registration CF-XLW. This purchase would be the first of many airplanes that would number over fifty by the time of the writing of this book, including six jet aircraft. McCulloch is obsessed with automobiles, and airplanes as will become apparent. He considers this a personality defect but doesn't plan to correct it. "It will be corrected when I die."

McCulloch now had an airplane but he still didn't have a license. Not that that would stop him. His brother Gordon was a licensed pilot. He would fly with McCulloch on his business trips. He was now a flying salesman if needs be.

McCulloch had an idea that he wanted to explore; an idea that was rooted in his earlier experiences while travelling and selling Paymaster in the outports and secluded towns and villages on the east coast of the country. Why not do the same in the west and more specifically; the north. McCulloch knew that the majority of the small communities and villages of the north were only accessible by air; possibly by sea in certain areas but accessibility was even less so in the 1960s compared to present day nearly 40 years later with weather changing the northern coasts and some areas barely accessible by roads.

McCulloch saw this as an untapped resource. But consider this; from Calgary to Dawson city-as the crow flies-is 1,800 miles (3,000 kms) of open wilderness, deep forests, lakes and the southern reaches of the tundra. Remote or not businesses still needed business machines and cheque security. Once again where others saw territory presenting little in opportunity he saw sales and commissions. And best of all, he was probably one of the few who could even access them. It was a no-brainer for the new aircraft owner. This was to be his first step in using airplanes and aviation to expand into what would become his business community. But back then he had little idea how much this would become one of the biggest tools in his business dealings. Now, Western Canada and the Northwest Territories lay before him.

Excited with his new acquisition, McCulloch contacted his brother Gordon in Winnipeg. Gordon had a flying license. This included a total of fifty hours of flying experience. He asked Gordon to come over to Calgary and they would fly back to his home.

Gordon arrived the next morning. "He came to Calgary and we fired up my new plane...we were excited. I was going to cover all of Canada by plane, with no expenses. We made numerous mistakes first flight."

The two brothers were so excited; so anxious to get airborne that they neglected to check to see if the Cessna's wing tanks were full. They took off from Calgary and headed east following the Trans-Canada Highway.

They figured they couldn't get lost if they followed that.

They were wrong.

They headed south from Calgary International and intercepted the Trans-Canada Highway and headed east. As is the case in the prairie provinces the roads are oriented east-west and north-south. They are laid out in grid fashion. The Trans-Canada tracked straight east as expected for about four and one half miles before dog-legging due south at the small town of Chesemere. However Township Road 244 continues straight off to the east as if it is an extension of the Trans-Canada.

Neither McCulloch or Gordon noticed this. They continued to follow the Township Road 244 as it tracked eastward into farming country. In the meantime-unbeknownst to the new plane owner and the licensed pilot the Trans-Canada Highway had resumed its eastward course two miles to the south of them. McCulloch and his brother, content that they were following the TCH, flew on.

The earlier model Cessna 150s carried 26 US gallons of fuel (13 gals. in each wing) of which only 24.5 is usable. The rest remains in the tank to prevent water and foreign material from being drawn into the fuel inlets. Normally full tanks would allow the Cessna 150 to fly for about three and one half hours. Having taken off with partially filled tanks, it soon became clear that they were badly in need of fuel.

By now they had flown deep into farming country and were lost. Anxious glances at the wing-root tank gauges were indicating they were running out of time and there were no airfields in sight.

Then the engine sputtered and quit. As one famous pilot once said, "Suddenly it became very quiet up at the sharp end."

They were now flying a glider with a ten to one glide ratio. At least that's what the handbook says. For non-pilots that ratio indicates that the plane is supposed to glide 10 times the distance as the airplane is from the ground; e.g. if at one mile of altitude the plane-properly set up and trimmed-should glide ten miles before reaching the ground. Or as Transport Canada puts it - Contacts the terrain. Most people call it crashing.

Sometimes the fates are kind to fools and brand new pilots. In this case the fate gods supplied the errant pilots with a huge landing area known locally as Alberta. Everywhere one looked was level terrain albeit covered in waist high wheat. McCulloch turned into the wind, picked a field and landed, mowing down a couple of acres of wheat in the process.

They exited the plane and were pleased to see that it had suffered no damage. Their relief turned to concern when they saw a tractor heading toward them. Obviously this was the owner of the wheat which they had just destroyed. But rather than being angry with McCulloch and Gordon the farmer seemed happy to have had them land there. Obviously they had broken the monotony of his day by adding a little excitement. Rather than anger and retribution he offered them his help. He took them to the farmhouse and they ate lunch, then he supplied them with enough tractor gasoline to fill their tanks. "He was a good man; he never charged us for the fuel." They cut a swath up to the farmhouse then taxied the plane down the driveway to the road passing the farm.

Power lines ran along the side of the road which could be a hazard during take-off. As it turned out the take-off from the road was a bit hairy because of the power lines. McCulloch recalls a wing passing between a couple of the power lines before he ruddered the plane away from them and then once more they were on their way eastward.

They successfully navigated their way east across the rest of Alberta and the nearly 400 miles (644 kilometers) across southern Saskatchewan headed for Brandon, Manitoba. They sighted the airport and landed and only then discovered they were at CFB Rivers, a Canadian military training base built during World War Two. They were met by an angry officer.

"After a chewing out by the base commander and confusing comments about our ancestors, we were filled with government gas for sixteen cents a gallon (just under four cents per liter)."

They were then sent on their merry way. They had landed slightly northwest of Brandon which was about 15 miles southeast of CFB, Rivers. The base closed three years later in 1971.

McCulloch and Gordon arrived in Winnipeg. After what McCulloch describes as embarrassing difficulties with radio and controlled airport procedures they landed. Learning from his mistakes, McCulloch remained at Winnipeg for a few days and took an additional eight hours of flight training with an instructor. He hired the instructor to fly back with him to Calgary. The entire journey amounted to some twenty-four hours of additional time on top of the eight hours he had from previously. "I figured I knew it all."

Another saying derived by pilots some 30 years of flying after the Wright Brothers that states; There are old pilots and bold pilots but there are no old, bold pilots.

McCulloch began racking up hours on his Cessna 150. Along with regular trips to other towns and cities in his territory that were serviced by highway infrastructure he began to put his plans to visit and sell to businesses in remote communities not linked to highways into play. If there was an airfield nearby, McCulloch would go there.

There was an additional perk to flying his own plane. The salesmen under his management were impressed by his flying salesman capabilities. He would often take one of them along on a trip and show them how to sell to businesses where other salesmen might not think the trip financially beneficial. McCulloch showed his salesmen time and again how this was not true. He continuously made sales where others saw no opportunities.

McCulloch was hiring and firing during this period. "If you had a negative attitude or low sales, you were fired!!! If you were breathing you were hired. It's unbelievable what giving a chance to a person who never had one can do." He had inherited fifty salesmen when he arrived to take over the western territory for Paymaster Corporation. During his tenure he increased that number to one hundred and fifty.

"I taught sales people, to be forceful, to look sharp... drive a good car and stay at the best hotel in town. There is nothing more depressing than a cheap salesman telling a customer what he should do."

Again and again McCulloch would demonstrate that appearances counted for a great deal when it came to selling to people who were in business. He had no doubts about the fact that when he arrived in a remote community cut off from the highways serving wealthier communities that the small businessmen there were impressed. The fact that he had his own plane made it obvious that he was not some fly-by-night salesman that had no roots or connections to his business other than to make a quick buck. He was heavily invested in his sales career because airplanes were not cheap-even in the 1960s. And people in remote communities relied heavily-even as they do today-on air travel and on the planes that bring in their supplies, their food, their medication, the fuel needed to survive the harsh winters of northern Canada.

Having that plane changed a lot in McCulloch's life. He was not only a terrific salesman but he was an adventurer. He was obviously successful in his staff's eyes and in the eyes of his own community and peers. And he was respected by the businessmen of the north who often based their assessment of others on their willingness to take on the north, the weather and the obvious danger of flying over desolate geography to sell his wares. He understood them and they understood him. He was in it as much for the adventure as the profit. He obviously loved what he did and he did it very well.

Cutting north to south through the western third of McCulloch's sales territory are the Rocky and Selkirk Mountains. To get to his sales territory in British Columbia using his airplane, McCulloch used the Rogers Pass as one way to get through the Selkirk Mountain west of the Rockies.

The pass was discovered in May of 1881, by Major Albert Bowman Rogers, a surveyor exploring that region looking for a route eastward through the mountains for the Canadian Pacific Railway. The route through the mountains was dangerous and not for the faint of heart. One wrong turn and you might end up in a box canyon, a canyon you could not turn around in and get back out. Climbing over the mountain was out of the question. The tops of the mountains were too high for a Cessna 150 and a Cardinal 177, and the reason why pilots including McCulloch chose the pass in the first place.

This was long before the days of electronic aids in the area such as AWOS-Automated Weather Observation Systems. The pilots of the day used Texaco road maps with which to navigate through the passes. Following the roads through the mountains was necessary for several reasons. The planes flew too low to pick up radio beacons, following the road was easier and most roads were constructed in the lowest of the mountain passes.. If an engine failed there was a good chance you could land on the road. McCulloch often landed on the roads for other reasons. Fatalistically, "If you crashed near the road, it was easier for the hearse to pick you up." On the upside, McCulloch saw the roads as leading to towns and possible sales prospects.

Once out on the coast McCulloch would fly out over the water, traveling from Vancouver to the Queen Charlotte Islands. He had to because the mountains rose up so steeply from the shore that it was impossible to fly over the land in his plane. Two to ten thousand foot high mountains climb upward on one side while three thousand miles of Pacific Ocean stretches off to the orient on the other side. The coast was as rugged as one could imagine; lush forests covered the steep slopes of the mountains and primitive forests populating the islands. It is a strangely beautiful but deadly tract to fly in a light airplane. But McCulloch loved it. It was places like this that gave him the high level of adventure he craved, matched by the commissions on sales that he made, by risking himself and the plane to get to these remote areas.

"Of course the ever waiting slippery side of failure awaited me. But no fear of failure has allowed a country boy to fly with the eagles." It was a dangerous element to be flying in using a poorly equipped Cessna 177 in VFR conditions. McCulloch was pushing the plane and himself to the limits.

McCulloch put three hundred hours on the Cessna 150. In 1969 he sold his Cessna 150 and purchased a one year old Cessna-177 Cardinal registration CF-WXH, a four seat aircraft capable of carrying more payload; it was faster and better equipped to handle the hostile territories he needed to cross. He decided to get a commercial license rather than a private ticket. He wrote his exams, did his flight test and passed.

McCulloch had crept further and further outside of his comfort zone with the Cessna 150, flying to more remote locations in the southern regions of his territory. With the Cardinal he now expanded further to the Northwest to the territories. Once he received his commercial ticket he decided there was nothing holding him back other than perhaps innate caution. But those that know McCulloch know that caution is not his middle name. His taste for new horizons and adventures overrides caution; but not common sense. He is not reckless; he just can't resist the urge to go.

"I always preferred the long way home. To me the journey is often more important than the destination."

McCulloch didn't put any barriers up for himself. If he decided he was going north, that meant all the way; right up to the Arctic Ocean.

The purchase of the Cessna Cardinal gave McCulloch longer legs. The increase in fuel range and speed increase-about 25 miles per hour-prompted him that summer to load his family aboard and fly back to Nova Scotia and visit their families and friends. From 1969 to 1973 he put 1,800 hours on the Cardinal flying the aircraft as his own sales conveyance-even more so than the Cessna 150. To him it was a no brainer-airplanes and sales went together in a perfect union of sales and spirit. Each sale was an experience, each flight an adventure all its own. But they were not without mishap and the constant element of danger when flying the wilderness of Canada. "A cat only has 9 lives , but I (must) have more and counting." He was living on the edge and going where others failed to tread. "This obsession has taken me to some very high levels of adventure; profit etc. and of course to the ever waiting slippery side of failure."

But not then because McCulloch was enjoying great success in sales. He had accumulated more salesmen and reaped the benefits of their sales as well as his own. His income was about $35,000.00 a year at this point-in 1969 and 1970. He had a plane, two vehicles and a four room house. By all intents he was successful during the years when six to eight thousand was average and a fifteen thousand dollar annual salary was considered very good.

McCulloch flew, and taught his salesmen how to make sales. Often he would take one of them along on one of his trips. He not only was impressing them but teaching them that there was more to sales than meeting clients, offering them the product and then waiting for a yes or no.

- *Telling is not selling, Don't educate...demonstrate.*

- *Know your ABCs, Always Be Closing*

- *Assume the prospect has bought!!*

- *Do NOT let the prospect sell you! It's depressing to see a salesperson leaving after the first no, with his tail between his legs.*

"The ONLY thing that a man MUST have between his legs are BIG BALLS."

McCulloch held sales meeting after sales meeting; on the job training was relentlessly pursued. Many well known salespeople (those in the business) improved and others - often the unknown ones - became top performers.

McCulloch taught and demonstrated, backing his training and selling philosophy with high volume sales. It was hard for his staff to argue or find fault with his method. "Flying gave me a leg up on most salesmen. I could be many places quickly." There were virtually no roads to most of these communities. They relied on airplanes for just about everything. As mentioned earlier, a salesman showing up to sell them a product was not only novel but a reason for some congenial conversation and interest as well. Often the pilots flying in cargo were coming from other northern locales south of their community. Their stock of information was not much more informed than their own. McCulloch on the other hand was flying in from Calgary – the big city – the thriving metropolis to the south. He regularly visited other southern cities and towns as well from Victoria to

Eastern Manitoba. But he had topics of interest from other remote communities around the north as well.

Regardless of what he had to offer in the way of news, he sold them his business machines, racking up sales all over the north. He was the flying salesman. He had the words *Flying Forger* painted on the front of his airplane. He was known all over the north.

McCulloch's flying came in handy in other ways. Many of his salesmen were caught sleeping…literally. McCulloch did aerial surveillance of some of the suspect salesmen's houses on a Monday morning (car still in the driveway at noon). "It told me if they were lazy, and when questioned told me when they left home. Sometimes they were lazy, liars or both. " He makes no apologies for this. His sales staff learned that it is no good to BS David McCulloch. When they slacked off it was money coming out of his pocket as well as their own. Additionally Paymaster Corporation would see this reflected in monthly sales statistics. It reflected back on McCulloch. He was in charge; he bore the brunt of any criticism.

With a Commercial Pilot's License to his name McCulloch was now free to indulge openly in practices denied the private pilot – particularly those who didn't actually have a license to begin with.

Chapter Six

One adventure stuck in McCulloch's mind. It was a sales trip to Alaska in August of 1971. It was one of a hundred trips all over the remote regions of Northern Canada and Alaska. This was another occasion when McCulloch had his brother Gordon along.

In the early morning of August 3 of 1971, the brothers lifted off the concrete and pavement of Calgary International in the Cessna Cardinal 177. They were loaded over gross (exceeding the maximum allowable take-off weight the plane was designed for) with business machines and their equipment, some of which was for survival purposes. McCulloch was certain he would be a welcome sight for the northern businessmen who rarely saw salesmen in their locales; and they would get premium prices for their business machines. Being overloaded might be sometimes employed for bush pilots however it was never recommended. To aggravate the problem the plane was taking off at Calgary International, an airport whose elevation is 3,650 feet (1113 meters) above sea-level. The Cardinal's manual and its performance figures were written for performance at sea-level not over a half mile above sea-level and in air that is thinner-though marginally so-than at mean sea-level. They knew that as they flew northward the terrain would drop closer to sea-level. But then, runways would get shorter as well.

The cardinal was equipped with a radio transceiver and a VOR. The panel contained few of the avionic perks in present day aircraft. GPS was unheard of while Loran C was still 15 years in the future. Even Emergency Locator Transmitters (ELTs-used to hopefully locate the aircraft if it crashed) were unavailable at that time. They would have been of little use in the Canadian north in any event as one got close to the Arctic Circle. Their only real navigational aid the VOR (VHF Omni-directional Radio Ranges) was useless north of Edmonton the next stop on their list. In order for them to work they needed the broadcasting stations on the ground (VORs) and there were none in the remote north in the late 1960s and the early 1970s.

McCulloch and Gordon were navigating using their aeronautical charts under visual flight rules (VFR). This meant that they used their magnetic compass and features on the ground to navigate their way northward.

Pilots have found that when they are using geographical details in the north they have little to go on. The north is so vast, so littered with lakes and rivers and prominences that it is difficult to tell one feature from another. It is only special features that stand out from the myriad of features that aid these navigators in their journeys around the north.

They landed at Edmonton International Airport 155 miles (250 kilometers) to the north of Calgary to take on fuel. The elevation at that airport was 1,200 feet lower than at Calgary. From there they flew northwestward 250 miles (400 kilometers) to Peace River. The airports were getting smaller and lower in elevation.

The terrain was getting interesting as well. As they proceeded further north and west, skirting well east of the Rockies, they encountered sprawling areas of unpopulated terrain. Evidence of the ever-present wheat farms of southern Alberta were giving way to rising terrain and deep valleys. Their little citified airplane would seem lost in the sprawling untracked regions of the north. Once they left for the flight from Peace River to Fort Simpson a distance of 400 miles (650 kilometers) the evidence of wheat farms lessened while the forests below began to take over. These were shot through with logging trails and survey lines that went in straight lines for many miles.

The latter portion of their flight track to Fort Simpson was over terrain that rose and fell into river valleys or rose to short plateaus. Rugged and empty back in the 1970s much as it still is today although business and industry have taken a small hold in the north. The brothers crossed the northern border of Alberta into the North West Territories arriving at Fort Simpson on the Mackenzie River. They were definitely out of their usual element.

And they were now headed northward to the Arctic Circle at 67 degrees North-570 miles lay ahead of them. To put that in perspective for American readers, that distance is about the same as from JFK in New York City, New York, across the states of Pennsylvania and Ohio to Fort Wayne, Indiana.

"The Cardinal we were flying was never meant to be a bush plane; it's a city slicker plane from down south." This was a place for heavy lifters such as the float equipped de Havilland DHC-2 Beaver or de Havilland Twin Otters, tail dragging Cessna 180s on wheels or equipped with floats or DC-3s left over from World War Two, the planes of choice in the north. "While flying in the north we got many looks from the locals implying; "These guys will never make it back down south. This country is for real men. BUSH PILOTS!"

This didn't deter McCulloch. The journey would be but one of a hundred trips in the Cardinal that he flew all over the north in his pursuit of sales and the adventures that came with it.

Words cannot adequately describe the panorama that pilots experience when flying in small aircraft. They can usually see in a large arc around their plane unlike that seen by passengers through the tiny port hole in a jet or similar passenger plane. The vista is one that keeps pilots coming back for more. The terrain unfolds below them, undulating as it passes beneath as the topography changes. There are thousands of details to absorb, some of which are important for navigation purposes. The pilots survey their surrounding with eyes always seeking a possible landing spot because that single engine up front; the heartbeat of the flight - is the only thing that keeps the plane from having to commit to landing in some of the harshest country on the planet. Most of it isn't friendly to aircraft that suddenly need to land somewhere because of engine failure.

McCulloch and his brother were comfortable with the plane; they didn't dwell on the single engine. They did what pilots do; they scanned – almost unconsciously – their instruments looking for any signs of an engine that might be experiencing some internal problem. Gauges indicating oil pressure, engine temperature, cylinder head temperatures, carburetor temperature, generator or alternator output, tachometer readings, manifold pressure were all scanned regularly as a matter of course. The ear was tuned to the engine; again automatically listening for any anomaly in its regularity. In the meantime the eyes were scanning the horizon looking for weather changes such as rain or snow showers, cloud buildup representing thunder storm activity, flocks of birds, even other aircraft remote as this possibility seemed in this great vastness.

Quite often it was sudden when things went 'south' a euphemism for 'to hell'. A tiny fracture in the prop could see a piece of it fly off so unbalancing the whirling fly-wheel up front that if the pilot couldn't shut down the engine quickly enough the severe shaking of the prop could literally tear the engine from the airplane. The plane would become tail heavy and uncontrollable. The plunge to the ground would be un-survivable. Chances are that the wreck would never be found.

The pilots and passengers would simply vanish into the wilderness and become part of the lore about flying the North Country.

If the engine quit and could not be re-started then the pilot had to use the height and the glide range available to try and find a spot level enough without serious obstructions such as rocks trees or mountains on which he could attempt a landing. Often in the wilderness the chances of finding this was not great. Perhaps then he could put it into the trees at such an attitude that the wings tearing off and the tail section coming apart might dissipate the energy sufficiently to allow the cabin to survive and perhaps the passengers as well. Surviving the crash was not always synonymous with getting out of the situation alive. Not in the wilderness. Injuries of a serious nature could take a life later than sooner. Surviving the wilderness was another matter. The chances of being found after a forced landing in a light aircraft in the 1970s in the northern territories were slim. Until one actually has the opportunity to search huge tracts of forest for downed aircraft they usually don't realize just how miniscule a plane can be when it is in the trees or half buried in a river. Even in present day planes equipped with an ELT are most likely not going to be found because of that piece of equipment in seventy-five percent of crashes. Often the ELT does not trigger or the antenna is buried or torn off during the crash; is submerged in water or the signal is blocked from satellite reception of the ELTs signal by terrain and the plane's location is not known.

The chances of discovery in 1971 were low. Sometimes, years later a plane is discovered by hunters or people working in the bush or in the mountains. An airliner - a converted Lancaster bomber - that went missing in the Andes in the late 1940s was only discovered in 2005 or 2006 by mountain climbers. These were the chances McCulloch and his brother Gordon were prepared to take. They didn't worry about the possibility because the odds were that they would be okay. They accepted this, trusted the engine and instruments and moved on.

From Fort Simpson they proceeded to Inuvik via Fort Good Hope and Fort McPherson. Once north of Fort Simpson they were above the Arctic Circle. They were following the Mackenzie River to the Arctic Ocean and the Beaufort Sea. Most of the strips were gravel strips this far north. From Inuvik they hopped the 75 miles to Tuktoyaktuk. They landed and were now within a few miles of seventy degrees north latitude. The trip ate up about 1,400 miles (2,350 kilometers) over one province and one territory. Yet this adventure was just beginning.

Tutoyaktuk was an afterthought. McCulloch wanted to go there so he could see the Arctic Ocean. There was no business there to be conducted. The runway was bad, constructed of substandard gravel. This was in the days before Dome Petroleum located out of "Tuk" to build a man-made island in the Bering Sea that supported a drilling rig. The island protected the rig from the monstrous ice-floes in the Arctic Ocean.

"Tuktoyaktuk was pretty much like hell but without the fire." McCulloch remembers. Even today the runway is still gravel but five thousand feet (1525 meters). Pilots have to be careful to avoid the edges of the runway which drops off as much as two meters on the sides.

They flew out over the Arctic Ocean for the experience and then from "Tuk" McCulloch flew 417 miles (670 kilometers) southwestward to Dawson City. Somewhere in between the two locations he remembers landing on the Dempster Highway and refueling at a gas station.

Now in Dawson City they were not far from Alaska. Eagle, Alaska was only 47 miles northwest of Dawson.

In 1971 only 762 people were recorded by census as living in Dawson City. By that time the population had plummeted from a peak of 40,000 people in 1898 at the height of the gold rush. At time of writing the population has doubled from the 1971 figures to just over thirteen hundred people; however that can climb to over fifty thousand during the tourist season.

They took a couple of days to relax and enjoy the childhood home of Pierre Burton and some of Jack London's writing about the north.

The Brothers McCulloch flew over to Eagle, Alaska and cleared customs there. Eagle is about 6 miles (9 kilometers) from the Canada, Alaska border. "You must be pretty much snowed in here during the winter." McCulloch observed to the Customs Man..

"Naw, we are alright, but everyone else is snowed out." The Customs officer quipped. This is typical of northern thinking. Often the people of the north see their isolation and the harsh winter climate as a plus rather than a negative. They don't fight it; they work with it and turn it to their advantage. These days Eagle, Alaska hosts a checkpoint for the long-distance Yukon Quest sled dog race and is home to less than two hundred people.

The brothers noted that all over their north country they had travelled that the black flies were numerous. "These weren't your garden variety black fly either, these were the twin engined types." McCulloch noted.

From there they flew to Fairbanks 190 miles (305 kilometers) to the west of Eagle. In 1971 Fairbanks boasted a population of some fifteen thousand people which was a large metropolitan community compared with most northern cities. Not content with the big city they continued on to Unalakleet, four hundred miles away over on the western shore of Alaska.

Unalakleet has gained fame recently on the History Channel's reality show, *Flying Wild Alaska* and the adventures of *Era Alaska's* Tweto family and bush pilot Jim Tweto. The community has a population now of some 750 people but in 1971 it was about half that.

"We pitched a tent and caught lots of salmon; cooked over an open fire. Flying, fishing and making money. Life was good." Except for the tenting part. The mosquitos were big and in thick swarms. The Flight Service operator in Unalakleet advised them to, put their sleeping bags in the flight service station. "Don't try and tent; you will be eaten alive, by the mosquitos." He told them. They ended up sleeping in an old military building. But they still caught salmon. McCulloch left his Rolex watch in an airport washroom. "A nice American found it and turned it in to lost and found. It was mailed back to me in Calgary."

Their next stop was Nome, 147 miles westward across Norton Sound. They skirted the coast rather than go direct then landed for the first time on grated runways left over from World War Two. These were necessary to make the runway surface hard enough to combat mushy Tundra surfaces in the warmer months.

McCulloch couldn't pass up the opportunity to fly as close to the Soviet Union as he could so they took a trip up to Diomede Island off the Russian coast to get a glimpse of the Russian Bear. "If they knew we have this .22 rifle on board they would probably go to Red Alert." I told Gordon.

From Nome they travelled back to the east to Moses Point east on Norton Sound. They were out of cash. They met the hotel owner there and asked if they could cash a cheque. "When he found out we were from Canada with a plane he said just help yourself to anything at the store restaurant etc. I own them all and I'll send you a bill." The spirit of the north was alive and well. They often found that getting fuel at remote airports was on the honor system. "You filled up, left your amount, name and address and they sent you a bill back home." They returned to Nome and from there decided to go to McGrath in the interior of Alaska. If you draw a line eastward from Nome to McGrath it passes practically right over Unalakleet.

They found that the track from Nome to McGrath was three hundred miles of mountains and brown bears and no sign of human habitation.

Naturally, that is when they ran into trouble.

Chapter Seven

"We were between the proverbial rock and a hard place."

Eighty miles out of McGrath the McCullochs ran into very low clouds. The mountains became obscure. They didn't have enough fuel to return or divert to another airport-few and far between as they were. They began to look for a place where they could make a forced landing but there was nothing but trees and rocks below them.

McGrath actually had a VOR broadcasting antenna array at their field and McCulloch had a VOR receiver on board but they were too low for the receiver to pick up a radial emanating for the VOR some eighty miles away. And as pilots know the Cessna 300 VOR receiver was prone to intermittent behavior. It might work if it had something to receive from.

McCulloch was an 1,100 hour pilot and he was not rated for instrument flight. That meant that he could not fly using just his instruments and no outside visual references. But he was running out of room, time and options. He was low with no navigating references from which to determine by his chart where the mountains were. The smart money was on mountains being just about everywhere. There could be one ahead of them right now. All that he did know was that any mountains in the vicinity topped out at about 8,000 feet (2,440 meters). He had to get up above that altitude at least to clear the highest mountain peaks in his vicinity. Once up there he hoped that the VOR would pick up the airport VOR in McGrath.

At one time or another every pilot has one of these experiences. In this case McCulloch was adding power and pulling the nose of the plane up slightly and climbing; but he was climbing into cloud and would lose any visual reference with a horizon. Other than using his instruments he would have no way of knowing if his wings were level; whether he was climbing or diving or the plane was slewing (Yawing) around its vertical axis.

"Don't talk to me until we clear eight thousand feet." He told his brother.

If you are trained on instruments you know how to use them properly. You have to trust that they are right and not believe the signals your inner ear is giving you-the human body's balancing sensor; or what is referred to as seat of your pants flying. It has been proven that even the most experienced pilots cannot hold a level state for more than about forty seconds. At some point your inner ear will give you a false signal because it relies on visual input and feet on the floor to keep you upright.

McCulloch was sweating this one. He concentrated on keeping his wings level in a climbing state and not exceeding a certain rate of climb that would make the aircraft lose lift over its wings and stall. He watched the artificial horizon (AH) to keep his wings level, the turn and bank as well. He kept the rate of climb steady at a shallow climb rate. This and the AH would assure him he was in a climb and still with the wings parallel to the ground.

Two things bothered him. He didn't know how close the mountains were and if his angle of climb or his direction was taking him toward one and he didn't know where the tops of the clouds were. He could literally climb above mountains and still be in cloud and even if he got a direction to McGrath; would it be free of cloud.

Neither pilot panicked. There was no point. The best state to be in was to be calm. If you hit, you hit. Not much you could do about it. There might be the briefest perception of some dark mass in front of the plane then it would impact at eighty or ninety miles per hour. The human body couldn't survive a 50 to 100 G impact. Over in a blink of an eye.

Under the best of conditions, the Cardinal had a service ceiling of about 12,700 feet above while its engine - which is ingesting much thinner air, producing less horsepower, slowing the airplane so that the wings could not sustain lift - would not take it. At that altitude another problem would be added, the possible onset of hypoxia. It was different for each pilot but certainly judgement could be impaired in conditions when the pilot needed to be extra sharp.

Suddenly they broke out of cloud at seven thousand feet. Relief flooded through them but that was short lived. They needed a radio bearing from McGrath so they could find it on the Earth's surface that was now blanketed in cloud.

And their fuel state hadn't changed. They were low and running out.

"Knowing what I know now we were on thin ice; there were several things that could make this our last flight. Our life depended on one radio signal and the devil was looking me in the eye."

All of a sudden the VOR's to/from flag switched to *from*. The Cessna 300 VOR had come through. McCulloch turned to line up on one of the radials. But they were not out of the soup yet… literally. Now they had to get down through the cloud hoping that the cloud didn't go right to the ground or through a peak.

The communications in McGrath weren't what they are in the present.

Once more, no talking in the cabin. McCulloch went on instruments but this time going downhill rather than up. They were guaranteed a hard bottom eventually unlike when they were climbing. They would reach the surface of the Earth eventually.

They descended and were rewarded with clear space between the cloud and the ground. They landed and found the airport's watering hole.

After that it was back to Fairbanks, then Northway, Whitehorse, Muncho Lake, Todd River, Fort Nelson south to Edmonton and home to Calgary.

Other than the scare during the low cloud encounter this was typical of many of the trips that McCulloch took into the north, sometimes with his brother, other times with other salesmen under his management. And it wasn't always during the summer months. He often flew north during the colder months. Along went the Eiderdown sleeping bag-good to 40 below Fahrenheit. There was also the rifle. Extra food in case you were stranded. A blanket or muff went along to keep the heat in the cowl when you could put a car warmer inside to heat up the engine block and jugs before trying to turn it over in the cold. Maybe one in the cockpit as well if you were lucky. That's if there was a power outlet around somewhere to plug into. Hangars were scarce or just too expensive to overnight in. But mostly they were just few and far between in the north back in the 1970s. One of the problems with travelling in the colder months was that it gets darker much earlier. It narrows the flight time during the day leaving long nights to wait out the cold-waiting for the Sun.

"Getting lost or having an engine failure was pretty much a guarantee that you would be in hell for breakfast." With that in mind the pilots and McCulloch did all they could to stave off that possibility. There are many bold pilots in the north but not many stupid ones.

Gas was very expensive in the north even in the 70s. The jaws of fellow pilots who hadn't flown north would drop when they learned that McCulloch paid as much as $8.00 a gallon for gas in the north. It wasn't that gas was that expensive back then but getting it up north in bulk was and still is a problem.

A gas dealer in the north once remarked to McCulloch, "It's only rich people and fools who fly way up here." Then he laughed. McCulloch wasn't rich back then but he was well off. He considered the fuel expense just the cost of doing business and he had no intention of stopping what he was doing.

Looking back, McCulloch realizes this was the beginning of many years of going past the usual boundaries set in place by every aviator. There was no real need to tackle these remote communities; he could have made as many sales-perhaps many more- in the south as he did ranging northward. Airplanes are expensive to operate as every pilot with a plane knows. Fuel costs and maintenance of the airplane in the 1970s might have been cheaper than today's but in the scheme of things it probably all works out. Too, most salesmen are not likely to die having slammed into the top of some mountain or from spiraling down through thousands of feet of dense cloud then impacting the ground.

You would never hear a travelling salesman say that "...the turbulence going through Kicking Horse Pass nearly tore the doors off my car." Or, "...the engine quit and I had no place to pull over." You can't pull an airplane over at five thousand feet, get out, raise the cowl and look for the problem. You got a problem, you solve it right now-or you will probably end up on the five o'clock news."

Airplane manufacturers in the fifties and sixties went to great pains to convince the public that anyone can fly an airplane. 'It's just like driving the family car.' They would say. Most pilots know that this is bullshit. If they don't they have no business flying in the first place.

Flying is serious business. An airline pilot once said "If God had meant man to fly He would have given him more money."

Damn straight. But you thought it was going to be the other one, right??

Money makes airplanes fly, make no mistake about it. Lots of money makes bigger airplanes fly faster and further in greater comfort. McCulloch knew this and in the back of his mind was a voice saying, "Learn more and earn more." Experience is to pilots what sea room is to sailors. The more you have the better your chances of avoiding the wreck.

Chapter Eight

Downward Spiral

One morning in Prince George, British Columbia, the Cardinal decided to be cranky. It had every right to be. It was a cold and icy morning late in the fall. Snow lay around the airport plowed up in piles. The Cardinal refused to start, the battery losing its power. McCulloch decided to hand-prop the engine. This has been done millions of times since the beginning of aviation, but every once in a while the plane bites back. In this case it involved a throttle setting that was a bit too high and a pair of leather soled shoes on a slippery tarmac. McCulloch dressed in his suit, overcoat, tie and aforementioned shoes spun the propeller with the magnetos live and the throttle set and the engine caught just as he lost his footing on the icy ramp. The Cardinal nearly ran him over on its trip across the tarmac, past a row of airplanes and buried itself in a snow bank on the other side of the ramp. His was the only plane damaged.

The local paper caught the story and reported that a pilot's airplane tried to leave Prince George without him. "I felt lower than a snake in a wagon wheel rut." It took $4,500.00 to get the plane back into shape. A lot of money in 1972 and even by today's standards.

McCulloch made an important decision late in 1972. He reviewed his personal life and it was clear to him that he was partying too much and despite his married status; his flirting was out of control. Something had to give. McCulloch gave up drinking. One of his salesmen, Pat Wood, showed McCulloch that you could fly more, have just as much fun without booze as with it. It took McCulloch many attempts to kick the alcohol habit but by the end of that year he was flying high. He hasn't touched a drop in over forty years.

The same could not be said about his love of partying and flirting and all that entails.

But business was good. McCulloch was selling and his staff of 150 were selling as well; increasing his income. His image as the flying salesman helped increase his visibility and not only impressed his sales staff but his clients as well. He flew the north accumulating over one hundred flights in the remote territories alone. In fact he flew so much that he was running the engine out in the Cardinal - it was supposed to be majored every 2,000 hours and he was at 1,800. Majoring an engine is expensive costing as much as half of the airplane's current value. He was thinking that his remote flying habit, his long distance runs, mountain flying and lack of navigation equipment required an airplane with longer legs, more speed and a built in 'safety' factor.

Then the proverbial crap hit the fan.

Chapter Nine

"If you don't get offered a job once a week you are not doing a good sales job." Dave McCulloch

By anyone's standards McCulloch was successful. He was making great money, his family was well off, he had a four bedroom house, two cars and an airplane that he flew all over his territory. His annual income in 1973 was in the $37,000.00 range. His sales staff looked up to him and to him for guidance. They trusted him because he was always upfront with them. No bullshit. And he expected none back from them. He was 100% loyal to them and expected the same in return. And he was convinced that he had that. These men were now strong and confident in their ability to succeed in any sales company. McCulloch was generous, often giving away prospects or pieces of territory that he could have easily sold. But his philosophy about giving rewarded him with returns; a philosophy which still holds true to this day.

This loyalty to McCulloch did not go un-noticed in the towers in Toronto. He was becoming a power in the company. His staff would listen to him before toeing the line for Toronto. Success is hard to ignore. His immediate boss was perhaps threatened by McCulloch's success out in the western territory.

To this day McCulloch believes that because of his perceived threat to his boss's position in the company his supervisor made a critical decision; he decided to cut McCulloch's empire in half. Cutting his territory by half would also cut his staff and perhaps

McCulloch's power and influence over those people working for him. In this way McCulloch's boss could insure that his own superiors would not look at McCulloch and see him as a possible replacement for himself or advance McCulloch to a position above him.

"A key lesson; there is usually only one King or one big company boss. It's a dilemma faced by many high achievers." McCulloch learned, "Governments practice the same thing secretly. They want to look down on their people; keeping them needy."

Later on in this biography McCulloch addresses how to manipulate this hurdle. But at the time he was so angry that he gave into his emotions and quit his job. Many of his top salesmen quit right along with him realizing that they would probably never advance beyond the position of Sales Manager of a now much smaller territory. High sales volume did not translate beyond monetary reward. That was the message the Toronto head office was sending.

McCulloch was learning. And this was one important message that had been sent. If you want to expand your horizons you could not rely on someone else's ability to see beyond the walls of their own domain-and certainly could not or would not help you get beyond yours.

"Shit happens it's true but sometimes stupid shit happens-someone else's stupid shit at that." The way around that was to ensure that there was no one in the way of you reaching the top. So why not just go straight for the top and eliminate the herky-jerky elevator ride to the lofty levels of ownership or something like it?

McCulloch had much going for him even though he had no job now. But he still had the responsibilities of before, the family, the house, the plane, the cars....all of this weighed heavily upon him. When he left Paymaster there were no rewards to carry him through for the next few months; the paychecks stopped along with his commissions when they were paid out. And in 1973 there was no unemployment insurance for commissioned sales people. The government assumed that everyone on the books of a sales-oriented company was making money-maybe not right now but they would receive commissions later for what they had sold right now.

The life's blood of any manufacturing company is the salespeople who get out there and sell their product. Few people realize just how much their jobs rely on some salesman or saleswoman somewhere selling something.

McCulloch took a job with another check-writing company; Canadian Checkwriters. He was confident in his ability to pick up where he left off. To prove it he did what he would do later on-he spit in the eye of possible failure and purchased another airplane; this time one with two engines. With a couple of hundred hours left on the Cardinal's engine he traded up to a PA-30 Piper Twin Comanche.

The Twin Comanche had two engines, each producing 160 horsepower. The Cardinal had just one engine which produced 150 horsepower. The Cardinal was fixed gear while the Comanche was retractable gear. Despite this the Light Twin as it was often referred to was not twice as fast as the Cardinal. Its combined 320 horsepower pulled it through the sky perhaps 50 miles per hour faster than the Cardinal. The safety factor was the extra engine which presumably would get the airplane to a safe landing if one of the two engines quit in flight.

Many older pilots believe, fatalistically, that 'the extra engine (on a light twin) just gets the plane to the scene-of-the-accident faster' than no engine working at all. In some cases this may be true but there is a psychological benefit and the Comanche could hold its own if one engine went out and was not the critical engine-the right engine in this case which if it did induced a powerful left turning moment that was hard to overcome with right rudder. This induced drag and slowed the airplane. Its wings could stall in a critical situation. The Twin Comanche was prone to flat spins at low power on one engine.

Pilots train for this and McCulloch's plane was built in 1964. He purchased it, as mentioned, in 1973; the flat-spin problem was well known by then. The plane not only had more speed, endurance and a heavier payload, it also had more navigation equipment. He now had an ADF, two radios and two VORs (see glossary of terms) to navigate with.

It was as if he was tempting fate, daring it to slap him down. Lose your job? Take on more debt. Maybe buying a twin engined plane was a little over the top but as we will see that was McCulloch's way. It wasn't the only time he did this. Years later he would purchase a business jet when similar circumstances presented themselves.

McCulloch had a new job. His brother Gordon quit Paymaster as well as Dave Yates (Yates stayed for a time then opened his own business and became a very successful businessman in his own right) and a dozen of Paymaster's top salesmen in the western territory. They too went to work for the new company. But the job didn't last long for McCulloch. Three months later he was off on another project that was entirely different from anything he had attempted before.

McCulloch entered the computer age.

McCulloch's first plane, a two seat 1965 Cessna 150 and his three children; Jeffery, Dawn and Stephanie (July' 68)

Gordon stands beside McCulloch's second plane, a 1968 Cessna Cardinal 177 - Flying Forger (1969)

A 1971 Corvette, McCulloch's first; one of 21 by 2014 (1971

*Linda and McCulloch first twin engined airplane a 1964 Piper PA 30
at Dulles Airport, Washington, DC (1973)*

Chapter Ten

"Do not build companies for others. If times are tough they will fire you and you won't be there to reap the benefits. If times become great, they become afraid of you." Dave McCulloch

With his territory cut in half by his boss at Paymaster, McCulloch had real expectations of his salary being diminished by that percentage as well. It was also an attack on his integrity, his power and his principles. He had been stabbed in the back and that pissed him off to no end. He knew he deserved more rather than less, otherwise what was the good of busting his ass and those of his sales staff if there was no reward for any of them. Getting the potential for making money cut in half was hardly an incentive. We now live in a time when CEOs and executives award themselves huge bonuses even when the company is applying for Chapter 11-or its equivalent so nearly 40 years later a territory cut (read downsizing)seems now to be just another day at the office. But McCulloch never forgot. He forgave his boss eventually but he never forgot. The next twin engined aircraft he purchased had a relief tube for the pilot. For years whenever McCulloch's flight path took him over his former boss's home he would relieve himself. The message was quite clear.

But maybe in hindsight this was to be a good thing. Had he stayed with Paymaster for years after, would the rest of this book have been written? Would he have moved on to even bigger business deals that would net him millions in later years?

The move to Canadian Check writer would have been a natural progression for himself and most sales people but for McCulloch it seemed that he was just repeating history. Something inside McCulloch just would not be fobbed off with more-of-the-same. Not then; not now. It was the Imperial Toronto tanker job all over again. Could he see himself doing the same thing for the rest of his working life?

He lasted three months. McCulloch got off the check-writing–machine ship; this time without a US immigration escort to the nearest Canadian border. He worked his way into a deal that had the promise of making him more money than ever before. Lots of it.

McCulloch's travels throughout eastern, central and western Canada had given him a resource that he hoped to tap into. He was connected all over the country to those who were in the money game; banks, entrepreneurs and sales.

"One of my heroes is Albert Einstein. He said, 'Imagination is more important than knowledge.' Well we had the imagination."

This is what they imagined-and the concept was brilliant for the times in 1973. McCulloch teamed up with a company named Pharma-Data based in Calgary. "I didn't start it (the company) I teamed with Ron Dunphy, it was his deal. My flying mobility and familiarization with Canada coast to coast landed me my marketing deal."

The plan was to tie all of the drug companies in Canada together via telephone lines and computer terminals. This would streamline prescription refills, billing and eliminate duplication abuse. McCulloch would be Director of Marketing. For his labours he would receive one cent for every prescription filled plus commissions on the computer terminals/data bases that were sold to the pharmacies. A rough estimate would see McCulloch realize some $100,000.00 a year in commissions. That's nearly a million dollars a year in 2016 dollars. This looked like a golden opportunity for McCulloch and the company he was associated with.

"It was an ambitious and imaginative idea. Computers were just being introduced and most pharmacists were amazed at our online-by-telephone demonstration set up with a shared program, at the University of Calgary."

It went smoothly enough at first. They had *Einstein* imagination. They flew around the country in McCulloch's Twin Comanche garnering interest. They set up an office at the Toronto Dominion Bank Center in Toronto.

He rented a penthouse to live in. McCulloch marketed the idea to everyone with the money to make the idea float. "But this country boy found it hard to convince the big boys to join." He recalls, "They all wanted a big piece of the company. Some of them wanted it all."

Pharmacies conglomerates such as Shoppers Drug Mart, CN Telecommunications with their control data were big and difficult to handle. Unlike these days when even a small company can either buy or rent server space and then set up their own databases, forty years ago this was unheard of. You relied on what was already in place.

McCulloch sank all of his money into the venture; it finally came to a point where he had to admit he was broke and had to back away from this deal. The idea was way ahead of its time. In the present the concept of high speed information distribution is so commonplace that one scarcely thinks about the times when this was not so. Millions of everyday people do their banking online through their home computers and their smart phones.

Coming down off the high of being a top salesman with a big company like Paymaster, being successful and well off, this latest failure was an ego crusher for McCulloch. But he had learned a hard lesson. McCulloch always learned from his mistakes. All he knew was selling and airplanes. So for now…he would sell airplanes.

Chapter Eleven

"There are two big imposters in this world, success and failure, and now I had met them both." Dave McCulloch.

It was 1974. McCulloch was at loose ends. He had sunk everything in Pharma Data and basically he was broke. He decided to stay in Toronto. It had a large population base and there was the promise of businessmen wanting to learn to fly as well as those who wanted to get their private license in order to fly for enjoyment. He started a small business, *Apache Airways*. He would sell Piper aircraft and give flying instruction; he had obtained his certificate to instruct while getting his commercial license. "All I really knew how to do was selling and flying so I opened a shoestring company called Apache Airways. I did a little flight instruction, and sold a few small airplanes. It was hand to mouth living." But not necessarily boring.

During the slow periods, McCulloch would take his family or friends to Florida in the Twin Comanche. By now he had purchased a second Twin Comanche capable of carrying five passengers and pilot. This model aircraft was considerably faster than the Cardinal by about 40 miles (70 kilometres) an hour.

To relieve the training boredom and weekly humdrum of just making a living he decided to fly the Comanche from Toronto to

Bermuda. It would be a bit pricy fuel-wise so he found five other people who would fly along and share the expenses.

They left Toronto and flew to Buffalo, New York to clear US Customs. From there they flew to Cape Cod.

Bermuda lies about 675 miles off the east coast of the United States with Pamlico Sound, North Carolina being the closest. Twin engines notwithstanding the PA-30 Comanche needed the added wingtip tanks to extend its range for over the water. On this flight they would fly from Cape Cod to the island in the Atlantic. They lifted off from Barnstable Municipal Airport on Cape Cod. Within a matter of minutes they would be flying exclusively over the water to Bermuda; a distance of 720 miles.

McCulloch was willing to risk it all, life and money, to fly the distance to what is now, L.F.Wade International Airport in Bermuda. In the 1970s the airport went under the name of Kindley Field. It was a joint construction project of the United States Army Air Force (USAAF) and the Royal Air Force (RAF) between 1941 and 1943. The RAF withdrew their forces at the end of World War Two converting their facilities into the Civil Air Terminal under the advisement of an RAF Commander.

The newer United States Air Force (USAF), inaugurated in 1947 maintained their control over their command as Kindley Air Force base until 1970 when it was turned over to the US Navy. It was then named US Naval Air Station, Bermuda. It was this command that gave McCulloch a great deal of trouble when they landed there in August of 1975.

"The small piper, fully loaded, points south east from Boston into the infamous Bermuda triangle. With only one ADF and one VOR, an electrical malfunction, would mean finding Bermuda a tiny speck in the middle of the western Atlantic; a near impossible task."

In the back of McCulloch's mind lurked the memory of Emilia Earhart who disappeared in the Pacific in 1937. She too was flying to a tiny speck of an island designated as Howland Island situated in the vastness of the Pacific Ocean. McCulloch was shooting for a hook shaped island about 15 miles (25 kilometers) long while flying only on his compasses now that he was out of range of the American mainland and the electronic aids at Kingsley Field in Bermuda. Basically he was out of range of the American navigational aids when he was some 75 miles out to sea and the same would hold true of the ranges in Bermuda. Neither his ADF or VOR would pick up nav-aids during a good portion of the flight amounting to about 550 miles (920 kilometers) of Atlantic Ocean's expanse. Cruising at an economical fuel rate to conserve av/gas they would spend three hours out of range of electronic guidance. "For hour after hour we flew on past our point of no return, we only had fuel to continue." They were at an altitude of 7,500 feet.

Hours spent in the air over water in a small airplane can lead the imagination in many directions. This trip was not only boring but a bit scary as well for some of the passengers. But there were no signs of panic. McCulloch was watching his instruments and spent a lot of time looking at the ADF and the VOR. He scanned them frequently looking for signs of life. Then one hundred miles out of Bermuda a flicker on the ADF. It was receiving an intermittent signal from the Non Directional Beacon (NDB) at Kindley Field. It got stronger and then suddenly they had radio contact at 100 miles out.

McCulloch contacted the tower at Kindley. They quickly informed him that he didn't have permission to land and that he would have to turn back. McCulloch radioed back that turning back was not an option, that he didn't have fuel for a return trip. Apparently he was supposed to have contacted Washington to get clearance into the military base at Kindley despite it being a commercial as well as military operational airport. They also informed him there was no fuel that he could use there despite the fact that the Navy was using gas driven helicopters which in those days would have been burning 100/130 octane gas, the same as McCulloch's airplane.

McCulloch is not one to suffer fools gladly and was in no mood for them now. "You natives aren't being very friendly." He replied to one transmission. "That did not improve the situation at all." He remembers in hindsight.

One way or the other I'm landing he told the controller and was informed that his airplane would be impounded if he did. A jeep loaded with military personnel showed up and escorted the plane to a parking spot.

Rather than spending a few days on an island paradise enjoying the scenery, the waters and other adventures, McCulloch spent the next three days trying to obtain fuel. Finally he talked a local Esso distributor into filling his tank with auto gas. It seemed his only option. However a telegram arrived from ESSO's head offices in New York requiring him to not take off. They sent a biz-jet over and the personnel there drained all of the auto-gas from the Twin Comanche. They were afraid of the liability that might arise if this plane were to go into the ocean using improper fuel.

Once more McCulloch was stuck. But fate was intervening. The media had gotten wind of the story of the Canadians stranded in Bermuda because he was refused fuel to leave the island. The Governor learned of this and received orders from Great Britain to act on it. He read the riot act to the American base CO and reminded him who owned the island and that if this Canadian needed aviation fuel he would receive it-no if ands or buts.

Receive it McCulloch did. By the time the plane was fueled and ready it was night time, but McCulloch undaunted by a night-flight over 770 miles of Atlantic Ocean pointed the nose of the PA-30B in the direction of Wilmington, North Carolina, south west of Pamlico Sound; the nearest land-fall. They were not to enjoy a peaceful flight to the coast of the United States.

It was not only a dark night it was a rainy dark night. Ahead of them lay thunderclouds. They would have to fly dead-reckoning in a pitch black sky. Only the odd bolt of lightning would illuminate the night. He had no choice but to reduce speed in the resulting turbulence, avoiding flight vertigo, trusting his instruments to keep him level and on course.

If a pilot gives into the false signals the brain generates in its attempt to make sense of a situation where there is no sensory input such as a visible horizon, the inner ear will soon take over and provide false sensations. If the pilot gives into the sensations rather than trusting the instruments which operate on gyroscopic principles-maintaining a constant reference to a fixed position in space; the plane will soon spiral downward and impact the ground; or in this case the surface of the Atlantic Ocean. Vertigo has killed more pilots than any other cause. It was responsible for the death of John Kennedy Jr. on July 19, 1999 not much further north off Martha's Vineyard. The real name for this condition is spatial disorientation.

McCulloch's butt was eating his seat for much of that flight across the dark waters that night. Maintain pitch, roll and yaw; each was critical while maintaining course and airspeed. The altimeter was king. Believe what it said and stay on it.

McCulloch was flying an aircraft that could quickly climb or descend in the narrow envelope of two miles he had allowed himself in altitude. Below lay the ocean, above rarer air and hypoxia. His navigation instruments-other than the compass and it's gyroscopically controlled Heading Indicator mate-were of no value to him; they were out of range of any signals from shore. No satellite navigation in those days. To make matters worse the weather disturbances, especially lightning being generated in the thunderclouds, degraded his radio signals. Rain scatters the incoming returns and outgoing radar pulses lessening its transmission strength, while lightning creates so much interference that it drowns out transmissions on the AM band aviation frequencies.

"Without radar we held a direct course through several thunderstorms."

He was blind to their existence in the dark, in the blackness.

He switched the fuel selector knob to a succession of six fuel tanks, draining each one to its minimum fuel quantity. Inevitably he switched to the sixth and final tank. When that ran out they would either have to ditch or land in the dark.

McCulloch's eyes were always looking to where he thought the horizon might be, looking for the lights of the United States and North Carolina while listening intently for a signal in the noise of the Aviation band of frequencies. Unseen lightning noise crackled and snapped from the cabin speaker.

Neither of the VORs or the ADF twitched in the glow of the instrument panel lights. McCulloch did not have Distance Measuring Equipment (DME) in his aircraft other than dead reckoning; computing the distance, divided by indicated airspeed against his compass readings. Additionally the winds aloft are factored in but as all pilots and mariners know, the winds are not to be trusted; they are wayward winds. Pilots can never be certain what the airplane's actual speed is over the ground because winds influence the readings. It takes GPS to compute real progress over the Earth's surface in whatever distance measuring standard you prefer; knots, miles-per-hour or kilometres.

Down to its last few gallons the twin Comanche, its five passengers and the pilot droned through the black void, each engine gobbling up fuel at the rate of seven to eight US gallons per hour. McCulloch took comfort in his instruments, their constancy, their familiarity, their ability to relay accurate information to his eyes and brain while his inner ears sent different signals; plotting against him and his instruments.

With no visual reference McCulloch had no choice but to take his chances with the thunderstorms stretching across the path before him. He could only tell that he was near and penetrating their cells, the terrible domain of some of the worst weather phenomenon on the planet by the battering they took, by the Vertical Speed Indicator (VSI) telling him he was suddenly climbing at hundreds or thousands of feet per minute; each interlude verified by the altimeter. He was in the lofty halls of the cloud mountain kings and they were unforgiving of intruders into their thirty thousand foot high realms. By his own estimation they had passed through several thunderstorms.

The clock on the panel was now becoming important. It was getting later and near the time when they should have made landfall. The fuel quantity was diminishing; McCulloch`s nerves were stretched like violin strings. It was the worst trip ever but it was a walk in the park compared to what was to come years into the future.

Suddenly the ADF twitched then swung to life indicating a None Directional Beacon (NDB) straight ahead. Not long after they could see the illumination from Wilmington. "Seeing the lights of Wilmington added new meaning to America being a shining light."

Chapter Twelve

Back in Toronto, change is in the air. McCulloch was tired of living hand to mouth. Sure he had some toys but the opportunity to play with them was limited by minimal cash flow. McCulloch's marriage wasn`t going well either. His constant travelling and womanizing were taking their toll.

McCulloch was going broke. "If you are going broke, you might as well go broke all the way." He had maybe a $1000.00 in cash and some credit cards that weren't maxed out-one of which was an American Express Platinum card that he has relied on for decades. He decided to take the Twin Comanche to Brazil. He would take his girlfriend Linda with him.

He took a pilot acquaintance-and his friend-along with him as co-pilot. On December 27, 1975 McCulloch flew twin Comanche C-GGIS from Toronto to Nassau, then to Trinidad. There were the usual amount of forms - in this case twelve - that had to be filled out for entry purposes. Their next stop was to be at Ogle Airport in Georgetown, British Guyana but when they contacted the tower there they were advised not to land because there was a riot going on in the city. Good idea. They diverted to French Guiana. Before landing they did a low circle over Devil's

Island, France's notorious penal colony, made famous by the book and movie Papillon.

They landed in Cayenne at Rochambeau airport. From there they flew on to Belem Brazil where trouble began. This time it was over the insurance coverage required to fly into that country. This glitch cost them a four day stay in Belem. "Working through the use of Telex machines I was able to work some mumble jumble up north by a few innovative people and some questionable manoeuvring that resulted in our getting forwarded some additional cash (in US Funds) via Western Union and we were rubber stamped out of there."

McCulloch flew on to Brasilia. "It was like flying over a sea of broccoli; just solid, jungle tree top canopy. In the back of your mind was this constant scenario that if you ever went down into that canopy you would just disappear; probably be in the stew pot that night. There were head hunters and tribesmen still living down there." You would never be found; even in the late '70s. Hundreds of planes and their occupants are still unaccounted for in the vast rainforests of Brazil and South America. But the 950 mile trip to Brasilia was uneventful.

That night it was raining but one of his pilot friends wanted to fly out to Rio de Janeiro to prove his prowess as an IFR pilot. It was 570 miles from Brasilia to Rio de Janiero; again over nothing but jungle. McCulloch quickly kiboshed that idea. "My airplane my rules." He told them. International Airport rather than their flight planned destination of Jacarepaqua Airport (or Santos Dumont Airport) in downtown Rio which was closer to the beach and some 15 miles to the southeast? I made some kind of sarcastic remark to the guy then apologized to him later but that friendship apparently ended right there." The two pilots flew home commercial. McCulloch and Linda were on their own.

They went to the famous Copacabana beach which is lined with hotels and condos along the Avenida Atlantica between the beach and the buildings. They went swimming. While at the water's edge, McCulloch spotted someone - a man- poking around their clothing. The man ran off with McCulloch's wallet and passport with Dave in hot pursuit. But the thief was faster- and younger-than the 37 year old pilot and got away. McCulloch went to the poliza with his story. They asked for a description. He told them he was black. "They just shrugged." There were hundreds of thousands of black people in Rio de Janeiro; the odds of finding the thief were slim to nothing.

That night they were in their motel room. "I was broke...no money or credit cards. "I had nearly $1,000.00 US dollars in that wallet. Everything was in the wallet" His only hope was to wire back home and get some more money transferred to him. It would take weeks or a month to renew the credit cards.

The phone rang. "Who would be calling me in Rio?" He wondered. No one knew that he was at this hotel. He answered the phone. There was a voice speaking in broken English on the other end. The voice said, "Dadid (presumably an attempt at pronouncing David) we may have something for you." It appears that they have his wallet. McCulloch thinks, "They want ransom for my wallet." The caller wants him to come to his place to get his wallet. "I figured-what the hell the bastards have my papers and my credit cards and I've got an airplane 10,000 miles from home and no money or resources. I needed that Platinum American Express card."

As far as McCulloch is concerned the Amex Platinum card is the only one you need when you are in a jam. He took down an address and left the hotel with Linda. Linda was to be his back-up. When he arrived there she would stay out in the street while he went inside and confronted whoever had his wallet. His problem was that he didn't have anything to negotiate with. He was playing this by ear. They asked for nothing and right then I had nothing to offer in the way of a reward. But I mailed them a small reward later when I was able to get my hands on some American dollars."

McCulloch was so relieved and grateful that he spent time speaking-with difficulty-to the Portuguese family and was well past his five minute deadline given to Linda. She was down in the street, panicking; thinking that the worst had happened. Her attractiveness already drawing male attention Linda's agitation about McCulloch's being past his deadline were related to the crowd that was forming around her. They were curious as to what this young attractive blond woman was carrying on about. McCulloch arrived back in the nick of time before the poliza showed up. He had his Amex card back and with that he could pay hotel bills, fuel his airplane, purchase meals. "Had it not been for that honest Portuguese boy I don't know what I would have done." It was a lesson learned for the future.

The couple's stay in Rio de Janeiro lasted five days. Even though McCulloch had been to Rio de Janeiro some twenty years earlier as a sailor on an ESSO tanker the city was still as vibrant and colourful with breathtaking scenery. Copacabana beach was world famous for its white sands bordered by the hotels on its west side. The city was an eclectic mix of races and hair colours. The young (and not so young) and the beautiful of each roamed the beaches in abbreviated beachwear. Once the haunting grounds of the wealthy back in the 1930s Rio de Janeiro once again became noticed by the general population as an exotic vacation spot in the mid 1960s when the song hit the music charts. It became a worldwide hit receiving a Grammy in 1965. Ipanema - a seaside community- is on the next beach a half mile southwest of Copacabana Beach. The carnivals, Sugar Loaf Mountain and the statue known as Christ the Redeemer are signature occasions and landmarks in that city.

But it was time to leave and head north to Canada. First a detour west to Campo Grande to be a tourist then northeast to

Jatai and onward to Brasilia. McCulloch retraced his steps to Belem, Cayenne, French Guiana. From there over the water to Trinidade and to Puerto Rico. He was burnt out from flying and putting up the constant harassment of South American officials. Everyone had their hands out. When he refuelled in Cayenne he knew they would not accept credit cards but all of his American cash had been stolen in Rio de Janeiro. A banker had advanced him Brazilian Reals from his American Express card. When the ramp operator in Cayenne asked how he was paying, McCulloch said 'in cash'.

Linda supervised the refuelling while Dave went inside and did the necessary paper work, greased the right palms so they could get out of there. The paperwork was stamped and it came time to pay the gas bill; McCulloch handed over Brazilian cash. The FBO was expecting American cash not Brazilian money and was pissed off because he had been tricked. It was legal tender after all but the FBO would have preferred American bucks; the currency in favour in South America. The FBO had no choice but to take the money and the Canadians left for Trinidad and Puerto Rico. McCulloch left the Twin Comanche in Puerto Rico and booked their flights back to Toronto on a commercial airliner. He was burnt out. And that would be reflected back in Toronto. His flight instruction business was not meeting his expectations. He decided to close down the business and moved back to Nova Scotia.

Chapter Thirteen

Once more from the bottom. `Promotion, promotion, promotion`.

McCulloch took the offer of a sales job with his brother Gordon's company which sold water treatment equipment. "You are a good salesman, before you know it you will be making five hundred a week." Gordon told him. He was back in his element. "It was easy for me to master sales. Before too long I was managing my own store." Soon he was training others to do the job. But in the fall of 1975 he and his wife Carole were divorced. He lasted two years in Nova Scotia before his restlessness got the better of him. Business-wise, Nova Scotia was just too small a venue to contain him. He moved back to the booming city of Calgary in 1977. He hadn`t owned or flown an airplane since July of 1976. McCulloch decided to stay in the water treatment business and opened his own store. He trademarked the business calling it *Water Doctor*.

At the outset it was a hand to mouth operation. He bootstrapped his sales from one sale to the next by installing a system, getting paid for it then purchasing another treatment system from the profits of the previous sale.

He had Gordon ship him a couple of units from Nova Scotia and worked from there. He used a borrowed truck to move the units to their new homes and installed them himself. Once again he was selling another company's product, but he had learned a valuable lesson with Paymaster. Rather than sell units and boost the manufacturer's bottom line and be manager of a sales division for the American owned company (Lindsay?) he would run his own business. Hence the name, *Water Doctor*. Any success he had in marketing would benefit McCulloch. The bigger the business got the more cash flow would accrue to him; *and* he could not have his sales territory split because this time *he* owned the business.

"We would set up a table at any number of malls in Calgary and then I had my salespeople dress in white smocks, just like the doctors wore. It gave the operation a look of professionalism."

McCulloch worked all day and many nights to complete an installation in a home or business so that he could get paid and then purchase the next unit. "I even plumbed in a few of the first installations. One installation we did had lots of leaks. The customer was suspicious; asked me if I'd been doing this very long."

Starting and bootstrapping a business together is a confidence game. The early customers would never have dealt with the company if they knew just how small and under-capitalized *Water Doctor* really was. "I basically sold, installed and ran to the bank with the cheque, depositing the money so I could buy another unit." It's a frenetic way of doing business; but in this case it worked.

McCulloch opened an office and had his girlfriend, Linda, staff it. For the most part she was looking after the books. Linda had been in his life for some five or six years at this point and would eventually become his wife.

McCulloch met Linda Stanmore on a blind date in Toronto. She had graduated from the University of London, England, with a degree in education and had immigrated to Canada as a school teacher. But she was then working for a personnel company in Toronto. She was 23 and McCulloch was 35. He enticed her with a plan to fly to Nassau for the weekend. Linda thought they were going commercial but he surprised her with his own airplane, the PA-30.

"Only the less fortunate travel by common carrier."

The trip developed into a relationship that included a lot of travel-including Bermuda and Brazil-eating interesting foods and other entertainment, "...something else we used to do but it's been so long ago I can't remember..." Has it been mentioned that McCulloch has an infectious smile?

"Linda, for the most part, began working in various companies with me. I hired her so her job wouldn't interfere with our travels."

They were married in Las Vegas in 1983. But that was a few years into the future. Over a period of two years and a half, McCulloch had worked his sales magic. He realized the value of marketing. He did everything he could to promote *Water Doctor* including having the company name painted on the side of his car- a V-12 Jaguar XJS. "I was putting in 18 hour days." McCulloch recalls. "I was soon hiring and building my sales force. Extra cash and a steady cash flow enabled many house deals to be flipped.`` This resulted in impressive revenue figures which led to progressively higher lines of credit. ``Soon I was expanding to nearby towns and cities, and charging a fee to other entrepreneurs to join and use my trade-marked name *Water Doctor*.

McCulloch was now franchising the business. He obtained a US working Visa and opened a store in Montana. During this brief period - with thirty stores opened – McCulloch worked to gain control of the water treatment business in western Canada and Montana. He began franchising the business. By 1979 he was making more money than ever before and was running a company that would be valued at $4.5 million in 1979 dollars. He was creating jobs, employing people to run individual stores and install the Lindsay water softening product. *Water Doctor* was a success. 'Rags to riches' in just under three years. Business was getting so good that after a flying hiatus of nearly three years , once again McCulloch plunged into aviation. He would never again be without an airplane or three.

In July of 1979, McCulloch purchased a 1962 model twin-engined Cessna 320. He credited that move with resulting in more contacts and the opening of more stores in western Canada. He would charge a fee for the use of the *Water Doctor* name. He used the plane to forge new friends and alliances in business, many of which he participated in and that have sustained themselves over the last 34 years.

McCulloch moved his head office from Calgary to Winnipeg to centralize his operation. "I used the Cessna 320 to fly around to the different stores, some of which were as far away as Winnipeg. Winnipeg was more in the middle of Canada. He opened a USA operation in Great Falls, Montana and obtained an American work visa to facilitate imports into Canada. "This didn't hurt me politically either. I was exporting and importing, creating jobs on both sides of the border; all the warm 'fuzzy' stuff governments like."

By this time McCulloch was doing commercial and industrial jobs; meeting and developing business with the Hutterite communities. *Water Doctor* installed - what was for its time - a large water treatment plant in the Decker, Manitoba Hutterite colony. "I was working with my Brandon, Manitoba *Water Doctor* dealer who heard they had a serious water problem out there, so we boarded the Cessna 320 and flew up there; 60 miles north of Brandon and landed in a stubble field next to a combine." McCulloch met Sam Waldner, a Hutterite Minister and his brother Albert "I tested the water and said if you have sick water I can fix it." This would be the beginning of a long business and personal journey over the years. "We have travelled the world and been associated in business ventures that included, salt, boilers, coal, wheels and water purification. This led to numerous flying trips to other Hutterian colonies in North America. They number in the hundreds." McCulloch earned their trust. Because of this initial contact and his treatment of this segment of our society, McCulloch continues to work with and invest with the Hutterites to this day.

McCulloch`s involvement with the Hutterites will arise from time to time in the future so a few words about this society is in order. The Hutterites (from the German, Hutterer) are a branch of the Anabaptists with roots going back to the 16th century in the Tyrol of Germany. Their founder Jakob Hutter died in 1536. Based on the texts of the New Testament, specifically the Acts of the Apostles (Chapters 2, Verse 44, 4, and 5 and 2 Corinthians, distinguishing them from the Amish and Mennonites) stemmed their belief in communal living and sharing and their strict adherence to pacifism. The latter in particular has seen them persecuted for their strict refusal to bear arms and serve in the military and therefore have been constantly moving from one country to another in Western Europe and Central Europe for much of four of the last five hundred years.

Between 1874 and 1879 three groups totalling 1,265 persons migrated to North America. They settled in the Dakota Territory and in parts of Montana. Their communal lifestyle was looked upon with suspicion by those governments and once more seeing persecution on the horizon many of them moved north to Canada, to Alberta and Saskatchewan. 17 of the 18 colonies moved northward to Alberta, Saskatchewan and Manitoba at the end of WWI due to persecution stateside resulting in torture and death. Some returned to the Dakotas in the 1930s while in 1942 Alberta enacted the Communal Properties Act restricting two of the colonies to limited tracts of land to farm. This eventually was rescinded but some moved back to the United States into Montana and the Dakotas to re-establish their communities there. Other colonies chose to stay in Canada.

By the 1950s these communities had stabilized into a part of the prairie landscape, just like any other farming community. McCulloch has been affiliated with the Schmiedeleut Hutterites -one of three such societies in North America. In present day, this particular Hutterite colony is known as the Decker Colony in Manitoba? They own about 10,000 acres all around this colony and about 130 people live there comprising twenty-five families. Farming and manufacturing is their vocation. They produce some 5,000 turkeys and 8,000 hogs. Wheat and sunflower seed are two staples they produce for the world market.

McCulloch's company built the colony a water treatment plant in 1980. It seemed big at the time; it was a $100,000.00 deal. In 1981 McCulloch upgraded his Cessna 320 to a Turbo-boosted model; the Cessna 320 "Skynight". This aircraft was capable of carrying as many as six passengers, had a longer range and a higher service ceiling which resulted in a faster cruise speed. Since his *Water Doctor* was expanding so rapidly, particularly the franchised portion he began to look to the future and where he wanted to head with this enterprise. One of his options was to expand his scope to include Western Europe. The seed of this idea would take root eventually and begin to grow. But in the meantime...

Second Twin Comanche (C-GGJS) in Bermuda. Note wing-tip tanks. (1975)

Toronto to Rio, "Typical airport in Brazil in the 70s; hot, public (curious kids) on the runways which were usually dirt strips." (Dec.'75-Jan.'76)

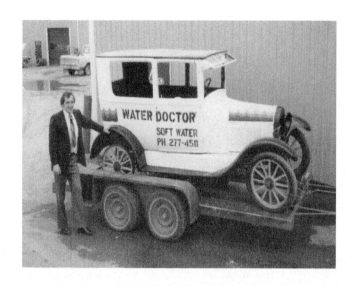

McCulloch stands beside one of his restored antiques . This and many others were often used in parades to promote Water Doctor

None of McCulloch's vehicles or airplanes escaped the brush of the sign-painter. McCulloch was/is a firm believer in saturation advertizing. Corvette lovers were shocked at this treatment of this classic '57 Corvette.

Cessna 320. This airplane served McCulloch through trips to South America and across the Atlantic via Iceland.

British Airways Concorde. Photo from Airliners. Copyright Harm Ruttan, Holland. The story below in Chapter 14

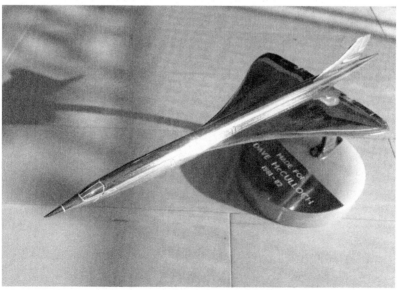

McCulloch's gold plated model of the Concorde dated 1981-1982

Chapter Fourteen

"All you need is money and airspeed!"

On December 30, 1981 McCulloch flew commercial airlines from Calgary to New York. In New York he was about to experience something new. Supersonic flight. He purchased a ticket to Paris on an Air France Concorde to that destination. He recalls the ticket price being somewhere in the $750.00 range in US funds. "There was talk of cancelling the Concorde in those days. The tree huggers were getting a lot of press and of course the politicians were ready to kiss whoever's ass that would get them the most votes."

There were several reasons for the trip. Linda was in London and McCulloch would get to fly on the world's fastest airliner to meet up with her. The two planned to meet in Paris, enjoy that city for a while (McCulloch is no snob but he likes good food) then from there fly to Egypt and see the pyramids and other points around the 'Med'.

First however, for McCulloch getting there was more than half the fun. "Travel on the Concorde was a high class operation. They didn't know I was a poor country boy. I was personally escorted to my seat and addressed as Mr. McCulloch, Sir."

The Concorde had arrived from Rio de Janeiro via Mexico "The champagne was flowing." Having imbibed-an infrequent pastime for him these days-he bullshitted a few of the passengers into thinking that he was an undercover, backup pilot on the jet. It didn't hurt his reputation any either when the Stewardess came and said, "Mr. McCulloch the pilots would be pleased if you would go to the cockpit." McCulloch never let on that he had mentioned to one of the 'Stews' earlier that he was a pilot and would like to visit the flight deck. You could do things like that before 9/11.

McCulloch stepped into the cockpit, the small narrow space lit by the glow of the instruments on the panel. There was no window in front of the pilots. There wasn't much need of a window anyway. In those days there were only two other aircraft flying at those altitudes. The Lockheed U-2 and the SR-71 Blackbird employed to spy on the Soviet Union and its allies; and even they were strictly confined to specific air spaces and regions.

The Concorde's cockpit was cramped but standard for the day. Duel instruments for captain and First Officer with instrument panels in front of them and overhead within easy reach. The Flight Engineer's instrument panel was on the right side behind the First officer. From there the FE managed the fuel and the four twin spool Rolls-Royce/Snecma Olympus 593 Turbojet engines originally designed for the Avro Vulcan Bomber. The long, sleek shielding nose cowl was in place to enable flight at Mach 2. On this flight, Mach 2.1 to be precise. At this speed without the stainless steel shield speed the window would have become red-hot then molten from the friction of the air molecules blasting past it. As it was even the exposed side windows were hot from a speed of 1,400 miles per hour-even through the thin air at Flight Level 660; or 66,000 feet. "The sky is a deep, almost purple colour and you can see the Earth's curvature." It was a happy moment for McCulloch. "This is really proof that all you need is money and airspeed!"

McCulloch spent part of the trip in the cockpit sitting in the small jump seat on the left side behind the captain jammed in between the circuit breaker panel banks and the back of the Flight engineer's chair.

The front seats are always better. "When I came back from the cockpit I had the SWAGGER." He had rock-star juice going. "If Linda had not been waiting in Paris this book would have needed a different chapter."

Perception is everything.

McCulloch and Linda spent two days in Paris, sightseeing and enjoying the cuisine before taking a commercial airliner to Cairo to see the pyramids. Like Brazil, Egypt was a pay as you go proposition. In those days you could actually go deep into the chambers as long as the American dollars held up. Grease this palm and that. The more you greased the deeper into the monolith you got. In this case all the way into the Pharos's chamber. Heavier with historical knowledge and lighter in US cash they departed Egypt. McCulloch noted one thing, however; "Those Pharaohs, they lived like our politicians do today."

They flew to Athens to see the Acropolis by Moonlight. It was in a deplorable condition in the early 1980s, however. Acid rain had been taking its toll since the industrial revolution began. "But those Greeks had their act together, centuries ago."

Back to London for McCulloch and Linda. They visited the Tower of London. "I checked out the crown jewels. Now that's a cache. Somewhere I heard the saying that ' It's good to be the King'."

One day while window shopping at one of the British Monarchy's jewellery outlets, Garrard's, McCulloch spotted a gold model of a Concorde on an Onyx base. He had to go in. "I foolishly asked how much and they said it was a private issue made for the heads of state, presidents and major airlines. I told him that mine must have been misplaced." A store official spotted him and asked McCulloch if he was from America. When he found out he was a Canadian he informed Dave that his daughter lived in Toronto. McCulloch informed the Garrad representative about his Concorde trip and his other flying adventures. He was impressed but informed McCulloch that the mold used to make the model had probably been destroyed but that he could probably make one for the recent Concorde passenger. "I explained that it would probably be too expensive." They exchanged cards and said their goodbyes. The trip over McCulloch and Linda returned to Canada.

There was a postscript to this trip. Eight weeks after their return a box arrived from Garrards in London. Inside was a gold model of the Concorde. A gold plate on its onyx base was inscribed Made for Dave McCulloch – 1981/1982. "It was beautiful." There was a bill inside for £2,200.00 or about $4,000.00 Canadian.

"I gulped, sent a check. Living rich is expensive when you are poor."

Chapter Fifteen

The best defense is an offence. Say, "Dish it up baby and don't be shy with the jalapenos."

In the early 1980s in Calgary, McCulloch is trying to expand his *Water Doctor* by increasing the number of stores he owns. He had a few stores, in western Canada and one in Montana.

Money is tight, everything financed; the house, the trucks, with a Royal Bank line of credit of only $60,000. "I used that to borrow another $50,000 for two weeks from a loan shark. It cost me $15,000 'vig' for those two weeks. I was trying to expand and needed inventory."

This was the time of runaway inflation in Canada. The Bank of Canada had increased its rate to high percentage points and the Canadian banks were cashing in on this. Housing quickly depressed with interest rates on mortgages in Calgary (and elsewhere) reaching as high as 21%. The banks were calling in loans; businesses were going under. "The banks were taking no prisoners, if your name came up they chopped your credit line. I was doing well, the cash flow was strong but without the credit line I would be finished."

McCulloch - who has had a problem with bank managers' thinking since the day he wanted to buy a car and the manager in Nova Scotia advised Dave's mother not to co-sign for him - decided to confront the Royal Bank of Canada who then controlled his line of credit. He went to his lawyer and explained his problem - one the lawyer had heard all too often in those troubled times. "What do you want me to do?" He asked. "I want to sue the Royal Bank!" McCulloch replied. "I want you to set it up." The lawyer probably thought McCulloch was crazy. He passed McCulloch pages with his letter head on them saying. "You write the letter. But I guarantee you that the bank will kick your ass."

"I wrote the letter and sent it registered mail to my bank and hand delivered a copy."

A couple of days later the phone rang, "Mister McCulloch it's the Royal Bank calling. I am Mister *Smith* (name changed). Please come on in to see me. I have been assigned your company account."

McCulloch went in. "I walked out with a $160,000.00 credit line and never looked back."

In a short time McCulloch had over 40 *Water Doctor* outlets. "I regularly flew from store to store teaching sales and advising them on how to handle bankers." Several of his dealers had airplanes also.

McCulloch put thousands of hours on his airplanes over the next few years. What had once been an adventure, travelling from one town or city to the next over the vastness of the Prairie Provinces, Montana and the Dakotas was now almost routine. His airplane was a business tool which he used to great advantage. It impressed his clients and his franchisees as well. He could be on site for a meeting in a matter of hours; often in small towns where the commercial jets could not go. This avoided flying commercially to a big city then renting a car to go the rest of the way to whatever small community he needed to visit. He could offer a client the convenience of a quick trip to his destination as a favour or fly in his experienced installers if the need arose. It was great for customer relations; and it translated into more sales.

One glitch popped up. "I was unable to renew my US work visa and had to move out of there and put my Montana operation up for sale." It was during this time that McCulloch relocated his head office to Winnipeg. *Water Doctor* continued to grow in size. It was the largest water dealer out of the 700 dealerships. Franchising was steadily becoming a key part of the business. He tried something new for the time-something that is a billion dollar business these days. "I tried to introduce bottled water, but it was a slow mover in the early eighties." Expand and grow. That was the procedure during the next three years. Meanwhile McCulloch's aviation ambitions had been regulated to business trips; to places he had been many times before. There was no challenge. He had upgraded his Turbo Charged 1968 Cessna 320. He had it modified to include long range fuel tanks and incorporated an oxygen system for high altitude work up to 29,000 feet to better take advantage of the turbo-boosted 280-hp engines. It had longer legs, a range of 845 miles and with the more powerful engines could cruise at 256 mph with a top speed of 275 mph. But without an Instrument Flight Rating (IFR) he could not take advantage of the increased speed and fuel economy available at altitudes over 12,500 feet. Nor could he fly in weather conditions that precluded visual contact with the ground. In August of 1983, McCulloch married his girlfriend of many years, Linda Stanmore. They were married in Las Vegas, Nevada. There was no honeymoon. "To me life is a MONEYMOON. It cost $39.00 bucks to get married and $39million to stay married for the next twenty-five years."

Chapter Sixteen

In May of 1984 McCulloch took instruction and ground school in order to get his Instrument Flight Rules (IFR) certificate and be rated as a multi-engine IFR pilot. "I got my IFR endorsement in Great Falls, Montana. It was a no brainer event because I had over 4,000 hours of pilot-in-command time and many of those were with other IFR pilots." However he still had to jump through the hoops. "I went through the full ground school, wrote the exams, and did the flight test procedure." By the end of June - his IFR endorsement in his back pocket - he had completed plans for a trip to Western Europe utilizing his Cessna 320. It was to be a voyage of business discovery.

McCulloch had been mulling the idea around in his head that it might be possible to expand his *Water Doctor* franchise overseas. This trip had been in the back of his mind for some time and he had been planning for it as a result. The IFR endorsement was part of that plan. There is no doubt that an expanded business in Western Europe was closely tied to McCulloch's sense of adventure and the use of his airplane to accomplish the enterprise. Certainly the airplane would give him a freedom of movement in Europe that was more attractive-not to mention faster-than regional airline travel or short trips on trains. Once again he was cognisant of the possibility that the mention of him flying his own plane across the Northern Atlantic to meet with European businessmen would give him a certain stature in their business community.

At any rate, McCulloch would accomplish two objectives on this trip. One was to make contact with European business interests and forge friendships that could be advantageous to him in the future and secondly feed his lust for air adventures; realizing a dream of his that had been formulating for years; flying his own plane across the Atlantic.

Even in the 1980s flying a light, twin-engined aircraft across the Atlantic was considered hazardous. And there were rules governing this type of general aviation flying. It wasn't like the days of Alcock and Brown or Charles Lindbergh where the pilots just planned the trips on their own, waved goodbye and were off into the serious blue with nothing but guts, luck, a wonky engine and their piloting skills contributing to their making it across the Atlantic Ocean.

Transport Canada's Air Regulations demanded that pilots flying the Atlantic in light aircraft have a life raft onboard the airplane. McCulloch purchased one. By this time he had the interest of another Canadian private pilot, Rick Boisselle who was enthusiastic about the idea of being McCulloch's co-pilot on the former's plan to fly across the Northern Atlantic. "He either thought or always said he would fly anywhere with me." It was hard for McCulloch to turn down that kind of confidence in him.

Boisselle was working on his private license and welcomed the opportunity to work with another pilot who would be using his IFR skills during the trip. They forged a lifelong friendship as a result.

The low-time pilot had a pool behind his house. The pair decided to inflate the life raft and test it out in the pool. It quickly became apparent that this was a dangerous business. "We nearly drowned in Rick's pool testing our life raft, and decided it was too dangerous to use. But regulations called for one on-board the aircraft." It was stowed aboard without much enthusiasm for its usefulness in an emergency, particularly in the North Atlantic waters that were in the near freezing range even in the month of June. Life expectancy was about five minutes without survival suits which were not available back then. That was hardly enough time to even drown. If one could climb into the life raft they would be in bad shape as they were, soaked in cold seawater. Back in the day, life jackets were required. A high frequency radio was required as well. McCulloch had a long antenna fixed from behind the cabin running back to the tip of the vertical stabilizer. His safety measures in place on June 28th they lifted off from Calgary, Alberta en-route to Churchill, Manitoba. From there they would cross over Hudson Bay to Frobisher Bay (now Iqaluit) and then over the Davis Strait to Sondrestrom air force base in Greenland. That first leg alone was 2,500 miles and they were just getting out of Canada. "First trip across the 'pond' in a private plane is a bit scary; not like today with GPS." McCulloch remembers. Compasses are practically useless that far north when the magnetic north pole is less than 1,500 miles off your left wing. The north pointing needle wants to bury itself in the face of the compass card. McCulloch had to rely on his ADF and the two VORs on his panel.

Sondrestrom was originally built in 1941 by the United States Army Air Force and was code named by the Allies during World War Two as Bluie West-8. It remained in service during the cold war but now the United States keeps only a small contingent of the Air National Guard there. It was turned over to the Danish Government and is now known as Kangerlussuaq Airport. It is situated about 80 miles inland from the Davis Strait at the end of Kangerlussuaq Fjord. At 60 miles above the Arctic Circle, Sondrestrom had earned a reputation of being a dangerous airport at which to land due to the height of sides of the Fjord leading up to the end of its runway. The mountains there reach as high as 2,200 feet and are at 650 feet just two miles from the west end of the runway. On a missed approach or a take-off to the east the terrain quickly rises with a 700 foot mountain five miles straight out but within 2,000 feet on either side of an easterly climb out. The terrain has reached 1,200 feet on the left and 700 feet on the right side. Add weather, such as fog or icing conditions that might prevail and it makes for a treacherous approach under IFR conditions or Instrument Meteorological Conditions (IMC); either of which could kill you.

McCulloch had icing; heavy icing. It appeared suddenly as he got to the lower altitudes and moisture laden air filled with super-cooled water droplets turned to ice adhering to the surface only when it hit his wings. It was building up on the leading edges of the Cessna 320. He had de-icing boots on his props but not on the leading edges of his wings or his horizontal stabilizer. It was not only destroying the lift over the wings but adding weight to the aircraft. Turbulence from the irregular ice on the outer leading edges would eventually decrease the effectiveness of his ailerons making lateral control (banking, turning) sloppy. You don't want sloppy when the Fjord walls are a short distance off to your left or right.

McCulloch asked the USAF controller at Sondrestrom for a precision approach. He didn't want to risk a regular approach because if he missed that he might not be able to climb high enough to clear the mountains to the east with the load of ice he was carrying. But there was another reason. A few miles to the east was the beginning of Greenland's ice cap. "It should be called Whiteland," McCulloch observed, "because you are faced with just one huge mass of white landscape in front of you. A problem arises because there is no frame of reference for the eye."

More than one airplane has landed accidentally-and usually with tragic results-on the icecap not realizing that they were that close to the surface of the glacier. It rises like a dome curving up from 700 feet on the west side to central Greenland at as much as 10,000 feet or two miles then drops back down on that same curve. Without normal visual references a pilot can be gently increasing altitude while the airplane is actually flying toward the face of the icecap. The landmass actually looks flat in front of you but is actually climbing steadily and gradually to its central spine. The USAF had good radar at Sondrestrom so a precision approach was available. McCulloch kept an eye on his airspeed, keeping it a bit higher on his approach to compensate for the ice on his wings decreasing his lift. The last thing he wanted to do was splash into the Fjord. "A missed approach was not an option."

They climbed out of Sondrestrom into bright sunny skies on their leg of 850 miles to Reykjavik, Iceland. About half that distance (430 miles) was over the glacier. The only speck on that great white tableau was the tiny American outpost of Sobstory. It was a hold-over from the old DEW Line network. The US military had a manned ice-camp there about halfway across the glacier. McCulloch talked to them briefly to establish a bearing but after that it was 'dead-reckoning' from there to Reykjavik for the next 600 miles. They climbed and travelled over the Greenland's icecap at 11,500 feet. That gave them a margin of over 2,000 feet of airspace between the belly of the twin-engined Cessna and the ice field below. The trip over water was uneventful, not a hiccup out of the engines. But they were well out over the North Atlantic and close to Iceland before they picked up any beacons. The ADF and the VORs began to twitch. Done with dead reckoning they could now take a bearing on Reykjavik.

"We are in heaven now!" Boisselle informed McCulloch. McCulloch asked him why. "Because all of the girls are blond." He quipped. Whether this was true or not, the pair spent a couple of nights partying there despite the high cost of food, and lodging before leaving once again to cross more open water; this time to Scotland. They landed in Prestwick, "The land of high landing fees and expensive gas." McCulloch recalls. "Even worse there in present day." After a brief stay in the United Kingdom, McCulloch flew over to Paris. He found out that flying as a private pilot engendered more regulatory oversight by the authority of each country. "It wasn't as free-wheeling as it is here in North America. Flight planning was much more strict and invasive in Western Europe-you had to flight plan for everything."

Quite by chance he bumped into a pilot flying a Mooney aircraft; a business acquaintance and friend, Charles Woolacott from Toronto. His business progress in Paris was proving to be fruitless. McCulloch was running up against regulations and limiting factors imposed by Lindsay, the manufacturer of the water treatment product that Water Doctor sold. He found he was restricted to being a North American dealer only. His hopes were dashed. Knowledge filed away for another time in the future. He decided to make the most of the trip however.

McCulloch and Boisselle flew south to Barcelona, Spain. To take a break from the flying McCulloch rented a car in Barcelona and the pair enjoyed the moderate temperatures of the eastern coast of Spain and drove northwards along the western coast of the Mediterranean to the south of France, making their way to Marseille and then southwestward to St. Tropez. He and Boisselle went to the beach. They spent a couple of days there sunning themselves on the beach enjoying the sun, sand and velvety azure waters of the Med. They enjoyed the scenery tremendously. "We discovered that the girls there were so poor they did not even have bathing suits." Ah life.

It had been a great vacation but as far as a successful business trip, it had been a bust. National and corporate laws were working against McCulloch no matter what approach he tried. He gave up-for then at least-and turned back toward the United kingdom and the long trip across the Atlantic; this time against the prevailing westerly winds.

On one of their refuelling stops the pilots landed in Stornaway, Scotland; their last landfall before the leg to Iceland. They met three pilots from Long Island, New York who had been weathered in there for a week. They were members of the New York Tall Tales Society.

"After a night of loud talk and flying expertise, we decided we would leave in the AM come hell or high water."

The three New York pilots figured their adventures flying across the North Atlantic would put them in good standing with the Society. They invited McCulloch to join the Society. His exploits to date would have made his acceptance a no-brainer.

As promised the two planes launched the next morning. "They followed us in the single engine Comanche, and made nervous calls to us every few moments." McCulloch recalls. Understandable flying the "wrong way" (against the prevailing westerly winds) across the North Atlantic with only one engine hammering away up front.

McCulloch and Boisselle clawed their way westward, retracing the course they had travelled ten days earlier. They eventually parted with the New York Comanche which headed south, down the eastern seaboard to the United States and home.

Once back home, McCulloch took some time to re-group. What had he gained from the trip to Europe? Not what one would expect.

"The biggest lesson I learned over there was that I needed to make a lot of money and go back and live on the French Riveria."

He was determined to expand his business, but once again he was up against restrictions and the limitations imposed on him by Lindsay's head offices. Like Paymaster they were determined to keep him in his place and not let him threaten their perceived standing in the business community. His *Water Doctor* franchise was getting big and they were afraid that he would become their only-or the very least-their largest outlet; that he would be able to dictate to them rather than the other way around.

The problem remained in the back of his mind.

Rick Boiselle (in raft) and McCulloch (behind) practice inflating the emergency raft in Rick's pool preparing for their flight across the Atlantic.

*McCulloch's black Cessna 320, Kangerlussuag airport Greenland (1984)
enroute to Europe via Iceland.*

*McCulloch (left), Rick Boiselle (right) 2 Tall Tales pilots-unidentified-from
New York in Stornaway, Scotland*

Chapter Seventeen

The Bungle in the Jungle

Once again, McCulloch's restlessness got the better of him. On December 29, 1984 he was wheels up in his Cessna Turbo 320 for South America. Linda went with him and his friend-and co-pilot-Doug Tomalin and his wife. This time he wanted to travel the length of the Amazon River from east to west and then land at the world's highest airport in La Paz, Bolivia.

They left from Winnipeg and hop-scotched to Florida. Once more over the Caribbean to the Grand Turk Islands, Puerto Rico to land at Val De Cans airport in Belem, Brazil. He was ready this time with "insurance papers" for the airplane to avoid the long delays he and Linda endured the last time he went through there on his way to Rio.

Belem is at the mouth of the mighty Amazon. They refueled there, spent the night then launched westward. McCulloch pointed the Cessna's nose inland and up the Amazon.

The Amazon (or Rio Amazonas as it's known in Brazil) was named after the Greek legend by Spanish conquistador Francisco Orellana. He claimed to have been attacked by a tribe of female and child warriors.

The Amazon's source is generally accepted as a waterfall near Arequipa in Peru called the Apacheta Cliff. 11,023 tributaries feed the Amazon River. It dumps some 18,000,000 cubic meters of water into the Atlantic Ocean every minute during the rainy season. Pilots can see the muddy evidence of the Amazon 100 miles out into the Atlantic Ocean.

"Once we were away from the coast I flew just above the trees and the Amazon. It was huge and beautiful. In some places it was as much as a mile and a half wide." McCulloch was headed for Manaus, 800 miles up the river.

The muddy brown waters slid by beneath them. Occasionally they passed over working boats and shallow-bottomed ferries. These were more in evidence downriver closer to the Amazon Delta and between Belem and Manaus at the juncture of the Amazon and the Rio Negro.

Upriver one sees more of the long thin boats with the engine on the stern with the long shaft terminating in a propeller. Others use canoes and small punts on the river. There is no shortage of boat types on the Amazon. It is a superhighway of boats, particularly around the ports and big cities and towns.

Many Brazilians consider the juncture of the dark Rio Negro and the muddy Amazon as the true beginning of the Amazon River. It is their river so who should argue.

"As you approach Manaus at the juncture of the two rivers you can see the contrast between the two. The Negro is dark, almost black while the Amazon is brown. Where they meet and flow eastward the two remain delineated for miles downstream before finally mingling into the muddy entity known as the Amazon."

McCulloch and company spent several days in Manaus. Manaus began as an European colonization in 1669 but it wasn't until the late 1800s that it was discovered that the area was the source of one of the world's most valuable commodities, the rubber tree. It became a British rubber manufacturing town-despite its Portuguese history-in its heyday toward the end of the 19th Century. They built huge opera houses and play houses in Manaus to provide entertainment for themselves. The city was a center of opulence for some years until the rubber tree plant seeds were smuggled out of the area and the land barons lost their rubber monopoly years later. The thriving city was readily accessible from downriver by the flat-bottomed riverboats.

McCulloch decided to take a swim in the river known to be inhabited by the infamous piranha fish. "My voice didn't get higher so I guess I escaped the worst that could happen." McCulloch has what can best be described as an impish smile.

Piranhas do bite, but the fishermen in that area consider them as more of a nuisance when they are fishing for other species because they will attack a sport fish that is already on a hook and damage the catch. They are less numerous than depicted in the movies and are actually timid and do not normally cluster in schools. Some have been found in ponds as far north as New York City and even in Lake Winnebago in Wisconsin.

They enjoyed the city for several days before they left southwestward for Bolivia. But they required fuel stops over such a long distance. McCulloch chose Rio Branco, a small city in the southwest of Brazil, over seven hundred miles from Manaus.

As airports go, the Rio Branco International Airport was pushing the limits of what anyone would expect of an airport. It was northwest of the city some 12 miles away but it did have a mile long runway running roughly east to west. McCulloch set up for the landing and while he was rolling out both he and his three passengers could see a truckload of soldiers off the left wing of the airplane. They circled the airplane when it came to a stop. Their guns were drawn and they were screaming in Portuguese. McCulloch warned his passengers to move slowly in case they started shooting. Suddenly a large Honda motorcycle arrived with what appeared to be the commander. He was better dressed than the others and was wearing an excessive amount of jewellery.

This officer spoke English. He said 'welcome gringos'. He told McCulloch that the tower would lower a bucket and that he should put some money in it. He also told them to be prepared to leave first thing in the morning. McCulloch dropped twenty US dollars in the bucket and it was lifted back up to the second story tower. A guy in the tower gave us a thumbs up.

McCulloch and his passengers secured a taxi and went into town where they found a hotel in which they could stay overnight. Early the next morning they returned to the airport and prepared for the flight to La Paz. Dave filed a flight plan which he knew full well would go nowhere but he carried it on the airplane with a rubber stamped approval to show on the next landing that he had filed to La Paz.

It was 454 air miles from Rio Branco, Brazil to La Paz, Bolivia. McCulloch, for one, was happy to see the end of Rio Branco. Being met by a truck full of soldiers brandishing rifles with a primary intent of extorting money from them did little to foster his good will toward the country. More jungle lay ahead of them but they were getting closer to the grandiose, snow-capped spine of South America, the Andes Mountains.

El Alto International Airport is on a plain east of the city of La Paz. It has the distinction of being the highest airport on the planet at 13,400 feet (4,087 meters). The peaks of Huayna Potosi Mountains, their top 2,000 feet covered in one hundred feet deep snow, are to the northeast of La Paz. They rise up in a barrier to 19,685 feet (6,003 meters) and were directly on line with McCulloch's course to La Paz.

McCulloch's Cessna 320 with its turbo-boosted engines could manage, at best, 21,000 feet. McCulloch was flight planned for

20,000 feet. There was no radar in the area and conditions were iffy at best. He had about a 400 foot cushion between his plane and the Huaya Potosi peaks. Everyone on board was on oxygen otherwise they would have blacked out from hypoxia and been rendered unconscious.

To make matters worse, warm, moist air pushing in from the Pacific 220 miles to the west flows inland and rises up the mountain slopes, condenses, often blanketing the mountains in cloud.

To illustrate the danger, one should consider that on January 1, 1985-the evening before McCulloch's approach to La Paz-Flight 980 an Eastern Airlines 727 crashed into these same mountain ranges - the Cordillera Oriental Mountains - to the southeast of La Paz impacting Mount Illimani (20,646 feet). All 19 passengers and 10 crew aboard the 727 were killed. The area was so inaccessible it wasn't until 21 years later in 2006 that the wreck was accidentally located by mountain climbers at an altitude of 19,600 feet (6000 meters). The bodies have yet to be recovered and the 'black boxes' have eluded investigators as well.

McCulloch and crew were blissfully unaware of the accident however until after they landed,. Investigators were already converging on the field and the NTSB was on their way from the United States.

McCulloch sweated the approach over the mountains then pointed the nose down to lose a mile and a half of altitude in order to land in El Alto because La Pas is located in a depression almost completely surrounded by the Andes Mountains. McCulloch was cleared for runway 10, a descent to 18,000 ft over the VOR, a procedure turn at 15,500 ft heading 097 then descent to the MDA (minimum descent altitude) of 13,420 ft then land on the 13,112 ft runway. An oxygen mask is required to be worn by the pilots of an unpressurized airplane, all the way to the ground. This approach is at heights beyond the ability of most planes to fly. It is a blow-your-mind approach.

While taxiing to the parking area, McCulloch noticed US Air Force aircraft parked on the field. He didn't think much of that at the time but would learn later that they had recently arrived as part of the search for Eastern Air Lines Flight 980. It was then he learned of the crash the night before on January 1st. After they got parked they dug their luggage out of the airplane and proceeded to walk the few hundred feet across the tarmac to the arrivals area. "We staggered to the terminal, walking was not easy." They were two and a half miles above sea-level and the air is much thinner up there.

It's no secret that people who live in the Andes Mountains are used to the thin air but most of the world's population are not. The hotels cater to this problem by providing oxygen and a mask for each bed in their rooms. Part of the reason is to make their guests more comfortable while sleeping. Any other exertion engaged in by lowlanders is a consideration as well. "You have to remove the mask to kiss though."

LaPaz in the early 1980s was suffering from rampant inflation. It literally took bricks of Pesos-as much as one million to purchase one dollar in US funds. "There was terrible poverty and run-away inflation. You could get stacks of Pecos Bolivanos tied in bunches of bills brick size on the street by vendors with their little tables stacked high with the nearly worthless currency. "Don't save money, has always been my battle cry. Don't trust your money to the Central Bank. If you trust central banks then dream on."

In a reversal of roles the poor were relegated to the foot hills around Le Paz on the north, east and south of the city while the wealthier population lived on in the depression of a large canyon bordered by the flat altiplano to the west. LaPaz was originally named *Nuestra Señora de La Paz (Our Lady of Peace)* and was founded by the Spanish Conquistadors in 1548. "The catholic churches certainly served themselves in South America. I don't know about the people." McCulloch and the others were amazed at the gold statues in the churches. "There was lots of real gold in the altars of these churches, even in the poor areas." He could only imagine the hard work these people had endured to ensure the churches altars were rich in gold while their own lives were one of eking out a meager living from a harsh land.

The climate in La Paz is normally dry except for the winter months when the rains come. The temperatures are cool, and frequently are in the 10 to 12 degree Celsius (50-54 F) range though there are periods when it gets up into the 30s.

Thirty miles to the North West are the shores of the famous Lake Titicaca, the highest navigable freshwater lake in the world. The lake is shared by Bolivia and Peru to the northwest. A visit there seemed to be in the cards. They arranged for a forty mile drive there then took a boat tour across the lake.

In 1970 Thor Heyerdahl had constructed his second reed boat (Ra II) from the totora reeds that grow in Peru and Bolivia (abundantly so on Lake Titicaca) and that he hoped to launch in Morocco and sail to Eastern South America. His aim was to prove that the early Egyptians had made contact with South American people long before the days of Columbus and the Spanish Conquistadors. This resulted in what Heyerdahl called the "Ra Expedition" named after the Egyptian Sun God Ra.

Heyerdahl had returned on occasion to the area in the 1980s. He was fascinated by the use of reed boats by the people of Lake Titicaca. They also took advantage of the floating reed's bouancy and used it to build small floating islands on which they live. `When we were at the lake we met some of the Limachi family of Lake Titicaca who were the builders of Ra II. Heyerdahl had taken them to Europe with him and they had pictures of the Ra II and the Tigris.

It is too bad that McCulloch and Heyerdhal had never met. In some respects both McCulloch and Heyerdahl were restless spirits who shared a desire to explore; to seek out new ideas and different ways of thinking. Once again - but still ahead of its time - McCulloch was looking into bottled water to sell. He eyed the snow-capped Andes Mountains to the east of Titicaca and La Paz and wondered about the possibility of obtaining water from these to sell; promoted as fresh mountain waters from the peaks of the Andes Mountains. Pay for water? Absurd. Who would even think of such a thing? You can get it out of the tap for free, why buy it? It is now a $3.5 billion dollar annual industry.

All too soon it was time to leave La Paz and head northeast back to Brazil and the trip home. Now fully aware of Eastern Air Line 980's crash into the mountains McCulloch picked his way over the peaks of the Andes and set course for Manaus, by-passing Rio Branco for the friendlier local of Manaus. It was a leg of 1,100 miles. They refuelled and over-nighted there and headed for their next stop which was in Venezuela.

The place was called Maturin. A half year after the incident the Winnipeg Free Press called it the *Bungle in the Jungle*. McCulloch had flight planned out of Manaus, Brazil for Caracas, Venezuela; a distance of 1,040 miles. But a couple of hours into the flight it soon became clear that they were getting a strong northwest headwind. Fighting it would erode the narrow margin of fuel (150 miles worth) they had in reserve to get to Caracas. Three quarters of the way to Caracas McCulloch decided to divert to an alternate off his right wing about 40 miles from the coast and south of the Island of Trinidad. The best bet for an alternate seemed to be Maturin. Maturin was about 920 miles from Manaus but they were diverting so the actual distance was much further. But they did have the wind quartering from the left rear of the aircraft which increased their speed while saving fuel.

McCulloch is bitter about what happened next. "Maturin is one of those mangy little equatorial towns. Back then you got used to being delayed as much as four hours in South American countries, being hassled over flight plans and permits…but we weren't ready for Maturin." They landed at Jose Tadeo Monagas International Airport. The International designation was a loose association to what one would expect from an International airport. It was noon and they were tired, hungry and hot. They were close to the Equator, just nine degrees north of it.

A truck loaded with soldiers was racing up to the plane. "When a truckload of federal military met us at the plane there was no doubt that something unpleasant was going to happen." Perhaps a repeat of their fuel stop in Rio Branco, Brazil?

Sadly no; this was worse. It was the start of an era; the beginning of the drug wars in South America. Combine the greed for drug money with an antipathy to human life and the lack of respect for same and you have a receipe for mayhem and mass murder. It was beginning in earnest in the mid 1980s and still rages today.

These were the thoughts running through the heads of the four Canadians. "It was a full scale search and interrogation." There was much yelling and seeming hysteria. An officer in combat fatigues had a pistol. His troops dressed in what appeared to be army surplus clothing were carrying automatic weapons. They waved the guns around. "Because we had been in Bolivia, we were suspected of carrying drugs." Two hours later they were finished. In perfect English the officer said, "You are free to go. Welcome to Venezuela!"

There were sighs of relief. They reloaded their luggage and McCulloch was preparing to go and file a flight plan to Puerto Rico. They were also waiting to be refuelled. This was not to be the case, however, because just then the local police arrived in several old cars. They were brandishing guns and yelling Polizia. "They looked more like Hell's Angels, like the Mexican bandits in the movie Treasure of the Sierra Madre than the Polizia but they claimed to be the law in Maturin."

This time the four Canadians were dragged out of the plane and held at gunpoint. "We search too!" the 'leader' yelled. "Compared to these guys the federal police were refined gentlemen."

The Policia took their wallets, purses and documents and started pulling the airplane apart. "Everything came out.. They removed panels including some that were not supposed to be removed. They took the fire extinguisher and removed the floor rugs. They piled everything on the runway. They opened Linda and Mary's bags and began prancing around holding up brassieres and lingerie. "If you tried to speak they stuck a gun in your neck." Things were heating up. "They kept calling us Gringo so I called them Spicks. The leader stuck a pistol against my jugular. My biggest fear was that they would plant drugs on us so they would have some excuse to hold us or extort money." They started screaming when they found the stash of $1,000.00 in American one dollar bills McCulloch had stashed in packets under the carpets to pay the bribes so frequently required in South America to get the paperwork done or just to get lodging or food. "We were in a precarious position. The ramp was empty of any other aircraft and there was no one around to see what was going on."

It was a very tense situation. And just when they thought it could not get any worse, it did. One of the banditos - as McCulloch called them - ran up to his superior holding a small brown paper bag with white powder in it. "I said 'shit, we have bought the farm, they have planted cocaine in the plane." That was the plant that McCulloch had feared - indeed expected - on more than one occasion.

The leader poked a wet finger in the bag and tasted the powder. He screwed up his face and demanded of McCulloch, what it was.

McCulloch looked closely at the bag and saw that it was from their survival kit. It had the words *Baking Soda* written on it. The four scrambled around looking for the Spanish/English translation book and found the translation *Bicarbonato de Sodio.* That crises was averted.

The Polizia took Linda and Mary to town to some rundown place that had a Police sign on it. Eventually Doug and McCulloch were also loaded into cars and taken in to town along with all of the stuff the local law had dragged out onto the runway.

"They sat us on a bench and we could see all of our stuff piled on the floor in another room. They were still picking through it. Then they gave it back to us loaded us into a car and took us back to the airport and saying Adios! they left us there."

The law required 21 copies of the customs declaration and they gave McCulloch only one. "For some reason they didn't steal all of the American money. They seemed leery of doing that, perhaps fearing recriminations. The whole exercise was one of intimidation, probably to frighten them enough so they could steal from the four. And they did. The 'Polizia' stole their cameras, sunglasses, some clothing and other valuables and most of their money. But the group didn't care. They loaded their stuff in the plane. It had been a long day and it didn't look like they were going to get airborne soon. The sun would be setting. He still needed a flight plan and fuel.

McCulloch used some of the remaining American money to take a taxi into town and copy off another 20 copies of the customs declaration. When he returned they climbed into the plane and locked the doors.

A female controller drove out to their plane in a pick-up truck and handed McCulloch his take-off clearance. Once airborne he was to contact Caracas Control.

Doug said to him, "Shall we do a run-up?" Running the engines up to full RPM while holding the brakes on and looking for engine problems-low RPM on one of two magnetos on each engine, high engine temperature increases, low oil pressure, etc.- by watching the engine instruments is a standard procedure on any airplane, particularly reciprocating engines. Better to find these problems while you are on the ground than well away from an airport and no place to land.

McCulloch replied, "Hell no. If the airplane doesn't work, we are going anyway." He was afraid that the local "police" would find some other excuse to harass them. He wasn't afraid of ponying up more American dollars but for any excuse they could impound his airplane.

Without a flight plan McCulloch flew directly to San Juan, Puerto Rico in the rain at night. They arrived exhausted at 2 am the next morning. It was the end to a 20 hour day. They cleared customs in 30 minutes. No search. "It was great to be back in American territory." When they arrived at the hotel, McCulloch crawled into bed and slept for twenty-four hours. He was drained. "We spent another day licking our wounds."

After he got up from his 24 hour nap McCulloch went back to the airplane. He remembered that when they had arrived he had dumped out the contents of the bag of baking soda. Even though it had rained he discovered the pile still sitting next to his plane. He fired up the plane and taxied it to another parking space.

There was a fear that pilots had about travelling in Central and South America that still applies even today. First that drugs will be planted by authorities while a plane is parked and then later discovered by the police with the result being that the pilot and his passengers are then held as drug traffickers. Later huge sums of money are extorted from them or their families before they are released. Pockets of various police officials and politicians are then lined with the riches of others. The other problem is that the drug traffickers themselves will hide drugs aboard a small plane headed to North America and once there the client on the other end finds some way of opening access panels on these aircraft and taking the drugs.

The not-so-easy solution to this is to carefully check your airplane before you leave and look for drugs. But what happens if you find them before you leave? Do you walk back into the terminal, find a security agent and say, *look what I found in my airplane?* Absolutely not. *You* get arrested anyway or at least detained for hours, days or weeks for being a good little pilot. No your best bet is to find a garbage can and drop it in there. Wear gloves. You can then return happily home having dodged that bullet only to have some thug show up at your home demanding that you turn over the drugs you stole from him. You report this to the police then they arrest you until they clear up the mess. Great options, huh?

Guilt by association.

"Àhhh, that doesn`t happen."You say. Really.

McCulloch and company arrived back in Winnipeg in the evening. They were exhausted. It was -30 Celsius. He was met at the plane on the ramp and detained while Canadian Customs, the Canadian version of the Venezuelan authorities, tore the plane apart. The only act of kindness and common sense shown here was that Canada Customs took McCulloch, Linda, Doug and Mary inside where it was warm before they were strip searched. "I even had some guy making me bend over while he looked at my rectum."

There was no justification for this action other than they had been flying a plane in South America. *Guilt by association.* How ludicrous this appears. Not that it couldn't happen today-right? In fact it could given the hysteria that seems to govern federal border services in Canada and the United States.

Remember this; McCulloch and his passengers landed *first* in Puerto Rico and were checked out by US Customs agents (it took 30 minutes) so one has to wonder just how slow and boring a day it was for some Canadian Government customs stooge to make the decision to strip search passengers who had already passed the test of the one country on the planet with the biggest federal agency in the world on the hunt for illegal drugs, the United States Drug Enforcement Agency. Canada's actions in this case were better suited to the border town mentality of Maturin in Brazil than in Canada. *We Stand On Guard For Thee.*

But then Canada's performance in its protection of its citizens abroad is practically non-existent, even today.

One final note about the ludicrous nature of what can happen when you deal with big government and big business; in this case the latter. McCulloch tried to file an insurance claim for the loss of the cameras, fire extinguisher, monies and clothing stolen by the Maturin Policia. The insurance adjuster wanted a copy of the police report that McCulloch was supposed to have. Apparently he was supposed to have reported to the same police that stole the items in the first place that they had stolen the items. File this one under live and learn.

"It was almost worth the inexcusable and needless invasion of our personal privacy to see what we saw in South America and be punished for the trip." McCulloch was referring to the vastness of the trackless jungles back in the 1980s. They were awed by the length and breadth of the Amazon River, the history and the splendor of South American architecture of cities. They wondered at how richness and opulence could exist cheek-by-jowl with extreme poverty; how some tribes in the jungles could still live as they had since the Stone Age.

"Angel Falls was incredible. Even viewed from the air." McCulloch flew low over this natural wonder whose overall height is twenty times higher than that of Niagara Falls. He did a low pass across the face of the falls. "At one point its source was nearly 2,000 feet above us."

Located on the Churun River in the Guiana Highlands of southeastern Venezuela it drops 2,640 feet (807 meters) to the jungle floor below from Auyan-Tepui (Devil's Mountain) Plateau. Other than the tribal peoples living near that location even the Venezuelans themselves were unaware of it until the 1930s. The jungle surrounding this plateau is so dense it is hard to navigate through and the top of the falls is usually wreathed in cloud from condensation. It wasn't until the advent of the airplane that it could be viewed at all.

American bush pilot James (Jimmie) Angel stumbled across this natural wonder-now known to be the highest falls in the world-while searching for ore beds on November 16, 1933. Four years later, on 9 October 1937, Jimmie Angel tried to land his Ryan Flamingo monoplane *El Río Caroní;* on the plateau. The Ryan Aeronautical Company was the same company in the United States that built Charles Lindbergh's "Spirit of Saint Louis".

Angel's plane was damaged when the wheels sank into a bog. Angel, his wife Marie and two other companions had no choice but to get down the mountain on foot and back to civilization. It took them eleven days. Once the press got hold of this adventure story the falls became known as Angel Falls in Jimmie Angel's honor. His plane remained on the plateau of Auyan-tepui for 33 years until the Venezuelan Air Force lifted it from atop the falls in 1970. It was restored to display condition and is now exhibited at Ciudad, Bolivar's airport. Bolivar State, Venezuela.

Several months later, the /Winnipeg Free Press did a story about McCulloch and company`s adventures in South America. The reporter asked McCulloch if he was going to give up flying after that.

"I said no...I am going all the way around the world next year, if I can find a co-pilot crazy enough to go with me."

And you know what, that is exactly what he did.

The Rio Negros joins the Amazon, delineated for miles down the Amazon.

*Manaus, Brazil Dec.1984. Setting up for a landing at Aeroporto
Internacional de Manaus.*

The Andes Mountains were between McCulloch's Cessna 320 and La Paz, Peru. La Paz is at 17,500 feet. The Andes at nearly 20,000 feet.

The altimeter (top right) indicates 22,420 feet. A comfortable margin usually but over the mountains with up and downdrafts and mountain waves...

Winnipeg Free Press
Sunday, September 8 1985
Pages 9-16

Bungle in the jungle

Winnipeggers at mercy of semi-military rabble

By John McManus

If it hadn't been for headwinds, Dave McCulloch's black Cessna would never have landed at Maturin.

Maturin is an insignificant, little-used alternate port of entry on the air routes off the South Atlantic in northeastern Venezuela.

McCulloch, wife Linda, co-pilot

erals were refined. They looked lik Mexican bandits out of Treasure Sierra Madre, that old Boga movie.

"They said 'we also do a search then they took our wallets and doc ments and started taking the ai plane apart.

"Everything came out, remo able panels, some that weren meant to be removed along wit

Self explanatory.

145

Returned home after a sometimes harrowing trip to Brazil. A grainy reproduction of a newspaper photo showing McCulloch (back) Linda McCulloch, Mary Tomalin and co-pilot Doug Tomalin in fore-front. Winnipeg Free Press article (September 8, 1985) Bungle in the Jungle

Chapter Eighteen

"If God had meant man to fly He would have given him more money."

McCulloch was once again back to the - by comparison - mundane routine of selling product and promoting his business. *Water Doctor* was doing well. And after several months, McCulloch was getting itchy feet again. He proposed a trip to Europe to his long-time friend, Dave Yates. McCulloch, Linda, Yates and his wife Kathy departed on June 14, 1985. McCulloch skipped over to Gimli, Manitoba and picked up Doug Tomalin to act as co-pilot. From there it was a course to Churchill, Frobisher Bay, Greenland, Iceland and England. They jumped over to Paris then Rome and Venice. They did everything that tourists normally do, they enjoyed the foods of both France and Italy, they visited the museums and historic sites while wondering at the culture of their peoples and the genius of their architecture. It was a wonderful trip but business demands back in Canada required their return home. McCulloch plotted his course back home, retracing their original. He was getting comfortable with these long trips. "This international flying was becoming a piece of cake."

Back to work, but also begin the process of realizing a dream McCulloch had inferred to the Winnipeg Free Press. With many long range trips to South America and Europe logged in his

Pilot`s Log Book, he decided it was time to stretch his aluminum wings and attempt an around-the-world flight. "My hero, Howard Hughes did it the year I was born."

Hughes departed New York flying eastward to Paris on July 10, 1938 in a Lockheed Lodestar Monoplane. He and his crew of four returned to New York on July 14, 1938 after "circling" the globe covering 24,672 miles in three days, nineteen hours, fourteen minutes and ten seconds. Hughes made sure the press would print that this was not a fly-by-night attempt but a carefully planned and exercised project to further the cause of aviation in general and airline flights in particular. His crew were some of the best radiomen and navigators of the time. The plane was loaded with the latest navigation equipment to keep him on course and powerful radios to stay in communication with the ground and New York. The idea was to show a potential air-travelling public that getting them to their destination would be as safe as possible and not some hit-and-miss endeavour.

Pilot McCulloch had another plan in mind. He would circumnavigate the globe but travelling westward against the prevailing winds. He shopped around, looking for a twin-engined plane that would fit the needs of his trip and eventually he settled on a plane that would fit his needs. "I purchased an eight passenger, pressurized Cessna 414 with two engines and began my modifications." It was July of 1985.

"The logistics involved in this record breaking attempt were massive." Modifications to the 414 *would* be needed. He upgraded the Continental 520 engines from 310 hp to 340 increasing his boost from 36 inches to 41 inches.

The 414 factory-built model could carry 160 US gallons of fuel. McCulloch crunched numbers and decided he needed 475 gallons of useable fuel to feed the larger engines and get the range he needed. He had those modifications done as well. He would get the much needed extra fuel from wingtip tanks, enlarged auxiliary tanks and wing locker tanks; four separate tanks in each wing. Inside the cabin, two bladder tanks one 150 gallon and one 100 gallon tank. "I now had 10 tanks; a plumber's nightmare."

McCulloch added a High Frequency (long range) radio, added another ADF to the existing one on the panel, a weather radar and a radar altimeter including a King IFR avionic package-duel everything. He packed food, a sun compass and sextant aboard, stowed life jackets and a raft as per safety regulations - and common sense.

"With us aboard, we were one hundred percent over gross weight."

But then, so was Charles Lindbergh-and-more-when he flew from New York to Paris.

In fact the airplane would not always be fully loaded with fuel; not while over populated mainland territories. The extra tanks were needed for the legs flown over the huge expanses of the Pacific and Atlantic oceans.

In September of 1985 the Winnipeg Free Press published a story about McCulloch's trip in Brazil nearly nine months earlier. A remark of McCulloch's therein that he would do the trip if he could find someone crazy enough to go with him had fired the imagination of the owner of Ford dealership in Russell, Manitoba. "Gerald Keating, said it was his dream to do such a trip. I said it takes cash to buy dreams; lots of people have them." McCulloch should know, he buys them and lives them.

"Keating showed up at my door with a cheque in hand. He apologized saying I am only a VFR pilot and I said 'no problem it only takes airspeed and money to fly'. We have both."

McCulloch estimated that he would be ready to make his westward, around-the-world trip by June of 1986. In the meantime, business wise, things were changing. McCulloch was beginning to feel the sharp edge of the knives of the parent company Lindsay in the United States. The president of the company was pulling down a large salary but not as large as McCulloch's. The company president was feeling threatened by the success of Water Doctor's sales and franchises. In an attempt to avoid once again losing the large territory he had built up through hard work and ingenuity, McCulloch decided to enlarge his Canadian franchising business. In July of 1985 he and his brother Gordon created a national company with the head office in Toronto. This would expand the business across Canada while setting its sights on expanding into the lucrative USA market. "The US factory was getting nervous. We were now the largest of their 700 dealer network, and their non-vision salaried president was getting jealous we were making more money than him."

As in the Paymaster International territorial splitting in order to clip McCulloch's wings, the US factory president was in fear of the tail wagging the dog.

In December of 1985 McCulloch sold his home in Winnipeg and moved himself and his now pregnant wife Linda to just north of Toronto. He did not realize it then but an era was ending for him and his family and a new, more involved (evolved) era was about to begin. He had purchased a 100 acre farm; one of several properties he purchased in the Toronto area. The farm was complete with an 1,800 foot long runway-twenty miles north of Toronto International Airport. He wanted to be close to the head office. With Linda about three months pregnant it seemed best to make the move then rather than later. McCulloch grew up in the country and now with a baby on the way a farm setting was a natural way for him to go. Whether he just wanted more space than provided in a four bedroom house or it was a throwback to his youth or both is probably moot.

Another opportunity arose. McCulloch had a chance to lease a portion of his farm out to a movie production company. They were shooting the fourth sequel to the popular *Police Academy* movies, *Police Academy 4-Citizens on Patrol* starring Steve Guttenberg, Bubba Smith, Michael Winslow and Sharon Stone as Officer Sweetchuck. "I got to have Sharon Stone in my barn." McCulloch quipped. This was six years before Stone would rocket to stardom in the movie thriller *Basic Instinct* opposite Michael Douglas.

Sharon Stone and other young starlets running about the property notwithstanding, the money from the lease would come in handy. By the end of Spring the Cessna 414 was ready for its around the world flight. McCulloch had invested $150,000.00 in upgrades and modifications and had it hangared in Niagara Falls, New York. "Transport Canada would never have approved the upgrades, despite Cessna and the country it was actually constructed in approving the changes." This record breaking attempt was sanctioned and approved by Federation Aeronautica in Paris, the USA National Aeronautical Association in Washington, DC and the Royal Canadian Flying Clubs in Ottawa, Canada.

However once again a complacent Canada would miss out on the opportunity of being the jump off point for a world record breaking achievement by a twin engined light aircraft travelling west around the world. That's called, *doin' it the hard way*; against the prevailing westerly winds.

Awww Canada.

But another event would take place before the Cessna was wheels up in Niagara Falls. On May, 8, 1986 Linda and David McCulloch announced the birth of their daughter, Kathryn. At time of writing Kathryn McCulloch is a lawyer practicing law in Toronto. She is a licensed pilot.

McCulloch could see no big future in the water filtering business. As mentioned earlier, his bottled water idea was not working out, which with hindsight the present day consumer must have to wonder why. His biggest concern was that he was seeing indications that the manufacturer of the product was looking for ways to clip his wings. His brain was turning over, "My radar was circling," as he puts it. He was looking for new opportunities. But for now his search would have to be put aside. Only a month would pass since the birth of his daughter and he would be attempting a trip only attempted by 18 other pilots since the birth of heavier than air flight. There was a chance he might not survive the trip. A trip that would take them across vast tracts of depthless oceans that Lindbergh himself would have shied away from.

The Cessna 414 was no airliner, just a light airplane never meant to travel such distances relying on engines that were not designed to run for hours on end and then do hours more again before landing. "The plane was not made to carry enough fuel for this feat so you must give up all the safety margins built into these aircraft. And then really all you have left is a wing and a prayer."

Thirty one days after his daughter was born McCulloch and Keating lifted off from Niagara Falls, New York. It would be the adventure of their lives. McCulloch wondered if he would return and see his wife and child again. But then again he wasn't being forced to make this attempt, unless you can make an argument for McCulloch's compulsion to do just what he was doing. The pressure on him arose only from within himself. It's always about seeing over the horizon whether that be while flying for pleasure or for business.

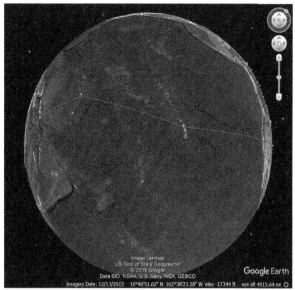

McCulloch's flight track across the Pacific, a distance of over 8,000 nautical miles. San Jose', California to Honolulu, Hawaii to Majuro Atoll, Marshall Islands to Honiara (Guadalcanal), Solomon Islands, to Brisbane Australia.(Google Earth image)

Chapter Nineteen

"It only takes airspeed and money to fly."

McCulloch had a grand adventure ahead of him; a trip around the world, westward, in a light, twin engined aircraft with hopes of achieving a speed record.

After receiving many good wishes and good byes, and just a month after his daughter was born, in the early morning of June 9, 1986, McCulloch and his co-pilot Keating climbed away from Niagara Falls International Airport in New York on the first leg of their around the world adventure. C-FASB's fuel tanks were filled to only half of their capacity. They would have to cross 2,300 miles of the United States to get to San Jose, California and they could refuel in many places along the way-a luxury denied them once they were out over the Pacific Ocean.

They refueled in Lincoln, Nebraska 980 miles from Niagara Falls. From Lincoln they travelled 500 miles over the relative flatlands of Nebraska and into Colorado before they flew the remaining 800 miles to San Jose over the rugged mountain country in Colorado, Utah, Nevada and the Sierra Mountains in eastern California. They arrived at their Pacific jumping off point of San Jose, California on June 10.

Sleep was almost impossible that night. McCulloch's mind kept grinding over details; mostly about fuel consumption and the ability to nail down a relatively small chain of islands in the Pacific Ocean.. They would be flying 1,900 nautical miles over open ocean with no place to refuel until they reached the Hawaiian Islands. McCulloch had supervised the refuelling of his aircraft. One gallon of fuel could make the difference between gliding to the end of a runway or force landing into rough terrain or even the Pacific a couple of miles or a few hundred meters short of it. McCulloch and Keating preferred the former option.

McCulloch did his engine run-ups looking for any hiccup, the slightest rpm reduction below the norm while begrudging the fuel he was burning and not getting anywhere. He received his taxi instructions to the active runway lined up and waited to be cleared for take-off by the tower at Norman Y Mineta San Jose International Airport. "You set?" he asked Keating. Keating nodded , "I'm ready." Keating was probably thinking of all the appointments and work at his own company that he had put off, which he shouldn't have been putting off, just to fly around the world.

Neither pilot was as concerned about the long over-water flight as they were aware that right now they were overloaded with fuel to twice the allowable take-off weight the airplane was designed for-and of that extra weight, nearly a ton or 2,000 pounds was highly inflammable, 100/130 high octane aviation fuel. "The plane was designed to carry 160 gallons of fuel and was loaded with over 520 US gallons. Literally, it was a flying gas bomb."

The first thing McCulloch and Keating had to do was survive the take-off, get enough altitude and at least a modest rate of climb before they even reached the Pacific Ocean. "The plane was not made to carry enough fuel for this feat. I used up all the safety margins built into this aircraft." He had gone well beyond it. "Really all you have is a wing and a prayer." He was about to attempt what his long time hero Howard Hughes had done the year he was born.

"I remembered thinking my daughter was born only a month before. I might never get to see her grow up. This is what the passion of flying will do to you."

The question in both their minds is whether the Cessna 414 will get off the runway or will it be an item on the five o'clock news across the United States and Canada-perhaps Europe. The possible fireball ending is a pretty interesting news story.

McCulloch pushed the throttles to their maximum limits on the quadrant. When he accelerated to maximum speed of 130 k (150 mph-241 kph), he rotated, pulling back gently on the control column-and waited. "With adrenaline pumping (and the devil watching) she finally lifts off the runway." The aircraft lumbered into the air. But it's not over yet. The aircraft is airborne but as every pilot knows there is something known as ground effect. A cushion of air builds up between the wing bottom and the runway surface when the plane is taking off. In an aircraft of this size this air cushion might exist up to ten or twelve feet. The plane might be flying but won't go higher.

Where the usual practice is to leave the gear down until the plane is out of ground effect, McCulloch was conscious of the drag the wheels were inducing. Where every knot of speed was important to ensure climb, he retracted the gear. This and another "trick" added another few knots of speed as well. He and Keating had re-adjusted the stops on the throttle allowing them to increase their manifold pressure from 36 inches of boost to 41 inches of boost.

McCulloch remembers the take-off as more like trying to stop the sink rate. "It was a long take-off run. We used up a lot of the runway." The 414's usual 110 knot speed rotate (wheels off) was not sufficient. He increased his speed to135 knots. "It required a lot of elevator to even get the nose up; all controls were slow to react. They were sluggish."

At this point they were balancing on the edge of stall, the engines at full fine pitch were screaming away outside. The screaming was good. As long as they were they were running. One hiccup out of the engines and the plane would pull to that bad engine and she would roll in.

Fireball.

If one of the props lost its governor and went flat the airplane would roll to that engine. Fireball. If one of the turbo boosts failed, same result. Fireball. Engine jug failure due to added boost....fireball.

All of McCulloch's options at this point-if he could not get altitude- would result in a colorful yellow/orange ball somewhere northwest of the field in a subdivision or in the Alviso Salt Marshes.

He climbed a bit more. Soon they figured they were out of ground effect but still he had to keep the wings level. Banking one way or the other would result in the loss of lift.

They climbed out straight ahead with McCulloch nursing the controls and the attitude of the airplane. As the Cessna twin burned off fuel it got a bit lighter. The lighter the better; better climb.

"We were holding our breath for so long it's a wonder we didn't pass out." Avoiding a fireball provides one with a lot of incentive particularly when you have two big fuel tanks loaded with high octane avgas right in the passenger compartment with you.

Satisfied finally that they were climbing, McCulloch still had to be mindful of the mountain barrier off to the west of him. The mountains climbed to nearly a half mile high but became gradually lower the further north they went tapering to nothing at the entrance to San Francisco Bay.

San Jose International was at an altitude of only 54 feet. McCulloch climbed out to the northwest and when he had the altitude he gently banked the aircraft left to the west and crossed over the mountains west of San Mateo.

"It was a long slow flight over the land to the Pacific. Once over the ocean I've traded one danger for another. Instead of burning now I will drown. My doctor friend says I am an adrenaline junkie."

Once over the ocean, McCulloch allowed the Cessna Twin to climb to an altitude of 4,000 then 6,000 feet, aiming, eventually for eight thousand feet. He then throttled the engines back to see a speed of 140 knots. This was 40 knots slower than the airplane's normal cruise. He had to maintain a slightly nose high attitude in order to maintain lift with all of that weight on board; but this slight increase in the wing's angle of attack also caused drag reducing the speed requiring an increase in throttle setting and diligent prop management.

McCulloch was doing a balancing act where attitude, fuel burn, distance and time were the main factors. The Pacific stretched away before them; massive, unbroken and unforgiving if he lost an engine at his present fuel state. Honolulu was out there somewhere 1,900 nautical (2,200 statute miles-3,520 km) miles in the distance.

They were on their way and on their own. There was no GPS to navigate by in 1986. They had Loran C a marine navigation aid but in this vast open expanse the broadcasting station chains were so far apart it made them unreliable. McCulloch had two very reliable ADFs on board the aircraft but they too were restricted by distance. With luck he might be able to pick up a radio station a couple of hundred miles out of the Hawaiian Islands but once they were away from the American mainland they were basically cut off and were navigating using dead reckoning, just like Fred Noonan, Amelia Earhart's navigator.

Basically, if you reckoned wrong, you were dead.

A total electrical failure would rob them of most of their navigation ability and deny them radio communications. The magneto driven engines would keep them running but they would have to rely on the sextant and the magnetic compass.

In any event, once they were away from shore navigation aids they were on their own; and 49 years of separation were stripped away. Both Earhart and McCulloch were trying to hit a tiny speck on the ocean with only dead reckoning to rely on. Earhart's navigator, Noonan was using a sextant to take bearings and in fact so was McCulloch. He had brought one along, the best he could lay his hands on. In his early life, McCulloch had been a sea dog, sailing around the world on ESSO Oil tankers. He was not intimidated by the ocean but he deeply respected it.

To do otherwise would be foolhardy.

Weather forecasting a few hundred miles offshore relied – even in the eighties with the emerging weather satellites – on long range ship transmissions and the observations of pilots. The latter was one luxury that McCulloch had that Earhart did not. He could communicate with the passenger jets at 32,000 to 40,000 feet. He could get weather and could update his estimated position to them and they could relay it to either Air Traffic Control or to their companies on their company frequencies. Since they could not see McCulloch's aircraft from their altitudes they could not give him accurate positions from their inertial navigation systems.

They were relying on IFR Jeppesen Charts. Using High and low level charts, they had at least the ATC intersections (and their Lat. and Longs.) to give them some indication if they were on course, but only if their navigation was accurate. Jeppesen is an American company that-among other services-specializes in navigational information. Jeppesen's aviation sector serves Commercial Aviation, Business Aviation, Military and General Aviation (airlines and private pilots).

Usually when McCulloch contacted a 'high flyer' and asked them to pass on their estimated position and altitude the cockpit crew would be more than helpful but would ask them if they were nuts. No one but another pilot could understand just how dangerous this attempt was.

And at an altitude of only 8,000 feet. There was no wiggle room for an airplane that low (even at a mile and a half altitude) overloaded as it was if an engine failed. In this configuration the second would just prove the old pilot adage; "Ahh...the second engine just gets you to the scene of the accident a bit sooner." they will say.

Pilots are fatalistic. That way you aren't disappointed when you 'buy the farm'. Complacency is killer stuff for pilots.

In this case the second engine-scene of the accident - jaded pilot motto would be true. The glide ratio (for every thousand feet of altitude of this Cessna 414) was considerably less - loaded as it was - than when within its specified FAA certified limits. No one expects to glide to land when the engine(s) quit [11], but the better the glide ratio (e.g. 10:1 as opposed to 4:1) gives the pilot and crew more decision making time before impact; more time to prepare before ditching. It also allows the pilot to attempt an engine restart or in the case of carb ice - not likely in this fuel injected airplane - time for the ice to melt and the engine to be re-started.

A steeper glide also includes a higher rate of descent and less time to slow the airplane down. Ditching at a slow speed beats the alternative every time. The airplane is less likely to break up on impact, cartwheel or pitch-pole over its nose.

The first few hundred miles had the pilots constantly checking their engine instruments; looking for oil pressure changes, increased cylinder head temperatures, for example. If the former drops and the latter increases; that's bad news. Any indication of these would require a 180 degree turn and nail biting, nursing the engine until landfall. There was no provision for dumping fuel on the 414 to lighten the load and gain the use of one engine flight. And there was always the possibility of putting the strain on the working engine and it failing.

There was a chance at least of making radio contact with someone on shore and getting closer to Search and Rescue assets such as a coastguard vessel or a helicopter. There was even a chance of being picked up by a recreational boat or even a commercial fishing vessel. Even a fairly accurate position fix could be possible. The possibilities thinned out once McCulloch and Keating were several hundred miles out over the Pacific.

The engines droned on without any hint of a problem. That didn't stop the continual scanning of the instruments; a practice as old as flying itself; looking for problems before they escalated and perhaps avoiding something more serious.

This early in the flight the plane was flying with an increased angle of attack, the nose raised slightly off-setting the tendency of the 414 to sink due to its weight. This slowed the plane as well due to drag. As the miles wore on and the fuel burned off McCulloch could trim the nose down and increase the airspeed without increasing his fuel burn. This whole flight would be a compromise of best speed and fuel consumption to ensure the longest range available. With good navigation, fuel management, best nominal altitude (drag verses speed verses fuel burn) and optimal speeds the plane should reach Honolulu with a comfortable fuel margin.

Hour after hour the view remained the same. Water, water everywhere...Gradually McCulloch increased his airspeed from 140 knots to 180 knots. "As each hour ticked away we got 210 lbs lighter as the fuel burned off. I regained the ability for the plane to stay airborne on one engine." They were flying normally once again with a safety margin. They were in a 1,000 nautical mile gap between the mainland and Hawaii where they had only the airliners to converse with. The weather was clear all the way to the Islands. The Sun was catching up with them. Where it had been behind at take-off it was finally overhead and then raced ahead at 868 knots per hour (1,000 mph) to their 180 knots. The golden orb would eventually reach the horizon ahead of them and sink below it. But this was expected. They would land in Honolulu at sunset if all worked out.

They passed Bingo; the point of no return. They were now committed to the Hawaiian Islands.

In 1973 Maurice and Maralyn Bailey were sailing across the Pacific in their small yacht bound from Southampton, England to New Zealand. They were holed by one of two Pilot whales shortly after motoring through the Panama Canal to the Pacific. Their boat sank. They were adrift in two small rubber dinghies on the Pacific Ocean between the Panama Canal and the Hawaiian islands for 117 days, three days short of four months, before being picked up by a Korean fishing boat The Weolmi which providentially was itself off course at the time. Eight vessels had passed them by during their four month trial; the one they didn't see found them.

The Pacific is so vast and the possibilities of spotting small rafts on the surface at much over a few hundred meters are so remote that being spotted without some visual aids back then were small. The Baileys were emaciated, had lost 40 pounds each (they were not overweight to begin with) were covered in salt-water sores and skin abrasions from sharks battering the bottom of their raft, and too weak to move when rescued. The Korean crew nursed them back to life as they transported the two to Honolulu.

Thirteen years later, in 1986, not much had changed that would aid those who were lost at sea for whatever the reason. Were they to successfully ditch the airplane, McCulloch and Keating had a raft and provisions and they might have been aided by carrying an air-band, hand held radio available back then- at least for as long as the batteries held out and the radio was protected from water: BUT they didn't have one of those aboard.

Thirteen hours went by. They were at critical fuel levels now. They were both bored and anxious at the same time. Bored with seeing nothing but water below and anxious about their fuel state and their position. Hitting the Hawaiian Islands by dead reckoning over a distance of 1,900 nautical miles was like hitting a house fly with a rifle bullet from a 1,000 meters. Then what they determined later was a distance of about three hundred nautical miles out the ADFs began to come alive however they did not necessarily agree with one another on direction. But initially this gave them a sense that they were closer than they really were. They were expecting to pick up ADF bearings much closer to the islands maybe 50 to 80 nautical miles (92 to 145 kilometres) out. Instead it took another hour to cover the distance to Honolulu with the Distance Measuring Equipment (DME) coming alive about eighty miles out.

Their first indication that they were approaching landfall was the appearance of the peak of Mauna Kea - a dead, 13,580 foot-high volcano on the Big Island of Hawaii - rising from the Pacific at their eleven o'clock position.

"We were in the right place." Shortly after the normally blue Pacific waters began to fade into aquamarine blue as they passed over the reefs off Bellows Beach on the Island of O'ahu-the home of Honolulu and Pearl Harbor. They flew almost directly over the abandoned Bellows Air Force Base and the city of Waimanoalo which surrounded it. Lights were beginning to appear in the shadows of the mountain range ahead, the lush, jungle-covered Koolau Mountain Range. This is shot through with canyons and small rivers and is a popular stock photo shot for any movie or documentary which depicts the beauty of Hawaii's beautiful mountains. The Koolaus rose up as much as 2,500 feet as they curved around them and were the last barrier before they had to quickly lose altitude on the back side of the range and slide down the glide-path on approach to Honolulu International Airport (AKA Hickham Airfield).

Off his left wing McCulloch saw the unmistakable circular crater of the extinct Diamond Head volcano. But then as his angle changed the well-defined outline of the world famous prominence of Diamond Head itself came into focus. South of Diamond Head he saw the chain of hotels along Waikiki Beach. Just to the northeast was Pearl Harbor.

They had little time for sightseeing unfortunately. They were too busy approaching and being vectored through Honolulu's busy traffic pattern.

It was near dusk (5:30 pm local) when they radioed "on final" to Honolulu Tower at Honolulu International Airport. The landing after the 13 hour flight was anti-climactic as the tower cleared them, gave them the winds and advised "check gear down and locked" just as McCulloch had heard many hundreds of times before. Runway length was not critical now where they were nearly exhausted of fuel, but the 12,000 foot runway there would be appreciated when they were fully loaded with fuel once again and on their way to Australia.

They were tired, cramped up and ready for brief rest, maybe even bed; but Honolulu beckoned. They rewarded themselves by staying at a luxury hotel that night. It was newly opened. They retired to the bar for a meal. McCulloch nursed a coke while Keating drank a cocktail.

They were winding down after a stressful 13 hours over the trackless Pacific Ocean. "Isn't that Kojak at the next table?" Keating said. Turning slightly McCulloch saw that indeed movie and TV actor, Telly Savalas was sitting at the table next to them.

For younger readers Savalas was a character actor who starred in high profile movies during the middle of a career spanning 40 years. He sometimes played the heavy or a good bad guy in movies such as the villain Blofeld in the James Bond movie *On Her Majesty's Secret Service*, in *Kelly's Heroes* with Clint Eastwood and Donald Sutherland, the *Dirty Dozen* with Lee Marvin but his star rose when he starred as New York City detective Lt. Theo Kojak on the long running and hard hitting television series, *Kojak* in the 1970s. He is credited with the line "Who loves you baby?"

They struck up a brief conversation with Savalas who was on his own. He was there as a celebrity for the opening of the new hotel. Eventually he asked them where they were from. McCulloch told him they were Canadians travelling around the world on what they hoped would be a record setting flight. Savalas wished them luck and told them they were 'crazy Canadians'.

Chapter Twenty

"I don't know where I am, but I know where I'm going."

Once again in the early morning, McCulloch lined the Cessna 414 on the runway. He was loaded with fuel for the next leg of 2,000 nautical miles across the Pacific to their destination west-northwest of Honolulu to Majuro Atoll in the Marshall Islands Or as McCulloch put it, "Another ball breaker flight from Honolulu to Majuro." Majuro is basically the rim of an extinct undersea volcano. Coral and the sands of time have gathered around this perimeter and made a habitable ribbon of land about 53 miles (88 kilometres) long but only approximately 600 feet in width. The sandy ring encloses a watery expanse with a deep ship anchorage in the northern enclosure of the atoll. The airport is on the southwestern ribbon of land and is bordered on both sides of the runway with the Pacific and the inner atoll. Houses pepper this odd rim of land. What really interested McCulloch was that Majuro Atoll had a paved 8,257 foot runway and aviation fuel; enough to accommodate McCulloch's thirsty, fuel-laden, Cessna 414. There was limited fuel there and real navigation concerns getting there. And on this leg of the trip he was out of touch with high flyers who were not flying regular airline routes like those from California to Hawaii.

En route McCulloch had to throw caution to the winds and penetrate several thunderstorms. "At one point during a severe shake down, or maybe it was a shake-up, we looked down at the churning seas below; we figured rough was better." The rain hammered the Cessna's cabin so hard that McCulloch told a Winnipeg Free Press reporter who was following their adventure, "I was surprised to see that the plane still had paint on it when we landed." The volume was unnerving. "The noise was something God awful. Like being inside a snare drum." He recalled these many years later. And there were always concerns about being hammered with hail (the hail forms internally at the tops of the thunder cell, sometimes as high as 70,000 feet) or struck by the lightning generated and embedded in the thunderclouds. The cabin was alternately pitch black-save for the red glowing dials of the instruments-and the blinding electric welding-like, blue-white flashes of nature's pyrotechnic display. Surprisingly they came out of the other side of the storm and shortly afterwards they arrived over Majuro Atoll and the Marshall Islands International Airport.

Unlike Hawaii there were no mountains like Mauna Kea or Diamond head to see far out over the ocean. Majuro Atoll is flat and in 1986 its highest elevation was not much above 10 feet (3 meters) above sea-level. It is part of the Marshall Island group, just seven degrees north of the Equator. Majuro's International Airport is built over the original World War Two US Army Air Force air field (see Google Earth). The original base was a major staging point for bombing raids on Japanese owned and held islands in the Pacific during WWII.

"A major conflict arose over fees. A Texas pilot who landed there as well was outraged because USA had built the airport (but not the new runway) during the war." Some American aircraft on a goodwill tour and some other aircraft in the same around the world attempt landed within hours of each other.

The airport crew wanted to charge the total overtime for refuelling rather than splitting the total among all of them. It was a money grab for pilots trapped there without fuel. The locals were making the best of this sudden influx of aircraft. Harsh words were uttered by the Texan with the end result being that the locals closed the airport until the next morning.

McCulloch and the other pilots were unable to get fuel until the next day. Basically they were shorting themselves because in the morning there would be no overtime income.

McCulloch who had learned the ways of the world and of lubrication had brought along his usual stash of American dollars. Canadian bills were treated with distain and were practically useless for bribing. In this case the American buck was of no help to him or the Texan. On another note, Majuro Atoll depends on the airport for its fresh water supply. The runway acts as a giant catchment basin for the rains it receives during the year.

Majuro has greater concerns these days a fate shared with many islands in the world's oceans. The island's make-up is a string of small sand bars on coral which built up over eons, strung like a necklace in and around the main atoll with the largest bulk of land to the east end and south side of the atoll. Majuro's population hovers around 21,000 people.

The local government has been seeking out options for the island where one would be hard pressed to find an elevation above 10 feet (3 meters). There is always the constant concern about Tsunamis which in any strength would wash completely over the island nation. For McCulloch and Keating it was port in the storm, a place for fuel and the jumping off point for their next destination, Guadalcanal's Henderson International Airport in the Solomon Islands 1,200 nautical miles (NM) to the southwest of Majuro Atoll.

If they had sweated the 1,900 NM range over fuel concerns from San Jose to Honolulu, or the 2,000 NM from Honolulu to Majuro Atoll, conversely this leg from Majuro to Henderson International Airport in Honiara on the Island of Guadalcanal was a meer 1,200 NM. Rather than dodge weather they flew through several tropical storms on this eight hour trip. Their arrival at Henderson was anti-climactic. They rested but departed the next morning for Brisbane, Australia.

Guadalcanal was an historic landmark and a significant and bloody battle ending in a defeat for the United States Marine Corp early in the Pacific War.

The leg from Guadalcanal to Brisbane would be a measly 1,300 nautical miles southwesterly over the historic Coral Sea, site of the naval clash between the US Navy and the Japanese Navy during Battle of the Coral Sea. Japan was threatening Australia during the Pacific War and this was an important battle that ensured the survival of this important part of what was then known as the British Commonwealth.

After another 1,260 NM over-water trek, McCulloch and Keating 'found' Brisbane through the use of the two Digital King ADFs on board. Surprisingly they contacted Brisbane Approach on their radio about 100 miles out from that airport. The tower asked them their position. Well they didn't know their exact position because they were using dead reckoning so McCulloch replied that he could not supply that information. Brisbane Approach said they had to know their position if they were coming to their airport. McCulloch replied, "I don't know where I am, but I know where I'm going." And that would be Brisbane. He wasn't about to be put off by a controller who obviously didn't understand the limitations of light aircraft flying over thousands of nautical miles of unforgiving ocean.

They resolved the issue when McCulloch said he would report in when he and Keating were closer to an identifiable landmark.

After that, things went smoothly. By the time McCulloch and Keating reached Brisbane in Queensland they were sick of seeing thousands of miles of water below them. "We were ready to swear off drinking water and bathing forever."

Brisbane is presently a city of some 2.15 million people, the capital city of and the largest in the State of Queensland. It ranks as the third largest city in Australia. It's located on a bend of the Brisbane River, approximately 23 km (14 mi) from its mouth at Moreton Bay on the east coast of Australia about 27.5 degrees south of the Equator. This is the southern latitude equivalent of Cape Canaveral Florida in the United States though they are 9,300 miles apart.

McCulloch landed at Brisbane Airport on July 16 after an 8.5 hour, 1,260 nautical mile trip from Guadalcanal. Apparently the media had gotten wind of their arrival and their adventure. "Surprisingly (despite their rather cold reception by Brisbane Approach) we were treated like brave adventurers; small planes from America, and all that." They were met by dignitaries who welcomed them to the country, the state and the city. Once again, McCulloch and Keating checked into a five star hotel, their first since Honolulu. Once again they encountered their former acquaintance, Telly Savalas who was making a tour of that chain of hotels. He remembered the "crazy Canadians" and expressed his pleasure at their having survived so far.

A reception followed in the evening which in turn led to making new friends who in turn-and in Aussie fashion-involved them in another pub crawling exercise through the town later that evening. McCulloch had not been drinking for over ten years at this point and it is probably fortunate that he was sober.

"The 'Sheilas' were all over us that night but I was a good boy with a wife at home and a newborn baby girl. Not sure I would have been able to resist if I'd been under the influence. It was tiring but we knew this time we didn't have to fly early the next morning."

They laid over the extra day to do some sightseeing in the twin and had also decided to dogleg it over to Ayers Rock rather than going directly to Darwin from Brisbane.

Then the weight of bureaucracy came down around him. Rules, Regulations and Safety, etc. They were about to cross the Australian Outback-a desert which accounted for three quarters of the Australian Continent; a territory where men have died etc. "*We must protect you from yourself.* A lot of people now make their paycheck by supposedly protecting others."

As a result of this protectiveness and before McCulloch could take-off on the next leg of his journey across the Outback to Darwin, he and Keating were required to sign documents absolving the Australian government from blame if they crashed in the hostile environment of the 'Outback". They were attempting to impress on McCulloch the dangers of the outback where "men had died". To McCulloch this seemed to be closing the gate after the horse had bolted. Northern Canada and the jungles of Brazil were no less intimidating than the Outback. Not much chance of freezing to death there at least.

"After negotiations, signing releases and waivers etc. I am gone, said goodbye to the control tower and didn't speak to anyone for 12 hours. Fuck that....I like Frankie's song, *I Did It My Way.*"

McCulloch wanted to fly low and at times, slow over the Outback, chasing kangaroos, see Ayers Rock and enjoy an orgasm of flying over this desolate region of Australia. The crow flight from Brisbane to Darwin is 1,500 nautical miles. Flying there with a detour over to Ayers Rock would add nearly 500 nautical miles to their trip and another 3 hours to their time. Record attempt aside; this was just too good an opportunity to pass up.

As luck would have it, flying the Outback of Australia is best done in the summer months when it is-conversely in Australia-cooler than during the fall, winter and spring.

Leaving Brisbane for the west they had to clear the Great Dividing range which rises up to about 1,800 feet then drops down to a plateau whose mean elevation is 100 feet give or take. This area for about 250 miles inland is cultivated farmland and some forest. Eventually the terrain drops away to a huge desert basin that was once an ocean that divided the continent as it was coming together and the sea bottom rose up to join the two separate parts of Australia. At times the terrain drops to 15 and 20 feet above sea level. This whole desert is dotted with the names of lakes which are for the most part dry lake beds for most of the year-or more; some of which hold water only for short periods of time during the sparse "rainy season".

For 800 nautical miles, McCulloch and Keating flew low; sometimes as low as 500 feet AGL. Once past the basin the ground began to rise gradually, once more. They saw more scrub vegetation that looked desolate but the terrain was inhabited by hundreds of different species of snakes, birds, animals and scattered human habitations. The vegetation is scant and dry comprised for the most part of spike grass and isolated bushes and trees. The latter are referred to by the Australians as Desert Oaks. Accumulated rainwater - albeit a rarity - collects at the base of rocks, in shaded canyons and crevices. There one will find rare flowers and plants which seem out of place for the harsh surroundings. But since rain is so infrequent -often a year can go by without precipitation - it is a wonder they grow at all. One of the stalwarts is the Stuarts Desert Rose, the escutcheon flower of the Northern Territory. The continued dried state of the stunted trees and vegetation often leads to brush fires on a monumental scale.

The two pilots made no radio contact with anyone. There was always some possibility of landing at one of many small airstrips that dot the Outback's landscape. That's if you could find them.

Airplanes are one of the best ways of getting around that vast expanse of territory. Air ambulances and medical services rely on aircraft in this region much the same way it does in northern Canada and Alaska. If they had an engine failure; overloaded with fuel as they were, the likelihood of the good engine getting them to a good airport was remote. They might have to force-land in the forbidding terrain below. As one famous Auzzie aviator once said, "The worst possible outcome of a crash landing in the Outback was to survive it." The meaning implied was that even worse was yet to come. "Just about everything there is poisonous when it bites, stings or claws you." Even the world renowned male, duckbilled Platypus-found predominantly in NSW, Australia-is venomous. It has spur-like appendages on its back flippers. If they choose to strike you with one of these it will cause excruciating pain and perhaps incapacitation for hours or days. Drowning is a real concern if a male platypus strikes you in the water. Not likely in the desert Outback however.

Ayers Rock also known by the aboriginals as Uluru (You-loo-roo) lies 280 (335kms) road miles (208 air miles) southwest of Alice Springs in the Northern Territory of central Australia. The "Rock" lies in some of the most hostile and desolate geography on the planet. It is almost as if nature was trying to hide this monolith from the rest of the world. Arresting, spectacular and downright weird are some of the adjectives that describe this sandstone edifice. But near and by the rock there are a great number of springs, waterholes, rock caves and ancient paintings that titillate and cause wonder about what the Anangu aboriginals in the area, who consider Uluru as sacred, were getting at when they made the drawings and glyphs hundreds and thousands of years ago. Indeed one would wonder why they would live in such desolation in the first place.

Uluru-Ayers Rock is located in Uluṟu-Kata Tjuṯa National Park and is designated a World Heritage Site.

One geological oddity that draws attention is the clean base around the perimeter of the rock. The sandstone is so hard that it does not flake off and cause tons of rubble around the base of the monolith. It's almost as if it pushed up through the Earth's surface a short time ago, but geologically that is incorrect. It is hundreds of millions of years old. At approximately 2,000 meters north to south by 3,000 meters, east to west it climbs up from the surrounding surface altitude of 1,700 feet over eleven hundred feet to an altitude of 2,828 feet. What makes the huge mound so impressive is just how abruptly it seems to rise from the plain below. From the air it dominates the surrounding landscape and can be seen from miles away as a bump on the horizon.

The early morning east light and the western sunset washes Ayers Rock in red light that is every science fiction writer's vision of what Mars must look like to an astronaut recently landed there. The combination of its size, make-up and the way it lights during the day must have awed the local Anangu who attributed it with magical properties and who considered it sacred.

It is almost impossible to walk up to the base of any mountain on level ground. Usually there is a rise in terrain and then a change gradually from treeline to boulders and gravel then the mountain rock itself. But it is different at Ayers Rock. Walking toward this piece of geology you are on the flat desert and encounter some bush and small trees then suddenly there it is rising right out of the desert floor like a giant wall right in front of you. In some places, it soars upward for over 300 meters as if nature had built a skyscraper in the middle of the desert. But the difference is, this skyscraper wall stretches off to your left and right for over a kilometer on either side of you.

In some places Ayers Rock slopes upward gently enough that if you have the legs for it you can make the trek to its flat summit eleven hundred feet above. It is as startling an apparition from the air as it is from the ground; perhaps even moreso since pilots can see the whole of the rock's 6,200 square meters from their altitude.

McCulloch could see the monolith from ten miles back. He was at a low altitude to begin with. He came up on it from the east, climbed to one thousand feet to stay above the edifice and then climbed some more but stayed low skimming over and then circling around the sacred rock.

They wondered at this monolith in the Australian desert as have thousands before them and since. They could see why the Aboriginals would think the place sacred. It had a special quality to it. It glowed in the Sun and was marvelous to see by Moonlight. But limited by fuel, they had to turn away.

McCulloch considered landing in Alice Springs and loading on more fuel but he had enough to make it to Darwin. Fuel in Alice Springs no doubt would be more expensive than in Darwin. They proceeded northward, crossing over Lake Amadeus on an 800 nautical mile trek to that port city.

Shortly after - off to the right of their course - they saw the arresting appearance of the layered domes of the once submerged mounts in Watarrka National Park. Within minutes they were passing by the Macdonnell Ranges hidden behind the layered mounts. Then the Outback settled down to flat desert once more dotted with the occasional growth of bushes or trees as they crossed into the western quadrant of the Tanami Desert. Flat it might be but the ground conditions were iffy at best for an emergency landing.

General aviation pilots-as opposed to commercial airline jets-are always looking for a place to land from the time they lift off from any runway; engine failures or other problems usually arise shortly after take-off when engines are asked to perform at maximum RPM and the plane is clawing its way up to higher altitude. In this case the desert floor is cut through with dry runnels and large rock outcroppings. Landing might be survivable but the plane would likely be wrecked.

McCulloch and Keating were not really concerned about this possibility. They were light on fuel at this juncture into the flight and had the second engine as a backup. And there were airports-more like airstrips-dotting the landscape right and left of them. The Tanami Desert was petering out; the topography changing over from desert to broken ground with greater periods of vegetation evident below them. The land dropped in altitude and gradually sloped down toward Darwin. The last four hundred miles of the flight was over greener territory which improved to lush as they got closer to the northern coast of Australia

They saw the azure-blue waters of Beagle Gulf long before Darwin appeared behind the treeline on it's the gulf's south-east coast. McCulloch made his calls and was surprised that he was not met with some comment on his being out of radio contact for 10 hours or more. They used normal VFR/tower procedures to land at Darwin International Airport. "I pulled in on long final at Darwin and was on top of them before they could crank up a *protect me* procedure."

They deplaned and stretched their legs with relief. "We had a great day viewing Aussie land. Of course if we had crashed out there we would have been in hell for breakfast."

The Australian pilots fly all over that territory on a daily basis and think nothing of it. But they respect its potential for ruining their whole day if they have to force land or crash there.

Despite the relative size of the Cessna's interior before fuel modifications-and with the cabin seats removed - the latter used up a lot of space. The extra fuel "tanks" in the cabin were really bladders. They are similar to water-bed mattresses. They were much sturdier than their water-bed equivalents, however. They had straps moulded to them that had metal re-enforced holes enabling them to be bolted to the floor. The seats were removed but provision was made for a port-a-potty type toilet. Additionally the pilots had relief tubes by their seats that allowed their urine to go overboard.

The cabin "tanks" were the first to be emptied. Better to have them empty if you had to force land than have them try to join you in the cockpit during a hard stop. "I took a snooze on them occasionally. They were quite comfortable." McCulloch recalls. Nothing like dozing on the 100/130 octane av-gas of the day.

Originally named Palmerston in 1869 it was officially renamed Darwin in 1911. The British naval ship HMS Beagle arrived in that area in 1839. Three years before that Charles Darwin had completed his historic five year voyage on the Beagle and returned to England. The Gulf area off Darwin was named Beagle Gulf because of that ship anchoring in that area.

Darwin-located on the Timor Sea-is the most northern city in Australia and is the capitol city of the Northern Territories; the smallest of Australia's cities. Today its population hovers around 130,000. Located in proximity to South East Asia, it is a natural gateway city between Asia and Australia. It is a modern, multi-cultural city that was bombed extensively by the Japanese during world war two. It was rebuilt but was devastated by Cyclone Tracy in 1974.

But the city was back in shape for their arrival. They had a late supper and went out to celebrate. The Sheilas were out and about as well. Promising rides in the Twin Cessna kept them close but once again discretion was in order. They took the following two days off, resorting to tourist activity.

Darwin is of course on the coast and in the lush rainforest area of Northern Australia boasting any number of exotic animals. It is also alligator country. The pilots heard about a Crocodile park the night before and decided to visit the place. It was located right in the center of the city. "There were some really vicious looking reptiles in their holding tanks. The stars of the Park were saltwater Crocodiles native to Australia. Visitors got to hold baby Crocs or view the 12 footers in the large glass walled tanks. These days a visitor can put on a bathing suit and slip into a large, water-filled, plastic cylinder that is situated in the crock tank and watch them swim around them. Once in the cylinder the glass walls aren't apparent.

The next day they prepared the airplane for the over ocean 960 nautical mile journey to Bali. They would be going from western to Asian cultures and the laws which accompany that culture. They pulled their inspection plates and using flashlights looked around inside the wings fuselage, fuel lockers, and engine compartments looking for evidence of drugs. They weren't looking for anything that might be illegal going from Australia because the flow would be in the opposite direction. But they wanted to assure themselves they were clear of any possible substance that could be misconstrued. McCulloch still had the baking soda incident fresh in his mind. It was also an opportunity to check out the airplane as well. Any number of things could go wrong and they would be flying through areas of the world that didn't have the expertise to deal with airplanes such as a Cessna 414. They could be delayed days and weeks waiting for parts or replacements for the airplane in Asia Minor in the mid-1980s.

On June 21st - once again loaded with fuel, they departed Darwin for Bali, a Province of Indonesia and one of several islands - Bali being the largest. It is located east of the larger island of Java in the Lesser Sunda Islands. Its capitol city of

Denpasar is at the island's southern tip. Java to the west is only 1.5 miles off Bali's western tip. South of their destination the Indonesian plate ends and the water depth quickly drops to 12,000 feet into the Lombok basin then a few miles further on drops down into the Gascony Abyssal plain four miles below the surface of the Pacific.

This is an active Vulcan area with volcanoes all along this chain of islands. The most famous is Krakatoa which is located 550 nautical miles to the west off the western tip of Java.

One hundred and three years before McCulloch's record breaking attempt, on May 26, 1883 a series of volcanic eruptions began a few days earlier. Magma buildup under this island gradually forced the terrain to a higher elevation over hundreds of years before the volcano finally released it's lava, spitting rocks and debris and poisonous gases over the island. At some point a massive crack formed and the Pacific poured in creating a superheated gas that blew two-thirds of the northern section of the island apart with a force estimated to be on the scale of a 200 megaton nuclear blast, 13,000 times the yield of the atom bomb blast at Hiroshima. According to the records of the Dutch East India company 297 villages and towns were destroyed or damaged. 36,417 people died and uncountable thousands were injured or drowned when the tsunamis rolled out from the island after the explosion. The northern section of Krakatoa disappeared below the Pacific but less than one hundred years later it began to rise again. The massive magma dome still exists below the island, swelling upward forming *Anak Krakatau*, or "Child of Krakatoa". No doubt it will blow again in a few thousand years.

It is worth noting that further along that chain of islands is the next in line, Sumatra. On Sunday, 26 December 2004, an undersea earthquake with its epicentre off the west coast of that island caused a tsunami that resulted in the deaths of over 250,000 people in Sumatra and around the Pacific.

But this was 1986 during a relatively peaceful era for that locale. McCulloch's destination was Ngurah Rai International Airport on Bali Province's big island. Once again they dodged weather, mostly thunderstorms that could spring up in a matter of minutes. They would sweep across the ocean towards you like a ragged, torn, gray curtain out of a clear blue sky; hammer the fuselage, threatening the paint and thin aluminum skin of the airplane and then be gone. The larger storms could require the plane an hour to go around or fly through only to be met again an hour later by another storm marching through the area. Lightning was another concern. Though it is not normally a threat to most airplanes it can destroy the avionics and on rare occasions has ignited the gaseous vapour at the top of airplane fuel tanks resulting in explosions.

They made landfall near dusk at Ngurah Rai International in the City of Bali situated on the Island of Bali (pop. 3.5 million) located just east of the much larger island of Java. It is home to most of Indonesia's Hindu minority.

The pilots cleared customs easily enough and took a cab to a five star hotel in town. The difference between a four and a five star hotel in some of these countries was cockroach infested bedrooms and real luxury. McCulloch and Keating made sure they went first class however on occasion they would be led astray.

"Bali was a lovely city, well-kept with tree lined roads and beautiful buildings. It left a good impression with us." They had a pleasant evening with no pub crawling. They stayed over an extra day leaving the following morning on June 24th for Kuala Lumpur in Malaysia.

Chapter Twenty-One

"The old fear is back."

Despite the 1084 nautical mile distance, the crossing from Bali to Kuala Lumpur in Malaysia was somewhat less intimidating than most of their overseas flights. This was due to having land all around them as they crossed over the Java Sea. Off to their left they had Java, Jakarta and then they passed over the Bangka-Belitung islands. Before that they were as close as 62 nautical miles from the coast of Borneo off their right wing. Of all the landfalls that may have been a possibility if an engine failed or a prop misbehaved, in 1986, Borneo would not be the first choice for a forced landing.

There are four locations on the planet that have been relatively untouched by modern influence, the Antarctic, the deepest Belgium Congo, the deepest jungles of Brazil and Borneo. As recently as 2007 fifty-two new species of plants and animals have been discovered in the latter and that is considered the tip of the iceberg. Although its present-day population is about 18 million that had doubled in just ten years.

In 1986 less than six million people inhabited the northern and eastern coasts of the island. The southern and central portion were nearly as pristine as they were at the dawn of man. Small tribal populations, not even suspected, inhabited the dense jungles of central Borneo. Fortunately the need for a forced landing had not arisen. Eventually they were briefly off the east coast of Sumatra.

Singapore and Kuala Lumpur are in the southern peninsular arm of Malaysia. "After flying over and past the relatively untouched lands of much of Indonesia suddenly coming upon Singapore is a real eye popper. Suddenly, there it is climbing out of Singapore Strait." Skyscrapers are jamb-packed on the island. The docks cover most of the waterfront and are the engines that drive Singapore's trade. It is an independent island state separated from the rest of Malaysia. It exudes wealth.

Likewise, Kuala Lumpur was a beautiful city. Its old history mixed with new architecture was refreshing. It was another city on the move toward the 21st Century as more recent developments in that cosmopolitan city will attest. It's skyscrapers have been the locations for more than a few movies in the last ten years.

McCulloch and Keating stayed an extra day to sample local cuisine and just be tourists. The two pilots were now following a pattern that left them a free day between flight legs. The long distance flights were taking a toll. They found they needed the extra day to relax, wind down, in order to stay sharp. Fatigue was a killer on long distance flights. And there were things to worry about other than avionic and engine problems, weather and fuel concerns and the tempers of local officials.

Drug smuggling. The old fear was back.

Private aircraft were usually searched to insure the pilots were not smuggling heroin or some other drugs. If you were caught there and convicted-possession being good enough; and ten points of the law-they usually tried, convicted and usually hanged you the same day-locals and international travellers alike. There was no tolerance for smuggling although these regions were responsible in many cases for producing the drugs in the first place.

As they had done in Bali, on the evening before they departed Kuala Lumpur, they made as thorough a check as possible of their airplane to make sure no one had tampered with the inspection plates, engine compartments and wing lockers. Pilots are always checking for possible problems in and around their airplanes so this activity would not raise the suspicions of local authorities. Despite this check they would make another hurried check before departure the next day. They had no idea of the level of security at the airport so had to rely on their own eyeballs. Even though McCulloch carried a couple of thousand in American currency (his international greasing agent) this would be of no value in the event of drugs being discovered in his plane.

There was/is no doubt that the authorities in these countries were as aware as the pilots of drugs being planted with innocent travellers – it appeared that they just didn't care. Pilots should be more aware of this problem when travelling in these countries because it is even worse nearly thirty years later. "You can still fly to these places but being aware of what is possible, the problems that pilots can encounter are a priority." The authorities in many of these countries are less than sympathetic toward westerners. Some are looking for bribes or revenge. Some are just doing their jobs as they see it.

McCulloch and Keating were wheels up from Kuala Lumpur early on the morning of June 25th; destination Madras (now Chennai) India. It would be a 1,400 nautical mile trek across Malacca Strait which separates Malaysia from Sumatra, over North Sumatra. Looking down at the lush rain forests and sandy beaches below they could not have envisioned the devastation that would result nearly eighteen years later as a result of the aforementioned 2004 Boxing Day sub-sea Earthquake measuring

Magnitudes of 9.1-9.3 on seismographs, the third largest event recorded in history. A 98 foot seismic wave (Tsunami) spread out across the Indian Ocean. Sumatra and Indonesia were the hardest-hit followed by Sri Lanka, India, and Thailand. Sumatra's landmass protected southern Malaya from the effect of the Tsunami.

They struck out over the Bay of Bengal which comprised nearly 1,100 nm of the total leg of the flight. Once again the engines performed admirably, the ADFs picked up signals when they should have. They endured typical weather for the area with tropical rain showers almost the norm. The Bay of Bengal stretched out before them, but by now they were inured to vast expanses of ocean.

McCulloch and Keating landed at Madras (now Chennai) Airport and once clear of the International Airport, were depressed to see streets crowded with beggars and the number of children begging in the streets. Their Four Star Hotel room was unclean, crawling with insects, the sheets clearly not laundered and downright depressing. They cut their losses and left for a reputed Five Star Hotel which was a magnitude better than the last. They could only imagine what a Three Star Hotel would be like.

People were everywhere. It is hard to imagine in North America just how crowded some cities in India are. "People actually live and die on the streets." They saw people, late at night sleeping in doorways and on window sills. "They picked up the dead in a wagon each day." The money beggars were everywhere, at the windows of the cab and on the street, some poor people look like death. "A feeling of sadness and guilt flows through your body; sadness because you can't help because there are just too many, and guilt because you are living in a 5 star hotel and flying your own plane."

McCulloch was thinking of the expense of just owning that plane, the cost of the fuel and the ancillary costs for this expedition. It probably would have kept a dozen families in clover for the rest of their lives in India.

McCulloch asked a cabby how he endured living there? He replied,

"I have my family here and my religion, I don't need anything else."

McCulloch learned the hard way that street food in India was a no-no. It would catch up with them later.

"The snake charmers were fascinating. I bought some gold-it was cheap then. The Indian people know that paper currency is a racket; North Americans will soon learn.

The westbound record seekers saw the folly of waiting an extra day in what is a much more modern city of Chennai today. They would have been mobbed by beggars all the time. Life was cheap and what difference to those who believed that this was just a hardship to be overcome to get to death's door and the better life thereafter. It seemed that the lifestyle of the time was very accommodating because life was short. "Religion has exacted a heavy price from people all over the world. I thank God , for my loose-goose, religious upbringing. I only went to Sunday school when forced - often hid in the woods, and said my prayers silently when allowed by mother."

They left Madras the next morning for the airport, did their inspections and then climbed into bad weather with IFR flightplan filed for Bombay (now Mumbai) 550 NMs to the northwest. The terrain on their track climbs rapidly to mountain peaks at 2,500 feet some 35 or forty miles from Chennai. This added a dangerous element exacerbated when they encountered numerous thunderstorms along their flight track. It would be the most harrowing flight in their around-the-world, record-setting attempt. "I swear it was monsoon season. ....we had hit India right at the beginning of the season." It was like flying underwater. "We got ten inches (254 millimetres) of rain in one twenty-four hour period – a submarine would have been better than a plane.

"The turbulence was so bad that we threatened to lose our breakfast and the already percolating street meals from the previous day."

Such is the romantic life of the intrepid pilot.

The wings stayed on despite the physics to the contrary. This southwestern sector of India is rugged but interrupted by farmlands, rivers, lush jungle tracts, canyons and gorges despite the terrain rapidly dropping down to an elevation of 750 feet just west of the mountain chain west of Chennai. But then it begins to climb gradually to over 1,500 feet and then rapidly rising to nearly three thousand just to the east of Mumbai requiring a rapid descent into that city; all of this in less than "marginal" weather.

The 550 NM track from Chennai was not to be enjoyed and required attention to detail throughout the entire flight. There was little time for sight-seeing.

"On approach and also when we were landing at Juhu Airport in Bombay-Mumbai, the visibility was near zero. The rain was hitting the runway so hard it was bouncing back up, like in a car wash, a real mess ricocheting four or five feet high off the paved surface. I had no choice but to just keep the flashing lights passing on each side as we flew into this watery soup." Hydroplaning was only a problem if one swerved off the runway. With two runways, one at 9,400 feet and the other at 11,300 feet there was plenty of runway using prudent braking.

Bombay of 1986 saw little in the way of private airplanes. They were either too expensive for the general population or government paranoia discouraged even the wealthy from owning their own aircraft. India's situation even today is of concern visa-vis its relationship with a nuclear weapon equipped Pakistan. It was even moreso in 1986. The situation was much more tense. The unknown target of a private aircraft close to the border could have triggered an incident.

So it was with some amazement for the pilots that the authorities received McCulloch's private plane and arranged a greeting party, welcoming them to the city. As a result, McCulloch saw his picture on the front page of the India Times the next morning. At this point they were 15,000 nautical miles from Niagara Falls, New York. This translates into 27,773 kilometers or 17,280 statute miles from their original departure site. They were well past the halfway mark around the world. They had been flying for thirteen days averaging 1153 nautical miles a day.

The Bombay, India of 1986 was much different than the Mumbai nearly thirty years later. Back then life was cheaper.

Unlike the modern metropolis of today with its modern architectural skyscrapers visited by hundreds of thousands of tourists, the 1986 city was noteworthy for its poverty.

The place was depressing in and of itself. The inner city and the surrounding area had a population of some eight million but boasts nearly 13 million people in the inner city and over 22 million in the sprawling urban extensions in present day.

McCulloch and Keating arranged a stay at another five star hotel. They stayed an extra day to wind down. The last leg had been brutal, after all.

Chapter Twenty-Two

"Bad weather is not so bad when landing is the only option."

The Canadian pilots enjoyed a tour of the city when the rains stopped the next day and then on the 28th they filed out of Bombay for the small country of Bahrain on the southwestern Persian Gulf and on the east coast of Saudi Arabia. But first they had to get off the runway in Bombay. Rules governing pedestrians and animals wandering freely on the runways were not rigidly enforced in Bombay of 1986.

During a telephone interview McCulloch told a reporter from the Winnipeg Free Press that the runway resembled a crowded Indian market with people, dogs and birds wandering freely about the tarmac.

The birds were usually Vultures, possibly waiting for their next meal after some disastrous prop strike. The authorities would do their best to clear the crowd but often dogs would get back out on the runway. "You took off and hoped everything got out of your way and those darn dogs weren't old and slow."

Leaving Bombay IFR for Bahrain, they understood that they were one of five planes leaving under one clearance. "I was cleared for take-off, the other four followed. The tower went nuts. The controller was still calling us an hour later.

We all dispersed going our separate ways. We set our own altitudes and proceeded to the Persian Gulf. Of course there was the trouble with Iran and we had to thread a small path between restricted no fly zones."

This was necessary to avoid Iran's airspace. Iran was cranky at just about everyone in 1986, pretty much as they are today. And they had no particular love for Canadians whose Ambassador, Ken Taylor, arranged the escape of six American diplomats on November 4, 1979 from the American Embassy. Taylor sheltered them for many weeks, arranged Canadian passports (with the help of the Canadian Government) for them before smuggling them out of the country using a cover story dreamed up by the CIA. Less than seven years had gone by when McCulloch and Keating did an end-run around Iran in their bid for their westward record. Best not to advertise their presence. They made an IFR approach into Bahrain International Airport, located in Manama, Bahrain. "We landed in another zero visibility situation." This time it was a sandstorm. "It's not good on the glass or paint."

McCulloch was fatalistic.

"Bad weather is not so bad when landing is the only option."

Their next leg of the flight would be to Cairo, Egypt. But to get there they would have to cross the considerable expanse of Saudi Arabia's deserts. Now they endured big hassles dealing with the Saudi's. There were paperwork delays while trying to get clearances to cross the country. "They couldn't understand why I would be flying if I was not military or government." Private aircraft were unheard of in Saudi Arabia, and still are for the rank and file citizens of that country. It was a sign of things to come.

Once the paperwork was approved they launched on a course that would take them to a position halfway up the Red Sea. The reason being, they did not want to do a large angle across the

Saudi Arabia desert and also risk entering Jordanian airspace. Then as now the Middle East was a volatile area.

"Getting shot down wasn't an option."

Fortunately the engines hummed as they always did and they came out on that body of water that has seen probably more history, possibly, than any other place on the planet.

McCulloch bisected the Red Sea half way along its length. They flew across this 130 nm expanse to the other side finally seeing the sandy desert shores of Egypt rise above the sea and crossing its western bank just north of Egypt's border with the Sudan. He turned right and flew northwest along its length until the Suez Canal was off their right wing. They tracked along in this manner until they banked left and covered the last few miles to Cairo. They travelled over 1,300 nautical miles on this journey leg but by now they could cover these distances routinely.

"A thousand nautical miles was a walk in the park after so many legs of nearly two thousand or twenty-three hundred." They spent a day of leisure in Cairo taking a camel ride around the pyramids. The monoliths were new to Keating while a repeat for McCulloch who had been there a year earlier.

Leaving Cairo was not as easy as entering it. "The red tape was at a high level here. I used the world's best lubricant (US dollars). It's made things slide into place all over the world. The tomato you get depends on the lettuce you got." McCulloch maintained.

They were wheels up the next day for another long flight out over the Mediterranean Sea and westward to the Island of Palma in the western end of the sea off the east coast of Spain. But there was one small problem. They had to skirt about 60 miles off-shore of Libya, a country known to violate their international limit and harass commercial aircraft in international airspace at what Colonel Gaddafi called his "Line of Death". This "Line of Death" was a known quantity so they were forewarned and allowed themselves to drift right of their best course to widen the distance between themselves and the shores of Libya.

On this day there were several private aircraft heading west along the Mediterranean-part of a goodwill tour started in Texas involving a half dozen airplanes. Not long after their departure from Cairo jets of the Libyan Air Force launched from the many bases along the shore that curved from their border with Egypt to Benghazi. A short time later - on the air to air radio frequency - they heard the fear in the voice of a pilot flying a light twin aircraft some 15 minutes ahead of them reporting being harassed by several unidentified jets which made fast, close passes at their airplane. Every pilot knows that the turbulence generated by the wings and fuselage of a fast moving plane can flip your own aircraft into an uncontrolled attitude possibly even over-stressing the airframe or wings. There was no doubt there were Libyan fighters whose pilots knew full well they could kill a crew with these cowardly actions. They might have been under orders but were enjoying themselves too. Not many years before some Libyan Mirages fired unwisely on two American F-15s. They missed and were subsequently blown out of the skies by the F-15s as their reward.

The pilot and his wife in the airplane ahead were fearful of being fired upon but there was not much they could do other than turn away from the coast and hope that distance from Libya's 12 mile limit-even though they were nearly 60 NMs off the coast to begin with - might deter the jets.

McCulloch and Keating wondered if theirs was to be the same fate. Bloated as they were with explosive, 100/130 high octane aviation fuel was not comforting. One hot tracer or 20 millimetre round through a fuel tank would result in a highly visible, yellow/red fireball in the morning sky. This would have been something new. They had always assumed that the fireball scenario would occur at the end of some runway while taking off over-gross due to fuel.

The plane ahead reported that the jets had flown away and they were unharmed, but still McCulloch and Keating spent an uncomfortable half hour twisting and turning their heads looking for harassing jets when they crossed through the same airspace. But nothing happened.

The Cessna 414 droned over the island of Malta, a strategic location protected by the British during World War two. The island was bombed unmercifully by the Luftwaffe during the Spring of 1942. Malta held out due to RAF air cover and continuous air battles to maintain supremacy. One pilot was Canadian ace George Frederick (Buzz) Beurling dubbed the *Falcon of Malta* and subsequently the Knight of Malta. Beurling shot down 27 Axis aircraft in just 14 days over the besieged Mediterranean island. Before the war ended his total climbed to thirty-one aircraft destroyed.

McCulloch skimmed along the southwest coast of Sicily. The original plan had been to land in Algiers in Algeria but considering the turmoil in that country they decided to fore-go a chance to be tourists for a day.

They flew onward to their next port of call, Palma de Mallorca off the east coast of Spain. "We spent a lovely night in Palma then left the next day for Lisbon, Portugal."

They overflew Spain, cutting across the lower third of Spanish airspace and overnighted in Lisbon. The next morning they were airborne once again and headed across 760 nautical miles of the Atlantic Ocean to Santa Maria Island in the Azores. They landed at Aero Porto de Santa Marie on that little island on July 2nd.

The next morning, - once again fat with fuel - they struck out for Sydney, Nova Scotia 1,720 nautical miles to the west northwest over the Atlantic Ocean. "It's a long haul, Azores to Halifax (via Sydney) my home town."

Originally they had advanced the information that they would be landing in St. John's, Newfoundland. "That was just in case

Transport Canada was going to be hard-nosed about my having the extra fuel modification and tanks. We changed our flight plan from that town to Sydney just in case."

The engines never skipped a beat. The weather was fair and they landed in Sydney in the late afternoon. "We took on fuel and headed for my home town of Halifax landing at Halifax International Airport a couple hours later.

News of their impending arrival had been broadcast from Sydney, consequently the major Canadian Networks of the day, the CBC and CTV and the Chronicle-Herald newspaper were waiting for them when they landed. They did their appearances and gave their stories. The media were interested in the *hometown boy makes good*, angle. The pilots contacted relieved wives and relatives. In McCulloch's case; "They never bought into my philosophy of; stay far from home - most people die near home."

McCulloch has a thing about horizons; he always wants to know what is on the other side of them whether it's the Earth's horizon or that of business.

"We have home in our sights. No wonder most planes never circle the earth; there is a lot of risk, a lot of work and a lot of what most of people die with – money. Me? I buy memories and live dreams. If I live rich it won't hurt to die poor."

That evening, exhausted they crashed. They were tired. It was an accumulated weariness from nearly a month of tension and sometimes real danger. Pilots will tell you that flying is often many hours of boredom punctuated by moments of stark terror. But it is a terror the pilot has to quickly suppress, not be frozen by panic, because there is a situation that has to be addressed and overcome if you want to live. Sometimes you win, sometimes you don't.

The next morning they were in the air for Niagara Falls, New York on the last leg of 680 nautical miles. It was July 7. Loaded light they made better speed to the "Falls". The landing was anti-climactic and no one showed up from the media. A day like any other day. They had crammed years of experiences into less than a month. Back to a normal life? It would be hard to wind down.

Not for McCulloch. He had other plans. There was the North Pole and the South Pole and more trips to Brazil yet to come.

Gerald Keating was lighter in the pocket by over sixteen thousand dollars but richer in spirit he recalls. McCulloch was out of pocket considerably more at $60-$70,000 when you factor in the expense of the aircraft modifications, etc. Not only did they have to cover the aircraft's fuel costs but meals and of course the extra expense of staying at Five Star Hotels. Then there was the cost of entertainment as well.

The Cessna 414 used for the record breaking attempt. McCulloch in navy blue blazer meets press in Toronto.

Pilot to try for speed record on global trip to, from Falls

By CAROLYN KUMA
Niagara Gazette

Dave McCulloch stood next to his 1970 Cessna 414 airplane, squinting from the sun as he peered at the sky above Niagara Falls Inter-national Airport.

time flying around the world. I've sailed it."

He will join nine other planes in California — one from Germany and eight from Texas. The Texans are making the same trip to celebrate that state's sesquicentennial, he said.

RON SCHIFFERLE — Niagara Gazette

Dave McCulloch checks out his Cessna 414 airplane at Niagara Falls International Airport. The Ontario man will take off Monday in an attempt to beat the 104-hour speed record for flying around the world.

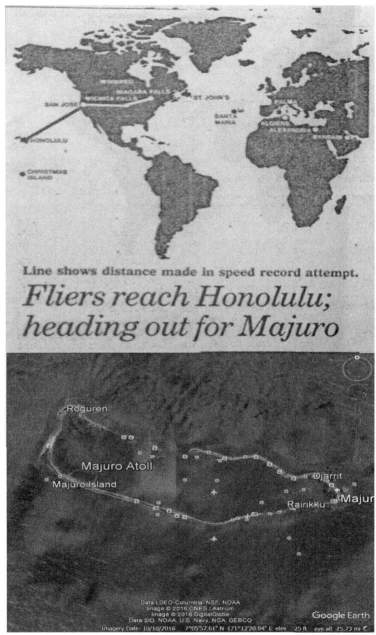

Majuro Atoll. An updated US WWII runway serves as the atoll's link to the rest of the world. Google Earth

Ayers Rock (Uluru) in Uluru-Kata Tjuta National Park, Australia.

Unidentified jets provided tension

B2 CALGARY HERALD   Tues., Aug. 5, 1986

Fighters buzz fliers near Gadhafi's Line of Death

Gerald Keating is back on the farm in Russell, Man., poorer in pocket by $16,000 but richer in spirit for his whirlwind tour of the globe, courtesy of the Water Doctor.

Keating was co-pilot for former Calgarian **Dave McCulloch** — the Water Doctor, or aqua-

Tom Keyser

Kevin Julian are just kicking into their second month of existence, so they don't know it yet. But theirs is already a sticky bond.

When Tara's mom, **Karen Ross**, realized her time would be quickly near, she sped off to Holy Cross Hospital, asking for and being granted a bed in the

Libya often deliberately harassed commercial and private aircraft in International Waters. It was a real concern for McCulloch and Keating.

Saturday, July 5, 1986   THE CHRONICLE-HERALD   THE MAIL-STAR   11

Aviators circling globe to top 21 international flying records

By TOM PETERS
Sackville Bureau

Pilot Dave McCulloch and co-pilot Gerald Keating leave Halifax International Airport today for Niagara Falls, N.Y., on the final leg of a round-the-world flight.

McCulloch, of Toronto, and Keating, of Russell, Man., left Niagara Falls, N.Y., June 9 in a twin-engine Cessna 414 in an attempt to break at least 21 international flying records, including the 23,757 mile, globe-circling odyssey.

The record attempts were all in the 3,000-kilogram category.

Although the two men should complete their trip today, McCulloch, formerly of Milford Station, Hants County, said it may be at least a year before they find out officially if they have established any records. He said it takes that long before all official documentation is filed from and approved by the various aviation agencies.

McCulloch, a water purification expert and a veteran flyer of some 20 years, said the trip was a once-in-a-lifetime experience. And it was expensive — costing $60,000 to $70,000, he said.

Keating, a road builder and operator of an implement agency in Manitoba, is also an experienced flyer. He said it was a difficult time of the year for him to leave his business but the opportunity became available so he seized it. "I'm not getting any younger . . ."

By the time they reached the Halifax International Airport Friday at approximately 1 p.m., the two flyers had already logged about 130 hours. Their flight had taken them to such places as San Jose, Calif., Honolulu, Brisbane, Darwin, Bombay, Cairo, and Santa Maria in the Azores.

McCulloch said he is planning other trips, among them another round-the-world flight — this time eastbound — in 1987, and flights to the Falkland Islands and the Antarctic.

Back in Nova Scotia and heading for Niagara Falls, New York to finish a successful attempt to break world records. See documents that follow. An original of above this skewed article was unavailable for copy. This photo saved from video archive.

Chapter Twenty-Three

The Numbers for the Around the World Westward Trip
June 9 to July 7, 1986
Pilot - David Donald McCulloch
Co-Pilot - Gerald Keating
Aircraft: Pressurized Cessna 414 (3000-6000 kgs)
(Canadian Registration - C-FASB)
Class C-1e Piston Engines
2 continental TSIO-520 engines – 340 HP each.

The Total Elapsed Time of the trip was 681 hours 18 minutes. (Includes air, ground and layover times)
Total Distance Flown: 40,563.93 Kilometers (21,904.52 Nautical Miles – 25,190.2 statute Miles)
When the total of 681R 18M is computed into distance flown the end result is 59.54 kms/hr but this is not a true record of actual in the air speed.

The engines were burning for a total of 129 hours. When the total distance of 40,563.93 is divided by 129 we get an airspeed of 314.45 kilometers per hour (195.27statute mph or 169 knots).

The reason the speeds are computed in kilometers per hour is because the world organization that keeps the recognized official records – Fédération Aéronautique Internationale - is in France and that country employs the metric system.

The record McCulloch set was a world speed record around the world, westbound. His was the 23rd twin engined aircraft to fly around the world and he accomplished this feat westbound against the prevailing winds (which most likely accounts for the extra hours) because he almost always had a headwind to contend with. Headwinds subtract from the airplane's ground speed, the actual progress/time that an aircraft makes over the terrain.

The biggest factor was the amount of fuel McCulloch had to carry to cover the distances over the water. As mentioned previously the longest leg was from Majuro Island to Honiara in Guadalcanal in the Solomon Islands, a distance of 2,640 nautical miles. 3042 statute miles (5149 kilometers) is a mind boggling distance for a light aircraft. There are biz-jets even today that do not have this range. The fact that McCulloch was able to pull this feat off is credit all on its own.

The Cessna 414 would never have been able to accomplish these over water legs without the extra fuel tanks McCulloch had installed in the aircraft. He would have been hopping from one small island to another and that would have eaten much more air time than he actually took, particularly when crossing the Pacific between the United States and Australia.

It would be another year before the Fédération Aéronautique Internationale would have the numbers tabulated and posted. In the meantime McCulloch and Keating would be receiving recognition from the national Aeronautic Association in the United States A formal presentation was being set up for the pilots depending on their availability. One such was to be on

May 15th, 1987 at the Air and Space Museum in Washington, DC. However McCulloch's schedule was showing him in Europe during this time frame so another time was being considered-perhaps in Oshkosh in 1987*.

In April of that year, McCulloch received a copy of a letter to the president of the National Aeronautic Association from Yan Whytlaw, NAA's Technical Counsellor informing him that David McCulloch was now recognized as holding a World Class Record for his and Keating's around the world record attempt which was now a reality.

*Author. More synchronicity. Had McCulloch received the award at Oshkosh it would have been done at the Theatre in the Woods at Oshkosh. Myself and several other pilots from Nova Scotia were tied down beside the theatre one hundred feet away.

McCulloch (center) and Keating (right) receive their record breaking award from the American National Aeronautic Assoc. at the Smithsonian Aerospace museum in Washington, DC. (Documents in following pages)

Awards and Documents

This diploma for the record-setting westward flight around the world in a light twin engine plane hangs on McCulloch's wall in his home in Valley, Nova Scotia. (Photo, David McCulloch)

Royal Canadian Flying Clubs Association

Canadian Aviation
RECORD
D'Aviation Canadien

SPEED AROUND THE WORLD (WESTBOUND)

NIAGARA FALLS, LINCOLN, ST. JOSE, HONOLULU, MAJURO, HONARIO, BRISBANE, DARWIN
BALI, KUALA LUMPUR, BOMBAY, BAHRAIN, CAIRO, PALMA, SANTA MARIA, SYDNEY, HALIFAX, NIAG/

CLASS / CLASSE	C.1.E GROUP II
AIRCRAFT / AVION	CESSNA 414 C-FASB
CREW / EQUIPAGE	DAVID McCULLOCH, PILOT; GERALD KEATING, CO-PILOT
DATE / DATE	JUNE 9, 1986 - JULY 7, 1986
RECORD / RECORD	61.84 KILOMETERS PER HOUR

PRESIDENT

NOVEMBER 3, 1986

The Canadian Award from The Royal Canadian Flying Clubs Association.

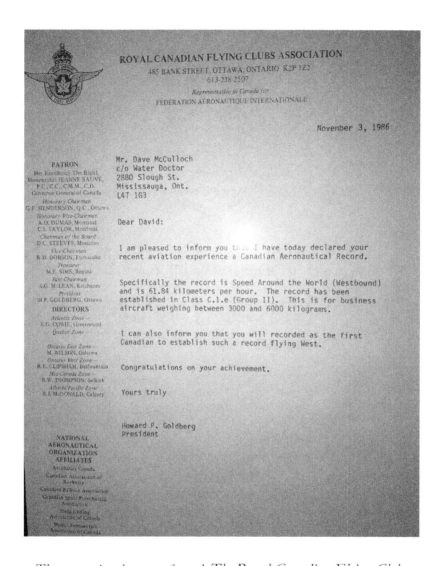

ROYAL CANADIAN FLYING CLUBS ASSOCIATION
485 BANK STREET, OTTAWA, ONTARIO K2P 1Z2
613-238-2507
Representative in Canada for
FÉDÉRATION AÉRONAUTIQUE INTERNATIONALE

November 3, 1986

Mr. Dave McCulloch
c/o Water Doctor
2880 Slough St.
Mississauga, Ont.
L4T 1G3

Dear David:

I am pleased to inform you that I have today declared your recent aviation experience a Canadian Aeronautical Record.

Specifically the record is Speed Around the World (Westbound) and is 61.84 kilometers per hour. The record has been established in Class C.1.e (Group II). This is for business aircraft weighing between 3000 and 6000 kilograms.

I can also inform you that you will recorded as the first Canadian to establish such a record flying West.

Congratulations on your achievement.

Yours truly

Howard P. Goldberg
President

The supporting document from theThe Royal Canadian Flying Clubs Association

National Aeronautic Association

Representing in the United States of America
The Federation Aeronautique Internationale
awards this

Certificate of Record

to
Dave McCulloch, Pilot
Gerald Keating, Copilot
for
U.S. National Record
Class C-1e, Piston Engine
Speed Around the World Westbound
Niagara Falls, Lincoln, San Jose, Honolulu,
Majuro, Guadalcanal, Brisbane, Darwin, Bali,
Kuala Lumpur, Madras, Bombay, Bahrain, Cairo,
Palma, Santa Maria, Sydney, Halifax, Niagara Falls
Cessna 414, C-FASB
Elapsed Time: 681 hours 18 minutes
June 9 - July 7, 1986

37.00mph
(59.54kmh)

President

Contest and Record Board

The American National Aeronautic Association's **Certificate of Record**
honouring McCulloch and Keating.

Riding The Fire

NATIONAL AERONAUTIC ASSOCIATION
"The Aero Club of America"

SUITE 550 • 1400 EYE ST., N.W. • WASHINGTON, D.C. 20005
AREA CODE 202-898-1313 • CABLE—NATAERO • TELEX 469170
UNITED STATES REPRESENTATIVE FEDERATION AERONAUTIQUE INTERNATIONALE

February 9, 1987

Mr. Dave McCulloch
2880 Slough Street
Mississauga Ontario
CANADA L4T 1G3

Dear Dave:

It is a pleasure to notify you that the dossier for your performance
June 9 - July 7, 1986 has been accepted as a U.S. National Record as
well as a Canadian record and forwarded to the FAI in Paris for
registration as a World record. Our computation showed a total
distance of 40,563.93 kms; elapsed time of 681 hrs 18 minutes and
speed of 59.54 km/h. The Royal Canadian Flying Club showed a speed
of 61.84 km/h and we are not sure which the FAI will accept so we'll
just have to wait and see.

I am not sure that the FAI will accept the group formation flight as
about 5600 kms of your flight was by yourself. That converts to
about 86% of the trip was in formation and 14% solo. We have
accepted that as a U.S. Record and asked the FAI for a ruling so
probably a year from now we'll get a decision.

An invoice for the sanction and registration fees is enclosed. We
will use the slide of you, Gerald and the aircraft for the 1987
Record Book, unless you want to send us a substitute photo. The
publisher says a Black and White glossy 8x10 shows up best but he
will use whatever we give him.

Enclosed are some pictures from the Air and Space Museum presen-
tations. We will have to arrange a formal presentation in the next
few weeks. Give us your ideas on that. We are tentatively planning
something in connection with the Collier trophy. We hope that Dick
Rutan and Jeana Yeager will win that and the Collier Dinner will be
May 15. You will probably be in Europe then so we we'll plan something else for you - maybe Oshkosh. Let us know your ideas and
we'll cooperate. Maybe a joint US/ Canadian ceremony in Ottawa,
Montreal, etc.

Let us know what we can do to help out in your next venture. If you
get desperate I'll go with you from Spitzbergen to the North Pole.
I've never been to Spitzbergen so it really intrigues me.

A faint copy of the support letter from the National Aeronautics Assoc. It's
author-Milton Brown-offered his services as a pilot as crew on McCulloch's
next adventure to the North Pole. McCulloch accepted.

Chapter Twenty-Four

Flying Into Earth's Deep-Freeze.

The remainder of 1986 was somewhat anti-climactic after a record setting adventure around the world in a light, twin engined airplane. Comparatively, flying around Canada and the United States was a bit blasé. McCulloch settled into business mode for a time.

He opened more *Water Doctor* Franchises bringing the total to forty-two. And business was good. But it wasn't too long before the old familiar itch was back.

It should be evident by now that McCulloch has something that drives him; something other than the need to succeed, to rise above the meager beginnings of his youth. There is no doubt that the aforementioned was always with him, but that can't be blamed on a miserable youth. Sure his family was poor but they were cohesive; they looked out for one another, made do and lived fairly comfortably within the limits of their parent's ability and income. They were close but this closeness did not impinge on young David McCulloch's need to see over horizons. A ship's horizon is about 16 miles away. As we have already discovered 16 miles is not far enough away for McCulloch. His four years at sea had partially inured him to its allure, the oft toted romance of its expanse. You don't see much from the bowels of an oil tanker in any event. "Down there it's pretty boring."

So it is no surprise that a man who would see far horizons would wish to climb above those near horizons to look twice that distance and then eventually as much as one hundred miles with the hell of a view afforded by the windscreen of an airplane; whether it be a Cessna 150 or a Learjet 23. And we have seen in recent chapters just what horizons and the land before, McCulloch has seen.

McCulloch now set his sights on a trip to the North Pole. "I wanted to see if there was a Santa Claus." More seriously however he decided that he wanted to retrace the steps of Commander Richard Evelyn Byrd, Jr. (USN) who made the flight on May 9, 1926. Byrd would be made a Rear Admiral in 1929 for his later forays into the Antarctic.

McCulloch believed it would make a more interesting adventure to retrace Byrd's steps. "Taking the same route on the same day appealed to me." But he needed a co-pilot or a navigator.

Not surprisingly McCulloch discovered that finding someone to share the journey on such a hazardous expedition was not easy. It was McCulloch's experience that "...most people will not live their dreams. They are hell bent on dying with a maximum amount of money in the bank."

At that time McCulloch still belonged to a group, the *Tall Tale Society of New York*. To be a member you have to have a tall tale or adventure. "I had no problem qualifying."

One of its members, Al Solomon, got wind of McCulloch's plan to fly to the North Pole. He offered his services to McCulloch who advised that it just required cash and a share in the expenses to get aboard.

Solomon flew to Toronto the next day with a cheque in hand and the deal was closed. They remained close friends until Solomon's death.

A communication document was sent to McCulloch by the National Aeronautic Association in Washington, DC confirming the organization had accepted McCulloch as achieving a world record on his Flight Around the World. The document's author, Vice-President (NAA) and pilot Milton M. Brown offered that organization's help in McCulloch's next venture. He added, "If you get desperate I'll go with you from Spitsbergen to the North Pole. I've never been to Spitsbergen so it really intrigues me."

As it turned out, during the process of arranging speed records and information on attempting a (first) formation flight around the North Pole McCulloch talked to Milt Brown at the NAA in Washington. "He was excited about our adventure and was FAI rep in the USA. I casually mentioned 'you should come with us'." Brown jumped at the chance and flew to meet McCulloch the next day. They remained friends until Brown's passing away. "He would figure in some of my future business adventures."

Preparations for the route from Toronto to the North Pole once again required the installation of ferry tanks to extend the Cessna 414's range, specifically the conversion to long-range tanks and the installation of long range High Frequency radio in addition to the normal UHF radio. There was no GPS navigation in 1987 so once McCulloch and his co-pilot left Tromsø for Spitsbergen and the North Pole he would have to rely on the old stand-bys; a stop watch, Sun compass and celestial navigation using a sextant.

On May 8, 1987, accompanied by two single engined aircraft (Model 35 Beech V-tail Bonanzas) one from Texas and one from Germany - taking part in a formation flight to the North Pole - and with much fanfare from the media, 49 year old McCulloch was airborne out of Toronto for a 950 nautical mile leg to Goose Bay, Labrador. He refuelled there. Once again McCulloch - and for the first time his co-pilot Al Solomon and navigator Milton Brown - would have to climb into their mandated, albeit, uncomfortable Immersion Suits for the trip across the Labrador Sea to Narsarsuag Airport, the infamous and dangerous airport 45 nautical miles up a fiord on the west coast of Greenland.

This leg was becoming a commonplace flight for McCulloch.

"It was nothing new. We crossed 700 miles of freezing cold water littered with small and monstrous icebergs." Still, it was no less dangerous. And this was in 1987, 27 years before ferry pilots on the current popular television program, *Dangerous Flights*, continually espoused their trepidations associated with light aircraft transits across this route; this despite their access to modern navigation aids such as GPS.

McCulloch refuelled and climbed away from Narsarsuag; climbing quickly to the east because the terrain of Greenland rises steeply on the eastern end of Narsarsuag. Within 50 miles the mountains top at 5,600 feet.

Reykjavik, Iceland waited 740 nautical miles in the distance. "We rested up and enjoyed the city."

Reykjavik is a frequent-and necessary fuel stop-over for ferry pilots moving planes back and forth to Europe. Other traffic in or out of Iceland is commercial traffic flying goods and passengers to or from that country. It is no longer a fuel stop for international airline traffic which has the ability to cross the Atlantic easily with their on-board fuel.

Their rest stop over, McCulloch and company had to depart for Oslo, Norway, a trip of some 800 nautical miles. But weather lay in their path. Icing conditions.

"When we left Iceland there was an event with one of our single engined Bonanzas. It was from Texas."

McCulloch departed for Oslo, Norway. Several other aircraft were making the trip as well so they departed together.

"Because I was expecting ice I departed first to relay reports to the two single bonanzas."

It was cloudy with light rain and a temperature of approximately 5C. "I experienced ice at 5,000 feet, but continued max climb rate and was using de-icing boots."

De-icing boots are thin rubber strips attached to the leading edges of the wings and the horizontal stabilizers. Air is fed behind the strips in pulses that causes them to expand and contract breaking the ice free in most conditions.

"I broke out on top at 11,000 ft and relayed to the others that they would require full power to climb all the way to 11,000 feet" One of the airplanes whose pilot was accompanied by a co-pilot pushed all the way through to the top. The other pilot lost confidence and attempted a return to Reykjavik. In doing so it accumulated a severe amount of ice on descending through heavier cloud with super-cooled water droplets which freeze upon contacting any surface. He was losing lift and talked about a forced landing.

McCulloch thought this was a bad idea, fearing the plane would get so heavy with ice and the wings' ability would be so deteriorated that their ability to produce lift would result in a stall. Depending on the airplane's attitude the result could end with a dive into the freezing cold waters of the North Atlantic.

"I gave him a stern 'never give up lecture' during his return to Reykjavik. He was very afraid and you could hear the fear in his voice." The pilot mentioned doing a forced landing on a beach. That was a no-no as far as McCulloch was concerned. The other bonanza went back down to comfort him and be at the airport. Both made it. The pilot abandoned his plane in Reykjavik and took an airliner home. What happened to the airplane after that is unclear but it was probably ferried back to the United States by an experienced Ferry Pilot. A day later the other Beech 35 showed up in Oslo.

McCulloch landed in Oslo, Norway. While over-nighting there and taking on full tanks of fuel he met up with two additional single V-tailed Bonanzas and returned to a formation of three aircraft including McCulloch's 414.

The first leg of their over ocean and pack ice trip to the North Pole would begin in Tromsø, Norway. The full distance from Oslo would be 2,000 nautical miles. This translates into 1,845 statute miles or just short of 3,000 kilometres. No matter which measure of distance you use it is a long way to travel to get to the top of the world. They left the next morning, flying some 650 NMs from Oslo to Tromsø, curving to the westward to avoid flying into Sweden's airspace. This was rugged terrain, remote, with snow and glacier capped mountains to the west of their track reaching up nearly 8,000 feet and to 2,500 feet further north. It is rocky terrain shot through with rivers and fiords and remote mountain lakes. The topography afforded little in the way of emergency landing space although present day Norway has provided a few airports along the spine of the country.

Staying to the east between the mountain chain and the border with Sweden meant fewer mountain tops but this was not a problem for the 414 which achieved better fuel economy and speeds at the higher altitudes.

They fueled up in Tromsø. Three aircraft would attempt the recreation of Admiral Byrd's historic flight to the North Pole; McCulloch's Cessna 414-a twin engine aircraft; Dr. Meisner (Texas) in his V-tailed Beech Bonanza and Rienhard Buculay of Germany in the other V-tailed Beech.

That night their supper consisted of vegetables and Reindeer meat. "It's a very lean meat. Very tasty. It reminded me of Moose meat." Reindeer are a small animal with large antlers. "They are not bulky however they are very strong. Perhaps that's why Santa uses them." McCulloch observed. "They are light. Makes them better for flight."

They were headed for the North Pole. "I wanted to see if Santa really lived there."

On the morning of May 9, 1987 the three aircraft departed Tromsø for Spitsbergen on Svalbard Island. The island then was controlled by Norway and the USSR. This would cause problems.

Sixty-two years later to the day, McCulloch and the other two crews were now at the point of duplicating Commander, Ret.d (later)Rear Admiral Richard E. Byrd's flight to the North Pole.

Byrd's airplane-sans wings-was towed on a barge from Norway to Spitsbergen through pack ice. Byrd did not want to risk flying from Norway to Svalbard Island. The point was to fly to the North Pole and back again, not make a long journey out of the venture.

The plane's wings were refitted to the fuselage and tests were performed, the fuel was loaded aboard. On May 9, 1926, Byrd as the navigator and his pilot Floydd Bennet took off from Spitsbergen (Svalbard) for the North Pole in a Fokker F-VII Tri-motor monoplane named *Josephine Ford*. They returned to Spitsbergen fifteen and one half hours later. Byrd claimed to have reached the North Pole.

Byrd received widespread acclaim in the United States-a country hungry for accomplishments during the time of the Great Depression and was later awarded the Medal of Honor. His fame enabled him to secure funding for future attempts to fly over the South Pole.

Byrd earned his pilot wings in August 1917, developing a passion for flight. He suffered a chronic injury to an ankle while playing sports that effectively curtailed his naval career and he was retired from active service while put on special duties. Despite being retired he managed to advance through the ranks until he was designated a Rear Admiral. Many of his subsequent exploits were privately funded including his attempt to reach the North Pole, which was underwritten by Edsel Ford, son of Henry Ford, founder of the Ford Motor Company. The Fokker

Tri-motor airplane was named in honor of Edsel Ford's wife, Josephine. Perhaps one of his greatest contributions to aviation was the pioneering of techniques for navigating airplanes over the open ocean using drift indicators and bubble sextants.

Unlike the South Pole, The North Pole is a fixed geological position almost three miles (6,240meters) below the chaotic ice surface of the Arctic Ocean which is frozen over for most of the year. In fact in 1987 it was frozen over all year long. This is the North Polar Ice-Cap; an ice cap that drifts around breaking into sections then rejoining in haphazard fashions due to the Earth's rotational forces and the effects of currents and winds. Because of this constant movement it has been impossible to locate a beacon of some description in place for navigation purposes. As a result McCulloch and his companions had to rely on pretty much the same technology as Admiral Byrd 62 years earlier.

As mentioned there was no GPS to rely on in 1987; at least not commercially or privately. The United States armed forces, in fact, had GPS at that point but it was a secret and used only by them and the armed forces of their closest allies. Within several years, however, the private sector and other countries on the planet had clued in on the fact that there were signals coming in from satellites in space that could be triangulated to fix positions on the surface of the Earth and its oceans.

The signals were scrambled signals however, but a signal is a signal whose time can be calculated. Scrambled or not their journey at the speed of light were a constant. It was the time differences that were important. The scrambled signals were good enough to get most navigators within a mile or so of their destination. It wasn't good enough for precision landings but for aviation, if you get within a mile of anything you are almost over top of it.

Four or five years after the Soviet Union collapsed the US gave up and unscrambled its GPS signals and now just about anyone could get their position fixed within a fifty foot (16 meter) circle.

McCulloch and company did not have this luxury however. Once they headed north from Spitsbergen they would have to rely on good old compass (the magnetic version relied on a fix with the Magnetic North Pole) a sextant and stop-watch navigation often called Dead Reckoning; an unfortunate choice of words for those who could end up dead if they didn't get the navigation right. Or in this case crashing on an ice floe or ditching in the freezing waters of the Arctic Ocean.

The navigation to Svalbard Island and the airport in Spitsbergen was more of the same for McCulloch. There were navigation beacons and the island was staying put not drifting around; a fixed location above the surface of the ocean. There was only one problem however. Neither the Norwegians nor the Soviets had much use for adventurers like McCulloch and company. The unlikely duo of Norway and the Soviet Union shared custody of the island and the Spitsbergen Airport. And they were jealous of their fuel supplies. Contrary to what he had been led to believe McCulloch was told that he and the two V-tailed Bonanzas would not be able to refuel there or anywhere else on the island of Svalbard. The fuel was reserved for military and government aircraft. And the same goes for food as well. No amount of posturing or the waving of American flags was going to help here; particularly with the Soviets.

One can only imagine the list of four letter words going through McCulloch's mind at this point. It was just like Brazil all over again; but with ice. No amount of American dollars was going to solve this problem.

Discouraged, McCulloch, Milton Brown and co-pilot Al Solomon went to their lodgings. "It was more like a barrack camp hotel than a hotel." Not content with the status quo, McCulloch, Solomon and Brown began nosing around. They asked questions, talked to some people, made inquiries. Someone mentioned that the local ESSO dealer had several barrels of 100 low lead fuel stashed away. "They were down over an embankment near the airport. Trouble was he was out of town." He had a hideaway fifty miles out of town at the top of a mountain. He claimed he had built it there to have a place where he could get away from it all. "To get away from it all? Christ we were in the most away-from-it-all place I had ever seen. It was so still and quiet that you freaked out." McCulloch shook his head.

The only option available to them was to rent a helicopter and find this ESSO dealer and get permission to purchase the aviation fuel. "Dr.Weisner, Col. Milt Brown, Al Solomon and myself climbed aboard the chopper and we went looking for the cabin in the sky on a snowy mountain top in Svalbard."

McCulloch thinks back to those men who are all deceased now. Like McCulloch they were men of adventure, not the types to let obstacles stand in their way. They were good friends. The price of poker – in this case adventure flying - was going up.

"My legacy is going to be adventure not left over money."

They went in search of the elusive and shy ESSO dealer. He was hidden away "… in a world of pure whiter mountains and wasteland. We spotted a small black spot on the side of a mountain." It was a log cabin.

The helicopter pilot landed on the side of the mountain in one of only a few flat spaces available. It was somewhat perilous. The chances of the chopper sliding over the edge was not something McCulloch wanted to think about.

A man and a woman came running out of the cabin alarmed at this intrusion and the noise and clatter of the helicopter. It was the ESSO dealer. His out-of-the-way and secluded hideaway was no more. At least for now. He demanded to know who McCulloch and his friends were but soon calmed down when he found out why they were there and their mission to fly over the

North Pole. "After a warm visit and our promise of money, free medical services, etc., they said take the gas." The wife added, "We don't need money up here." Perhaps she was happy for the company.

They returned to Longyear, a town 4.5 kilometres southeast of the airport. The next day was a hard day. They had only five gallon jerry cans with which to transfer 100LL octane gas from the 45 gallon drums to the tanks in their planes. They had to climb up the embankment and carry the jerry-cans over to the three airplanes. It was cold and slow work, but they got it done.

The following day the private pilots were prepared to leave at dawn-or near dawn because the Sun never really set at that time of the year.
Fat with fuel they were comforted by the 7,500 foot runway they would use to launch.

"We told the officials that like good little boys we would return to Norway." But after they got airborne, they swung to the north on a heading for the 1600 mile (2576 kilometres) round trip to the top of the world.

Chapter Twenty-Five

In search of a barber pole and a jolly old fat man.

"We had an ace in the hole. His name was Rienhard Buculay, the pilot of the V-tailed Bonanza from Germany." It turns out that Buculay had managed to cram a state of the art Inertial Guidance System (IGS)-well as much Inertial Guidance System that one could decently carry-into his single engine V-Tail. Nine thousand dollars' worth as a matter of fact; and that was back when $9,000.00 US dollars was $9,000.00.

I'm not going into the workings of this most modern of guidance systems initially developed for the US Navy; in particular their nuclear subs armed with nuclear guided missiles. But airlines used it as well. It was built on gyros and sensing devices that sensed every turn, climb or decent of an aircraft or a sub. Basically it knew where it was within a kilometre of its actual position.

So McCulloch, Doc Meisner and of course Buculay could rely on reasonable position. The problem is, IGS is dependent on gyros and slip indicators that record the most minute of influences on the aircraft after it has been pre-set to a precise position on the Earth's surface to accurately predict the aircraft's course and position as it travels to its destination. It works well in the relatively stable environments of airliners at altitude, submarines in still waters and large naval vessels, to name a few.

Small aircraft like a Beech Bonanza are susceptible to turbulence and easily pushed around by the winds at the lower altitudes they ply. A few feet of drift here could very well result in a large variation in the course one hour later.

It has been known for 150 years that magnetic compasses are highly unreliable above the Arctic Circle. The Earth's magnetic lines of force dip steeply down into the Earth's magnetic pole which in 1987 was somewhere at the north end of Ellesmere Island in northern Canada. It is not a single point delineating the magnetic north pole but rather a massive area that confused compasses as to its location, allowing for large variations amounting to course swings of 20-30 degrees or more, the closer you get to the location. Additionally, because the magnetic lines of force dip down into the Earth, at this point the compass needle wants to point down as well and causes the needle to jamb against the casing or bind on the axis shaft around which the needle swings.

Once north of Svalbard there are no other islands by which to navigate. Within a couple of hundred miles on his northerly track McCulloch was seeing large and small icebergs. Some were impressive in size. In the spring one could expect to see these conglomerations of fresh water adrift in a sea of salt; some as large as aircraft carriers or even small islands. As immense as they may appear above the surface this is only ten percent of their mass. Ninety percent remains hidden below in the murky depths. Oil companies exploring the Continental shelf off Newfoundland, Canada found deep, parallel gouges in the ocean floor as deep as 200 meters. This puzzled geologists for some time until they discovered it was the bottoms of icebergs grinding along the sea-floor causing the trenches. Often they would come to a grating halt, anchored in place until the seawater melted them enough to allow them to move on when the tides and winds accomplished this task.

As they progressed towards the Pole the pilots began to see more ice floes, relatively flat, interspersed with icebergs scattered across the surface of the Arctic Sea. Once they approached the Polar Ice cap these relatively flat cakes of ice became a solid mass of broken and tortured plates forming the pressure ridges along the "coast" of the cap.

Every hour along their track the planes would turn one hundred eighty degrees according to their compasses; take a new sighting of the Sun's angle to that course and its position above the horizon, turn back one hundred eighty degrees to that course having reset approximately 15 degrees from the former course. A check with the inertial guidance system in German pilot Buculay's Bonanza gave them a second point of reference.

The closer they got to the ice-clamper mantle of the North Polar Icecap the more they noticed the presence of polar bears. They swam from flat ice floe to flat floe hunting seals, fish or anything that was edible.

Polar bears were not a new animal for McCulloch. They populate northern Canada in large numbers. They can grow to a weight of 1,500 pounds or 680 kilograms. Whether you calculate in Imperial measure or metric that is one large animal. And despite their (particularly the cute little cubs) popularity with southerners who see them in zoo locations around the world Polar Bears are one of the very few animals around the world that will track and kill a human for food. And they aren't finicky about how they do it either. They usually overpower their prey, knock it to the ground (or snowy surface) place a large paw with hundreds of pounds of weight bearing down on the victim and start feeding. Apparently they are too impatient to make sure their meal is dead first.

"Land here and you could be lunch."

This was another threat to life and limb should one of the planes have to make a forced landing somewhere on the ice cap. That is assuming they survived the landing. McCulloch noted very few areas on the icecap that looked smooth and flat enough to land on. Pressure ridges - large mile long jumbled lines of ice forced upward by the Polar Ice Cap's constant movement and large plates of the ice came together, neither giving quarter to the other - resulted in the ice being forced upward in these long ridges, some of which could reach a height of 30 meters (approx. 100 feet). Further along their track they might see the exact opposite effect as the icecap tore apart in long leads of just a few meters to a couple of hundred.

The exact position of the North Pole is 13,900 feet (4,240 meters) below the surface of the mean Arctic Ocean surface. The temperature at 8,000 feet was -30 Celsius (-22 F). McCulloch's Cessna 414 had a heater in the nose of the aircraft that was fueled by avgas from one of the wing tanks. "It kept the cabin comfortable."

Assuming that the plane made a successful forced landing, pilot and passengers would have the killer temperatures, and the marauding Polar bears to contend with. Assuming they survived the landing their most immediate concern was staying warm. The cabin of an airplane constructed of aluminum is considered one of the worst structures in which to seek protection from the cold because the aluminum fuselage quickly adjusts to the ambient temperature. It affords protection from the winds but little else as the hull and interior quickly become cold soaked.

McCulloch had a rifle along for the attempt. Other than that they had their survival suits for protection. They were rated to allow those who went into Arctic waters forty-five minutes of time for rescue. Considering their location there was little chance of survival if they went into the water. It would take many hours for a boat to get to them. They would just be prolonging the inevitable.

Should they land on the icecap and survive there would be a delay of perhaps days while a ship with a helicopter could get close to their position and start looking for them. At least-depending on which plane was down-they would have two others to mark their position, perhaps stay with the down plane before they headed back to Spitsbergen, but they would not be able to wait for the rescue to arrive.

Hour after hour they made their position checks using their Sun compasses, verifying with Buculay's Inertial Guidance System.

They droned onward, McCulloch and his crew always vigilant for hiccups in engine performance. The chunk of articulated metal on each wing, their life's blood, the engine oil that combated friction and heat and their sustaining 100 LL aviation fuel, were the three key ingredients to a successful flight. The unending vista of pressure ridges, drifts and tantalizing flat areas, often shot through with saltwater leads rolled below them. Below the North Polar Ice Cap the Arctic Ocean teamed with sea life, schools of fish and squid; seals and Beluga whales although the latter do not often venture very far in from the ice-cap's 'coast'. They are air breathers and if caught too far in under the cap with no open lead available they could drown.

One other creature not reliant on air is often found under that great mass of ice; the nuclear submarines of the United States and Soviet Russia. There is no way of knowing if either of these were present under the ice cap back on May, 9, 1987 but the odds were that perhaps one or two were during the hey-day of the cold war.

After a fraction under eight hours of flight time from Spitsbergen at an average speed of 160 NM (295kilometers) per hour, the radios of the three aircraft were exchanging excited messages. At 11:02 Zulu (GMT) the Sun fixes from the three airplanes and Buculay's EGS confirmed they were over the Geographic North Pole. They pulled into a tight grouping and flew in formation around this fixed point, circling it three times; the first in history to have done this while setting a record for the shortest time flown from Spitsbergen to the pole. "We lined up and did several tight formation flights around the North Pole." And other myths were shattered. "There was no North Pole to see and we didn't see any evidence of Santa Claus."

McCulloch opened the small window beside him and pushed his business card, a small brass name-tag and a furled Canadian flag through the opening. The slipstream grabbed and flung the items rearward before they dropped to the frozen surface of the North Pole. "Maybe someday a scientist or some explorer might find the items, frozen in a chunk of ice and wonder how they got there." McCulloch mused.

From his position over the pole every direction in which you looked was a different time zone and was south; and not necessarily toward Norway. So since 'the lucky old Sun had nothing to do' they used it and the time to fix a track back to Spitsbergen. They set their Directional Gyros and turned on course to their destination over 800 miles of ice and sub-zero seawater.

It was just over six hours from the North Pole on an uneventful flight south when McCulloch's ADFs started to come alive and he could get a good fix on Spitsbergen. Fifteen hours and fifty-two minutes after taking off from Spitsbergen the Cessna 414's wheels kissed the runway setting a new world record for the time flown from there to the North Pole and back.

To say that the Norwegian and Russian authorities in Spitsbergen were angry would have been an understatement. "They were really pissed off." McCulloch recalled. "They thought we had left for Norway and once we were airborne they forgot about us. But suddenly, nearly 16 hours later we were back...looking for aviation fuel."

The airport officials refused to sell them fuel and washed their hands of the three planes. They would not waste fuel on a few adventurous private pilots. They apparently forgot that it was a group of adventurous private pilots that began and fostered aviation to begin with. Once the hard work was out of the way the military and the commercial sectors moved in and took over so that the military powers could flex their muscles and the commercial sector could make fortunes from it. Such has been the fate of general aviation.

"It's look after yourself at this time in history, a position I've been in many times in business and during hairy and scary flying conditions." McCulloch thrives on adversity and challenges.

If it had not been for the Norwegians sharing that field and only the Soviets were involved the pilots might have been treated even less friendly. They could have been arrested. Thankfully that option was out.

But they needed fuel. They had exhausted their other option having used all of the fuel the ESSO dealer had. They had one alternative; MO gas. The civilian population calls it car gas and that's what it is. It has a lower octane rating and in some cases the additives in this fuel can cause the deterioration of O-rings and other seals in an airplane engine. Auto fuel still contained lead in 1987 so they had that going for them and high-test gasoline was rated at 97 octane in North America.

It was their only option. McCulloch's long range tank supply still had a considerable amount available so he was mixing the two together which lessened his likelihood of seal and O-ring damage. The two Bonanzas had less fuel but were able to mix their tanks as well.

"I probably could have made it to Tromsø but decided to take on some additional and fly straight to Oslo." The two Bonanzas opted for Tromsø in order to take on 100 Octane.

"We got airborne assuring the officials at Spitsbergen that this time we really were going back to Norway." McCulloch's flight track to Oslo was 1,100 NM, more than twice that of the distance to Tromsø however it was 'old hat' for McCulloch's Cessna.

The three airplanes remained in touch for the first leg of the flight but then McCulloch's course was further southwestward from that of the Bonanzas. He was able to fly at faster cruise speeds now that he didn't have to maintain an airspeed more in keeping with the Bonanza's cruise speed to maintain formation.

They landed in Oslo, refueled, rested and then pushed on to London. There McCulloch parted ways with his co-pilot, Al Solomon and Navigator, Milton Brown. But he had new passengers; his wife Linda and his one year old daughter Kathryn. He rested briefly then went for a holiday in Madrid, Spain then to Lisbon, Portugal. He used this as a prolonged rest period, toured the cities, enjoying the food before the inevitable return to his business back in Canada.

No rest for the weary; at least not much. Time and money.... McCulloch would like to spend more time vacationing, perhaps explore a new destination while in Western Europe but he has a business to run.

Once again and for the second time in a year McCulloch flight plans from Lisbon to the Azores, a distance of 760 NM. They land, rest and McCulloch tops off his tanks.

It's a 1,760 nautical mile trip from Santa Maria to Halifax, Nova Scotia. He wanted to visit his siblings and relatives near Truro. But first there was a 12 hour haul from the Azores to Nova Scotia. At the halfway point, McCulloch's wife, Linda was asleep in the co-pilot's seat while baby Kathryn is asleep in her bed strapped to the top of one of the fuel bladders Once again the plane drones over the featureless Atlantic. Expecting this trip will be uneventful like the others McCulloch discovers at the half-way point fuel is not transferring from his reserve tanks in the cabin to the wing tanks. It appears one of the transfer pumps is not working. And McCulloch wants that fuel.

The situation was disturbing obviously but on this trip he had his wife and baby girl on board. It is one thing when you forecast for disaster and have only yourself to worry about but an entirely different thing when the lives of your one year old baby and your wife rely on your ability to successfully manage the situation. Any mistakes made are something a pilot will have to live with for the rest of his or her life-if they survive. Without waking Linda and with the plane already on auto-pilot McCulloch went to the tanks in the back of the cabin to assess the situation and see what he could do. One of the pumps was not functioning properly or at all. It looked to be an electrical problem.

McCulloch knew his systems. The pilots that know all aspects of their airplanes are better able to handle problems-at least work around them using alternate resources. In this case while his passengers were oblivious to what was happening, McCulloch did some quick rewiring - eliminating the faulty pump. But having done that he suffered a penalty; you don't get something for nothing.

He was putting the work of the whole fuel transfer on one pump and that restricted the fuel rate to the main tanks which slowed the transfer down. The engines, however, were sucking fuel from the wing tanks at a greater rate than the one pump could handle. The only solution to that was to reduce speed so he could transfer fuel to match the rate of his fuel burn. It took longer to complete the remaining leg of the journey, all the while McCulloch hoped the remaining fuel pump would hold up.

When he arrived at Halifax International to clear customs Linda was still unaware of the problem that had arisen over one of the deepest parts of the Atlantic Ocean. After a pleasant stay with his siblings and relatives in Nova Scotia they flew from Halifax home to Toronto.

The Flight Around The North Pole

'YOU STAY ON THE OUTER EDGE'

Flight into 'nowhere'

By MICHELE MANDEL
Toronto Sun

Pilot Dave McCulloch — Canada's own Indiana Jones — will take off tomorrow morning to re-enact the aerial crossing of the North Pole by Admiral Richard Byrd 61 years ago.

All McCulloch and his two pals will use in his Cessna 414 are turn-of-the-century navigation aids and survival suits — just in case.

Their route, similar to Byrd's in 1926, runs Toronto-Iceland-Norway-the Arctic-Norway-Finland-West

bound trip around the world.

"When you get old the only way you can get excited is by doing things that are risky," McCulloch, 49, said. "When you get old you've got to stay on the outside edge."

He gets a twinkle in his eye when asked whether he and co-pilot Al Solomon, 61, of New York and navigator Milt Brown, 67, of Washington will be landing on some ice patch in the Arctic for a little bubbly on May 9, the date of their crossing.

"We have to have a few secrets."

"You need a lot of luck," he said. "If you get lost up there, there's nowhere to go."

And in that remote stretch, there isn't anyone close enough to radio.

The cornerstone of aerial navigation is the magnetic north pole, but that's 1,000 miles south, he said. Their navigator will have to use an old-fashioned sextant and astrocompass. "We'll have to rely on the sun and the moon," McCulloch said.

"It's like a guy who wants to climb mountains b_____ ___ _

From The Sunday Toronto Sun by Michele Mandel' May 3, 1987. Canada's own Indiana Jones, David McCulloch, Al Solomon, co-pilot and Milton Brown, Navigator prepare to cross the Atlantic to Oslo, Norway, their launch-point to the North Pole via Tromso and Spitsbergen Airports.

The Cessna 414's right wingtip tank points out Spitsbergen, a desolate island bound by a frozen Barents Sea. 850 nautical miles to North Pole.

Aircraft Circle North Pole To Commemorate Byrd's Flight

A formation of three aircraft circled the North Pole on May 9th, the 61st anniversary of Admiral Byrd's first flight to the Pole in 1926. Crew members included, from left, Dr. William Wisner; Al Solomon; Cheryl Davis; Dave McCulloch; Rheinhard Buchaly; his wife, Andrea, and Milt Brown.

FOR THE RECORD

NATIONAL AERONAUTIC ASSOCIATION
The Aero Club of America
1763 R Street, N.W.
Washington, D.C. 20009

McCulloch's crew (3 of 7 in photo) Al Solomon stands on McCulloch's right (with cigarette). Milt Brown, far right. Partially blocking McCulloch is Rheinhard Buchaly. His plane's Inertial Guidance System allowed the three planes to pin down the geographical location of the North Pole and provide navigation where navigation by compass and dead reckoning was virtually impossible. McCulloch's Cessna 414 in background.

Chapter Twenty-Six

From Polar Bears to Penguins

Despite the fact that *Water Doctor* was in full swing; that McCulloch had been able to use the money he made from the operation and the franchises for his insatiable world travelling habit, he was still bored with the business. It was not challenging him. No one could argue at this point that David McCulloch avoided a challenge. If anything he charged full tilt toward them when they presented themselves. Most of this biography has been a testament to that very fact.

One of the things that bothered McCulloch about his association with the supplier of the components for his home and industry business was his inability to control that side of it. He was feeling pressure from the company that McCulloch felt was as a result of his success in the business. They saw him as a threat to their visibility to the consumer. His franchises were paying a franchise fee to Water Doctor while the supplier was relying on their markups on the product for their end. Why this would be so is a puzzle. It would be like beef suppliers being resentful of MacDonald's for marketing their products as Big Macs et al, and franchising it.

McCulloch was growing ever more suspicious of his supplier Lindsay as the months rolled on. He was now actively looking for a venture that he could own or at least control; an industry that had no over-seeing manufacturing hierarchy that could threaten him with the use of their product. His adventures in his small aircraft trading company were not proving sufficiently lucrative for the time and energy he was putting into it. It was time to pull the plug on that business and Water Doctor.

McCulloch sold out the major portion of his interest in Water Doctor to his partner and bother, Gordon. He retained only two of the stores for himself; one each in Barrie and Brampton, Ontario.

The move had been building over a couple of years as previous mentions of his restlessness in these pages will attest. And now the time seemed right. With that deal done McCulloch turned his attention to another adventure. He had already flown to and around the North Pole so it only seemed right that he do the same with the South Pole.

The planned attempt was for November of 1987. This was his way of clearing his head of old business and preparing for the new venture; one that would involve trips to Europe and Australia and an attempt at the Earth's South Pole later that year. This would be another adventure re-enacting Rear-Admiral (USN Ret.) Richard Byrd's flight around the South Pole on November 29, 1929. Three planes were shipped by boat to the Ross Ice Shelf and a base camp dubbed Little America was built. From there one of three planes would make the attempt to the South Pole on November 29th. Byrd and his pilot Bernt Balchen, co-pilot and radioman Harold June and photographer Ashley McKinley took off in the Ford Tri-motor airplane. They flew to the south pole and back in 18 hours, 41 minutes. Their chief problem during the attempt was getting the over weighted Tri-Motor to a sufficient height to climb to altitude of the South Polar Plateau. They threw used fuel tanks overboard and sacrificed some of their survival gear to maintain altitude and then climb when they had burnt off more fuel.

To an American reporter, in Lunken, Ohio McCulloch stated, "I tell people I'm making a commemorative trip (e.g. Adm. Byrd), eh, but really I'm going for the hell of it. You'd better get your licks in while you are still able."

In the living room of McCulloch's home north of Toronto in East Caledon stood a globe of the Earth. McCulloch pulled the pins on the ball and flipped it upside down so that Antarctic was now the 'top' of the world. He began planning a route to that continent while formulating a plan for the adventure.

McCulloch was 49 years old. Once again the attempt at the South Pole would be made using his Cessna 414. But on a trip of this caliber he wanted to make sure that the 414's engines were still up to the task. If he launched from Toronto the trip would entail a crow's flight of 8,200 nautical miles. But more realistically that could extend to 9,000 nautical (10,368 statute) miles with the jigging around pilots have to do to avoid weather, terrain and undesirable landing facilities.

McCulloch trusted only one engine shop to do the work on his plane; T.W Smith Co., an engine shop at Cincinnati Municipal Lunken Airport in Ohio. At that time they had been in business for 35 years. He flew the plane there to have the engines overhauled and returned home to continue his planning.

This new adventure would require the adding on of 2,000 nautical miles to the trip each leg far exceeding the legs flown to the North Pole, even launching as he would from Lunken-a suburb of Cinncinati, Ohio.

The temperatures were much lower and the distances over water were greater. Add to that the crazy winds one would encounter over the Drake Passage, the open stretch of water that separated the southernmost tip of South America and the northern islands off Grahams Land of Antarctica, and you had a dangerous situation. "It's about 3,000 miles from Marimba Island to the South Pole. Bung it up anywhere along the way and you are a dead man." McCulloch told reporter, David Wecker. "It's probably the longest, most dangerous trip you can make from anywhere."

Like his trip around the North Pole, McCulloch and his co-pilot would have to rely on celestial navigation using the bubble sextant and an astro compass. There would be no inertial guidance system to fall back on in another adventurer's airplane on this trip, however, McCulloch was having a primitive version of GPS, the accuracy of which was nothing like that of the GPS systems available to pilots in the second decade of the 21st Century. He was inclined to trust to his Astro Compass and his time keeper.

McCulloch had to do his homework. He needed airports with fuel, clearances and permission all the way down the South American coast to the arctic sub-continent. More than this he had to get familiar with Antarctica itself. In 1987 information was not as readily available as it is today thanks to the powerful search engines of the internet.

You don't just get into an airplane and fly to the South Pole. Between 1967 and 1987 only two light aircraft flew to the South Pole and only one of them made it back. The other is still there. "There's no radar, no support, no nothing." McCulloch told a reporter from Cincinnati, shortly before he left for the points south.

McCulloch was well aware of the dangers of flying over the continent assuming they survived the flight over the Drake Passage to the Bridgeman Islands where they would take on fuel. The Drake Passage has wrecked more than its share of sailing vessel over the last three centuries with its unpredictable winds and ocean currents. It is a narrow passage where two of the world's great oceans collide; the Atlantic and the Pacific. The winds howl through this passage at tremendous speeds, the seas are huge topping 30 plus meters on occasion. One can only imagine the courage of those sailors who endured weeks of the weather and steep seas while battling their way through the passage in the relatively small wooden vessels with little to navigate with.

McCulloch had to be concerned with the same winds but only about sea state if he lost his engines and had to ditch into those hellish waters. Once they made landfall, refuelled and made their bid for the South Pole the crew had to contend with the cold, the weather and the terrain. "It wasn't as if you just looked down to the surface to make sure you didn't hit it. The wind stirred up the surface snow and blended the surface to the horizon in such a way that one's perception was thrown off. In broad daylight you still had to rely on instruments to tell you if you were flying straight and level."

It was very easy to fly right onto the surface in the huge plateaus with no mountain outcroppings to give you a hint of where the terrain was below. Lose your attitude references and the next thing you know you are scattered all over the 2 mile thick glacier.

Recalling that accident, McCulloch observed, "If New Zealand Air could be lured into this trap with all of their computers and flight guidance systems, our chances of the same happening were even greater."

Air New Zealand Flight 901, a MacDonnell Douglas DC-10-30, registration ZK-NZP was one of that company's scheduled sightseeing junkets for those who want to experience a trip over the South Pole. Originating from Auckland Airport, New Zealand, FL 901 left at 8:00 am local on November 28, 1979. It was that aircraft's fourteenth flight to Antarctica. It had 20 crew and 237 passengers on board. After a few hours crossing the 2,500 nautical miles of the southern Pacific it used a regular approach into McMurdo Sound. Instead it slammed into Mount Erebus-an extinct volcano-killing all 257 on board. The accident was originally blamed on the pilot but later a Commission of Inquiry discovered that the night before the flight corrections had been made to the flight computer. The pilot and first officer were never informed of the change.

Rather than the DC-10 being directed down McMurdo Sound where an onboard tourist guide would regale the passengers-through the cabin public address- about landmarks and history during a low sweeping flight around McMurdo Sound, as they were used to, the flight track took them directly into the slopes of Mount Erebus. To date it was New Zealand's worst air disaster. Most of the wreckage is still there to this day.

On December 30, 1946 a United States Navy, Martin PBM Mariner (Designated as a Canso in Canada) crashed on Thurston Island during whiteout conditions. Three of the nine crewmembers were killed. The six survivors were rescued 13 days later. The three fatalities were buried at the site.

In November of 2008 and 2009 attempts were made to get to the site and retrieve the bodies of the three crewmen who would most likely be very well preserved in Earth's biggest deepfreeze. However the accumulation of snow over the last 62 and 63 years respectively found the bodies of the deceased now down some 150 feet in the glacier. The snow from above compacts the snow below into near ice consistency. They remain there still. It will take a major effort to recover those bodies.

Numerous marine vessels including some fishing vessels have ended badly in the ice-packed sounds and bays surrounding the continent. Helicopters and conventional aircraft have also crashed after McCulloch's attempt in 1987.

McCulloch's Cessna 414 lifted off in Toronto bound for New York City. On board were passengers Rick Boisselle and John Donaldson. They cleared customs at JFK and picked up an additional passenger, Al Solomon, McCulloch's navigator on the North Pole adventure. The next port of call was Wilmington, North Carolina where they refueled and prepared for a long trip over Atlantic waters to San Juan, Puerto Rico. Rather than waste time McCulloch elected to leave Wilmington and do the trip over water later in the day and into the night. Their course would take them over 1,350 nautical miles of ocean; a tract that is for the most void of land of any description. At its closest point Bermuda was 500 nm off to the east. "There were storms out there. We radared our way around them. But we could see lightning illuminating the horizon." One of the men remarked that they were flying through the so-called Bermuda Triangle. "We got a chuckle out of that. Then the planes magnetic compass flopped on its side and stayed there. It just died. Never saw that happen before." They laughed about that then exchanged stories about the planes that were reported lost in that area.

Not only planes were lost but ships as well. There is some reason to believe that hydrate strata-a frozen ice like layer- in layers deep below the ocean occasionally are uncovered by sea-quakes which when it interacts with seawater gives off methane gas in huge volumes. When this reaches the surface the water loses buoyancy-bubbling and roiling- and any vessel sailing into it will basically sink into a pit of rising gas. There is evidence that this gas will then form a low-lying bubble of volatile gas that lays on the surface before dissipating into the atmosphere. If flown into the gas can be set off by the spark from reciprocating engines.

The Flight 19 disappearance of five TBM Grumman Avenger Torpedo Bombers - each with a crew of three save one plane who's navigator was grounded by the flight surgeon on that fateful day due to a bad cold – is one of the most famous occurrences in the "Devil's Triangle" or "The Limbo of the Lost". The flight of five aircraft vanished somewhere off Chicken Shoals on December 5, 1945 during a United States Navy overwater navigation training flight from Naval Air Station Fort Lauderdale, Florida. 13 crew members of a USN PBM Mariner flying boat was assumed to have exploded in mid-air while searching for Flight 19. A US Navy board could not determine the cause of the loss of Flight 19. It is believed that the airmen may have become disoriented and ditched in rough seas after running out of fuel. The case has never been solved. The ocean in that area can drop to a depth of 3.5 miles (5,636 meters)

Perhaps even more concerning is the loss of a civilian registered aircraft flown by Jose Torres. Torres was a flight instructor in San Juan, Puerto Rico. On June 28, 1980 Torres was flying a small two-seat Ercoupe (N3808H) back from Santa Domingo, Dominican Republic to San Juan. He has one passenger, Jose Santos. While over the Mona Strait, 35 miles from the west coast of Puerto Rico he transmitted a Mayday. "Mayday, Mayday, Ercoup November three, eight, zero, eight Hotel. We can see a strange object in our course, we are lost, Mayday, Mayday." Torres was too far from San Juan for San Juan International to pick him up, but a high-flyer, Iberia Airlines Flight IB-976 en route from Santo Domingo to Spain picked up his transmission and relayed the information to SJI's tower. Basically Torres complained of a weird object that kept getting in front of their airplane forcing them to change course. They were now lost at an altitude of only 1,500 feet above the Strait. Torres made several transmissions complaining that this object was harassing them and then his transmissions were lost as was the airplane. A search for two days turned up nothing and nothing has been found since. An American Naval Air Station base in Puerto Rico recorded the exchanges between the Iberia Airliner and pilot Torres which is free to be viewed on the American National Transportation Safety Board's aviation accident site.

"I knew the devil didn't want me, and I was right. We landed in San Juan." McCulloch quipped. The compass had leaked its stabilizing fluid and was replaced.

The fabled, infamous Bermuda Triangle behind them they launched again the following day. "Fat with fuel we were off to French Guyana the next day, then the day after that we were off to Belem, Brazil." Belem was familiar territory for McCulloch. He had landed there before.

"I let each of the guys have a go at flying." The next leg of their trip took them from Belem to Brasilia a distance of 992 miles. Once again McCulloch was over the vast jungles of that country.

Brasilia was founded on April 21, 1960, to serve as the new national capital of Brazil. The national seat of the federal government was moved from the then capitol of Rio de Janeiro. Unlike other cities in Brazil it did not exist before that date. It was literally designed to be the Capitol city of an emerging nation that has become a powerhouse in the world in its own right. It went from a population of zero to 2,852,000 people by 2014. It is now a World heritage city because of its rich architecture and bold artistic structures. When I write literally designed I mean exactly that. It was designed from the ground up by architects and artists. So when McCulloch landed there for the second time in his life the city was virtually new, a scant 27 years of age. The city might have been new but the bureaucracy was not. Once again he ran into the same grindingly slow bureaucracy that he had before in Brazil. McCulloch's wife Linda told a reporter that her husband was stuck on the ground until he could get the proper papers and permission to fly in Brazilian airspace. And it wasn't just himself that was targeted, many pilots found themselves in the same boat, the authorities caring little about the cost due to delays.

"He waited a day and heard nothing...so he left." Linda reported.

Those of us that know David McCulloch are well aware of this restlessness that lives within him. The word *wait* is not high on the list of favorite words in his vocabulary. And waiting for the wheels of a bureaucracy that is hopelessly bound up in inefficiency with a tendency to being lubricated with bribery is not a worthy pastime for the man. Of course he left. If he had to return home without going through Brazil he would cross the Atlantic to Africa to gain the northern latitudes or fly up the crusty spine of Chile off the western edge of the Andes Mountains. There is always another way for McCulloch whether that is in flying or in business as we will see in upcoming chapters. Canada's Indiana Jones would not be stopped.

Apparently McCulloch was forgotten by the authorities or just got lost in the system because when McCulloch decided that he and crew needed some R and R the most obvious city place for that was Rio de Janeiro. McCulloch and company veered left from their north-south course and literally flew off to Rio. He never heard another word about documents of permission needed to fly through that fantastically beautiful and diverse region of the planet known as Brazil.

"We didn't get much rest and recuperation there but it broke the monotony of the jungle over-flights." The next stop was Buenos Aires, 1,040 nautical miles to the southwest. Then another "short" hop of 1,230 nm further southwest, most of it off the coast over the South Atlantic before making land and traversing the low Andes Mountains of southern Chile to land at Presidente Carlos Ibáñez del Campo Airport, ten miles northeast of the city of Punta Arenas in Chile. This airport had the kind of runways that McCulloch was looking for; long runways. When they made their bid for southern continent they would be heavily loaded with fuel, heavy clothing, and survival equipment for both land and water. Long runways were of great importance.

They had arrived at the jumping off point for Antarctica. The geopolitical importance of Punta Arenas has remained high in the 20th and 21st centuries because of its logistic importance in accessing the Antarctic Peninsula. The city's name in English means sandy point. The city itself is medium sized with a present day population of over 600,000 and as noted is a popular staging area for expeditions to Antarctica.

Christine Wolff, a reporter for the *Cincinnati Enquirer* wrote "Come dawn Nov. 29, David McCulloch plans on waking up in a tent pitched on the edge of Antarctica." But that was not to happen. In a rare display of weather gymnastics the temperatures that should have been in the -34 degree Celsius range keeping the runway at Tini Aria Marsh on the Antarctic icecap in the Bridgeman Islands in a frozen mud state did not happen. The years passing and vagaries of the world climate deemed it the temps would rise; so much so that the temperature would soar above the freezing mark of 0 Celsius and the frozen packed runways would become a muddy strip making it impossible to land. Gone were the hopes of landing there and refueling for the long haul to the South Pole and back (2,778 nm or 5,150 kilometers) or for that matter returning to Tini Aria Marsh after a hopefully successful Pole attempt to refuel for the trip back to Punta Arenas. "We thought it was frozen enough down there but the seasons are the reverse from ours." McCulloch's wife Linda told one reporter.

McCulloch and his crew were disappointed to say the least. They were so close only to be let down by the pilot's constant enemy; the weather; the biggest killer of them all. There was nothing to do but return home.

But McCulloch would not end it there. He would try again.

The Cessna 414. With long -range tanks and extra avionics McCulloch flew west around the world, flew around the Earth's geographic North Pole and now McCullock holds a globe upside down to show where he will ask the 414 to fly yet again - to the South Pole. (Note: there is a aerodynamic nose on the plane but it is lost in the dark background as are the leading edges of the fuel tanks on the wing tips.)

John Donaldson, left, looks on as McCulloch unfolds a navigation chart. They are preparing for the first leg of their flight from Canada to the South pole. Petro Canada fuel truck tops off their Cessena 414's fuel tanks.

Pilot flies on in face of trouble

DARYL-LYNN CARLSON
Toronto Sun

Caledon adventurer Dave McCulloch has had his ups and downs on the first week of his flight to the South Pole.

The upside of his trip is the good weather and great flying he's had since he left Caledon on Nov. 14, his wife Linda said last night.

But the downside is the problems he's had getting off the ground each day as he battles South American bureaucracy, she said.

"He can't get off the ground until noon. He has problems getting fuel and

DAVE McCULLOCH
Headed to South Pole

getting things done."

The 49-year-old pilot was stuck in Brazil after authorities grounded him

until he received permission to use their air space, said Linda.

"He waited a day and heard nothing, so he left," she said.

Otherwise, McCulloch is almost on schedule for his flight over the South Pole, which will commemorate Admiral Richard Byrd's trip over the icy polar line 58 years ago Nov. 29.

He expects to arrive at the southernmost tip of Chile by this afternoon, and he'll have one more stop before heading out for his 15-hour flight over the Pole.

MUDDY BUMMER

Polar pilot quits: It's too warm!

By MARJORIE SIM
Toronto Sun

Intrepid Caledon pilot David McCulloch has aborted an attempt to fly over the South Pole.

McCulloch, 49, was unable to land his twin-engined Cessna 414 at a final refuelling station because the dirt runway had turned to mud.

"They just can't land there," his wife Linda said last night. "He's very disappointed."

DAVID McCULLOCH
"A month too late"

McCulloch had to refuel at Tiniaria Marsh on the Antarctic ice cap for his fuel to last the 5,150-km (3,200-mile) round trip over the pole.

"We thought it was still frozen enough down there but the seasons are the reverse from ours. They're just going into spring," said Linda.

"He's about a month too late."

McCulloch hoped to fly over the South Pole on Nov. 29 — commemorat-

Chapter Twenty-Seven

On the way back from their two week stay in Puntas Arenas the Cessna 414 crawled northward above the Chilean coast. McCulloch had time to enjoy the disparity in the various regions of this intriguing continent called South America; a land mass he had now flown over a half dozen times. And still he saw things that were new to him. "We landed and overnighted in a place called Arica." The Brazilian jungle was ripe, lush from constant rains and the rivers fed by the snow and ice melts in the Andes Mountains.

"Arica is on record-or was back then-as the driest place on Earth. The annual rainfall in Arica was 0.03 (three-one hundreds) of an inch."

Due to the lack of precipitation some of Arica's inhabitants do not construct their dwellings with a roof added. There is no need since it never rains. And obviously it kept down the cost of construction.

They were in a hotel that night which had a roof but one can imagine the lifestyle change a transplanted traveler would go through each night when crawling into bed and lights were extinguished. The heavenly vista above would be captivating.

The next day McCulloch took off later than usual and pointed the plane's nose in the direction of Lima, Peru 650 miles to the northwest. The weather was rough; windy rain showers and thunderclouds spotting the horizon along the precipitous Pacific coasts of Chile and Peru.

To top off this adventure northwards they had been forewarned there was rioting in the city itself and the airport was closed down at night and in complete darkness due to an imposed, blanketed blackout by the authorities.

Peru had been rocked by rioting and violent confrontations through much of 1987 and 1988. Imprisoned rioters, many of whom were students, continued to riot while in the prisons. There were several massacres in various prisons which heated up the already hot South American blood of the population. Additionally, Peru's monetary problems fueled by austerity, a devalued currency and higher taxes exacerbated the problem.

The memory of these terrible and bloody riots is still fresh in the minds of many Peruvians. The political turmoil of that nation is deeper and more intricate than can be related in these pages. Despite the usual pleasant demeanor of the people in most Latin American countries there was always a sense there were tensions and old hatreds brewing just below the surface of much of the populations in the countries in South America. Officials and the authorities were often distant; confrontational, making life difficult often with unnecessary road blocks that would only go away with the offer of a bribe. This was true with most foreigners and in particular the Nord Americanos; a distrust that continues to this day. McCulloch had found this distrust and suspicion could be nullified or at least off-set by liberal uses of American dollars.

Sometimes the infusion of the American greenback did not help. One of McCulloch's co-pilots Rick Boisselle who accompanied McCulloch to South America and went across the

North Atlantic with him remembers one South American incident that could have gone south when McCulloch's temper snapped at another of constant delays imposed by airport authorities and the police or army.

McCulloch had landed to refuel at one of the many jungle airstrips in the northern sector of South America. They completed the task having taken on full fuel in the planes six fuel tanks. They were heavy, and it was hot. They were taxiing, back-tracking a long runway. Their nerves were already on edge with the heat and fully conscious of the fact that they were once again a potential bomb on wheels. Although the runway was acceptably long, the heat and their elevation combined to impose a higher density altitude. In other words, the increased elevation meant thinner air and heated air makes it even thinner; particularly above a paved, black, asphalt runway that can increase the heat factor several feet above its surface by as much as a few degrees Celsius or 10 degrees Fahrenheit. The asphalt gets softer and a bit sticky and the ground effect-an air cushion generated during the take-off where pressurized air gets trapped between the bottom of the wings and the runway surface that pilots rely on to get airborne in these situations-is thinner in volume and therefore less effective. Ground control radios McCulloch and tells him to return to the airport's tarmac. "We should ignore that and just go." McCulloch was pissed off. The engines were hot enough as it was. He increased his speed.

Boisselle recalled that, "Just as he begins to roll (take-off run) a military jeep comes out of the jungle in front of us." They effectively blocked his take-off run and they were escorted back to the terminal. More heat as no cool breeze is being forced into the non-air conditioned cabin via the vents due to the slow taxi. "Many more minutes (pass) for Dave to get hotter than the engine...(he) jumps out of the plane, swearing at the officials.

They try to calm him down saying that they need to spray for bugs!"

McCulloch, frustrated throws their baggage on the ground all of the time he is calling the soldiers f---ing so and sos. "They all had guns. I thought we were done." Boisselle related.

The ground crew sprayed for insects that were a problem in various countries around South America. It was a system used to prevent the spread of these insects. It was typical of some of these countries that the authorities had neglected to mention this fact while they were still on the airport's ramp and before McCulloch and Boisselle had climbed aboard and were on the roll. It had been forgotten or possibly the information was withheld until the last moment just to piss off another Nord Americano. Fuel was wasted in taxiing three times. Precious fuel that might be needed later.

They were not shot. The ground crew sprayed everything, papers were signed and the Cessna 414 was deemed bug free.

Due to their late departure McCulloch and company arrived off the south coast of Lima in darkness. The radar at Lima Internacional was shut down as were the runway lights. The whole city was just one black, blanket of airspace with no hint of where the airport was situated. They did 360s off the coast while McCulloch negotiated with the tower urging them to use their emergency generator to light the runway so they could make an approach.

The tower personnel gave in and lit some portions of the runways. And there it was situated northwest of the center of the riot-torn city. The airport boasted a long runway even in 1989. The tower advised they would leave the runway lights on for a very brief time so McCulloch made a fast approach to limit the time the lights would have to be illuminated. He was on final approach when suddenly there was a white flash in the upper portion of his windshield and then bang! They had struck something. "There was no option other than to continue the approach." He remembers. There was no time to assess the reason for the loud noise even though a large bird was suspected. He was under a time constraint. He needed those runway lights. And Lima Internacional was the only available airport for landing now. "A town in the middle of a riot was better than crashing in the mountains." McCulloch reasoned.

Lima, the capitol of Peru, is situated on a coastal plain on the west side of that country. The Cordillera Central Mountains formed a semi-circular danger curving around from the south, to the west and north of Lima ramping up from 1,200 feet to one or two miles high 25 miles inland or five to ten minutes of flying time away in the inky black darkness.

They landed uneventfully and found a place to park. Using a flashlight they discovered that some type of large bird had struck the tail plane which was covered in blood, feathers and guts. The bird's impact had torn the High Frequency radio antenna off the airplane's rear fuselage. Fortunately the tail feathers had suffered no damage; at least none that could be seen using a flashlight.

McCulloch and his crew were tired. They needed a place to spend the night. They would explore the bird impact damage the next morning. Rest and sleep without fear of the possible dangers posed by the riots and the blackouts were a priority.

They were able to get a ride to a hotel. Rick Boisselle recalls, "We caught a cab, asked where our hotel was and the driver said not too far.

"Not too far turned into a one hour drive or it seemed like it, anyway."

The cab proceeded for some time on four lane highways but soon the crew found they were down to two lanes and were now concerned for their safety. They were nervous. Boisselle had visions of them being kidnapped. They would just disappear into the jungle, robbed of their money and possessions; abandoned or killed was an option.

Then suddenly they were *there*, wherever *there* was. "...we saw a guy outside waving a lighter or a candle." Boisselle recalls. "It was impossible to see anything but an outline of a doorway, and we had no clue as to what the place was."

The "guy" was the hotel manager. He led them through inky black hallways with no sense of definition. McCulloch remembers that he could not see a hand in front of his face.

The manager who spoke very good English explained that terrorists had just blown up a power generating station a few blocks away. Comforting to know. Only a few blocks away?

"It was difficult to tell if we were in a reasonably nice hotel or a flop house, it was that dark. What was creepy for me," Boisselle said, "was when I was getting under the covers I had no idea what condition the bed was in." What lay beneath the sheets besides Boisselle and his partners? They had no flashlights or candles.

McCulloch recalls, "I remember it was a dark, overcast night. The hotel was black. You could not see your hand!"

They heard explosions all night long. It was hot and humid and of course there was no electricity so the air conditioning was off. "We didn't get much sleep that night."

When the Sun arose the next morning they were surprised to discover that they were in a nicely kept, well-appointed, 6-8 story hotel surrounded by good landscaping. They hired another cab to take them to the airport.

"On our way back to the airport, we drove past the generating station, and it was a mess!!" says Boisselle. Disturbing images, but better to see it after the fact rather than before and make a bad night even moreso with vivid pictures to go with an active imagination. Maybe the terrorists didn't like fancy hotels either.

At the airport early that morning they had a better look at the High Frequency (HF) antenna. There was no chance of them making repairs to it on their own and little chance that local air mechanics could do likewise so they cleaned up the blood, guts and feathers and then reluctantly cut away the rest of the trailing aerial wire. McCulloch fueled up and took off for Panama City, Panama. They would be flying over dangerous ground lacking their long range radio. If they got into trouble once away from the populated areas the plane's UHF radios would not transmit much further than 50-60 miles with the mountains making long range transmissions even more difficult. The HF radio could transmit across continents.

The Lima to Panama City leg of their return journey was uneventful.

"Panama City was full of Chinese gamblers." McCulloch recalls. "They now own the place."

Airborne once again they headed north across the Caribbean Sea 620 NM to the Cayman Islands. "The land of hiddenmoney…40,000 people and 600 banks. A bank can be a well-dressed man with a briefcase."

From there they hopped over Cuba to the Florida Keys, specifically, Key West International Airport in Key West. Once again McCulloch waited while the police gave the airplane a complete shakedown looking for drugs, specifically cocaine; the only drug the cartels thought worth smuggling in small amounts. All aircraft coming from South America endured this special treatment.

It is little known by the public that during those years and years to follow that the cartels would hi-jack aircraft, often killing the owners, then loading the planes up with cocaine and flying them to the United States. They would approach and land without clearances at airports such as Miami International in the dead of night without lights; with their transponders turned off and in complete radio silence. They would make their landing and roll out near some remote area of the airport and off-load their contraband to a waiting van, ditch the airplane and escape. Over the years Florida would auction off-or try to-hundreds of stolen aircraft whose journals were lost and which could never fly again until it had received a complete overhaul and re-certification. The list ranged from light twin engined aircraft to large business jets and even small airliners that had been stolen in some airport in South America. Sometimes the recertification cost more than the aircraft was worth. Pilots and companies would not purchase aircraft at auction when they had no idea of the engine (and prop) maintenance records, the hull history or even the number of times the aircraft had taken off and landed.

No continent can be more vindictive about this pirating practice and the use of private aircraft to move drugs around at the expense of the owners than South America. Its countries are chiefly responsible for producing the product in the first place. Their police and armed forces can't catch the suppliers. Oft times this is due to local corruption, bribery and plain fear of the cartels but they can arrest some helpless, unsuspecting pilot and make an "example" of him or her and extort money from them or at least impound the aircraft and either sell it back to the innocent owner or someone else.

McCulloch recalled the trauma he and his wife and their friends went through when the authorities found baking soda in his airplane's survival package. Guns were pointed at them and their property was stolen. This time he breathed a sigh of relief when the Key West police found no drugs hidden away aboard his airplane. "What if the druggies had stashed stuff on my plane? Tell it to the judge!" The police would not care. Let the courts figure it out. The defence lawyers win and McCulloch is out an airplane which could be impounded for months or perhaps years. Not only the plane but McCulloch and company might be impounded too. Hefty bails and expensive court appearances could ensue. McCulloch might not be able to leave the country as a supposed flight risk.

These were the days of the Barry Seal/CIA/DEA/ Colombia's Medellín Cartel scandals after all; a subject too large to explore in these pages. Seal was murdered by the Medellin Cartel in Baton Rouge, Louisiana in March of 1986.

Such were the lovely airways and bureaucratic obstacles that McCulloch had to traverse and avoid in those days. But now he was on his way back to Canada. He was about to make a lifestyle change.

Chapter Twenty-Eight

Multi-million dollar deals and jets.
Where the 'rubber' meets the road; all eight of them.

It is a new year back in Canada. 1988.
McCulloch, ever restless was chaffing over his need to move on regardless of what endeavour. The poor country boy from Hants East, Nova Scotia has developed an expensive and seemingly in exhaustive thirst for adventure whether that be in business or in aviation. The two co-existed for him. The business fed his expensive addiction to flying while flying assisted his business to thrive. When you get to know McCulloch you discover when it is time for him to go anywhere, he goes. He did and does his planning on his feet.

In recent years this writer has experienced this fluidity of movement more than a few times. If the weather prohibits him from using one of his own aircraft, he books a commercial flight-in couch mind you-right at the back, "The safest place on any commercial flight." he stated.

The flight booking he might have made that afternoon or evening due to pressure of business commitments or the purchase of equipment needed for the next venture might be cancelled. McCulloch cancels his flight and takes the hit, perhaps losing a grand or more for a non-refundable ticket only to re-book a couple of days later; and he's gone.

With the foregoing in mind, principally McCulloch's need for cash to finance his flying passion, and his decision to invest in big business; a chance comment by his friend and recent crew member to Antarctica, Al Solomon, McCulloch was about to make a major change in his life and life style.

Initially however he kicked around the idea of moving to Australia. He had expertise in the water filtration business and considered opening a chain of water stores as he did in Canada. "I wanted to avoid the mistakes of not being in control of the actual filtering system." Perhaps he could purchase the rights to existing technology or explore another option such as having his own engineered product.

He had given up on immigrating to the United States. "At the time it appeared they were only taking in people who drifted ashore on life-rafts and who could not speak English." Australia was attractive to him because it was warm; they spoke English and had laws. "You didn't have a gun pointed at you periodically when you landed at an airport."

It was then that Al Solomon called.

"Hey McCulloch you like things that are different. I saw a car with 8 tyres on it." Solomon went on to say it's incredible. It can stop fast on wet payment, drive with one tire flat, perfect for police and emergency vehicles. It's patented and comes out of Australia.

McCulloch was interested. "I said I would check it out."

Of course McCulloch had been to Australia before during his record setting flight around the world westward in his Cessna 414, albeit these were for short periods of time. His stop-overs for R&R and refuelling had lasted only a few days at most. He was up against a time constraint after all.

Notwithstanding his short stays, McCulloch had gained some insight into the frontier spirit of that country and a fierce independence born of its pioneering spirit.

"I am off to Australia on a commercial airline." He landed in Sydney and visited with an old friend, Richard Harold "Dick" Smith; a famed pilot in his own right.

McCulloch first met Dick in Punta Arenas, Chile when he was preparing for the hop to Antarctica in the Cessna 414. Smith, curious, had spotted McCulloch's plane with a fellow British Commonwealth Canadian registration on the ramp and wandered over to it. McCulloch explained that he and his crew were heading for the South Pole. Smith expressed doubts. He said to McCulloch that in his opinion McCulloch's 414 could not make the trip across the Drake Passage to Bridgeman Island off the north tip of Antarctica. It didn't have the range.

McCulloch explained that he had made certain alterations.

"You've got to show me what you have done."

"He laughed when I showed him the extra tanks and the fuel transfer system. He kept saying, 'I love it, it's so illegal.' We both knew that our slave master in our home countries would not approve of such modifications."

It was an exciting exchange between two explorers.

In many regards, Smith is an Auzzie version of McCulloch. They both started small businesses and then grew these businesses into large companies. Smith had started a small car radio installation business in 1986. In 1982 he sold the business to Woolworth's for $22,000,000.00.

In the meantime Smith satisfied his thirst for flight and like McCulloch he set world records of his own, normally using helicopters. Smith got his flying license in 1972 and flew a conventional twin engined Beech baron aircraft. He purchased a Jet Ranger in 1978 and used the helicopter to set world records not envisioned before. He started Dick Smith Foods and being a leader in Australia First entrepreneurial activism has become an iconic name in that country. He received the *Australian of the Year* award in 1986. Like McCulloch he has not let his age interfere with starting new businesses or interfere with his flying, business spirit and political activism.

His visit with Smith completed, McCulloch continued to Western Australia to check into the twin-tire deal. It turned out that company in this instance was a Motorcycle dealership that used the twin tire on their cycles. He was given a "hair-raising" ride in a Porsche equipped with the tires as a demonstration for McCulloch to prove the worthiness of the product. That followed with a police trial of the same technology against conventional tires and the twin tires won hands down by a wide margin in stopping, cornering and running with the tires flat. The twin tires shared a special common wheel rim that allowed each tire to be inflated independently of the other.

"My fertile mind was beginning to see a deal."

McCulloch discovered that the Australian motorcycle dealership was only a licenced user of the product, not the owner of the process. He was told that the inventor and the patent owner lived in Geneva, Switzerland.

McCulloch took an airliner back to Canada. He fired up his Cessna 414 (Deja Vu) and flew to Europe making his way via Labrador, Greenland, Iceland, England and France to Geneva. There he'd arranged to meet the twin tire inventor, Jerry J. Juhan.

Juhan was a Czechoslovakian. He was wealthy with multiple homes and married to a very rich Swiss heiress. "I won him over a bit with my crooked smile, straight teeth and country boy demeanor."

Juhan was apparently impressed that McCulloch just jumped in his plane and flew across the Atlantic Ocean just to meet with him.

Juhan said that he loved my spend-money, have fun approach and his sell something and close sales everyday attitude. Juhan explained that he had two dealers in the United States; one in California and one in Missouri. McCulloch explained to him that he wanted exclusive rights to all of North America. Juhan, however, was a man of honour and would not dump the two dealers.

McCulloch countered, "Okay then, I will buy them out… lock, stock and barrel."

Juhan replied, "Money talks and bullshit walks, David."

Two weeks later McCulloch was back in Geneva and once again across a table from Juhan.

"Jerry, I am your man. I own every tire and wheel that your dealers had in America. I bought them out completely. Let's make a deal."

There was further discussion and McCulloch presented Juhan with his business plan. "I'd sell to the car manufacturers and make it OEM equipment on the big three; General Motors, Ford and Chrysler."

They signed a contract and McCulloch hurried back to the states to implement his business plan. He knew he had been talking big and now he had to back up his claims. But he was thinking big too. He knew that he was a small player in the big leagues. His private funds, banks accounts and assets were now stretched to the limits. "I was in over my head, and I knew it."

At stake was a market that could see the sale of millions of tires and with the result of many millions of dollars in sale. He enlisted the aid of some high profile people close to the Vice-president of sales for General Motors. Through them he gave the VP a set of his tires. He contacted one of the most famous race car drivers of that time, Mario Andretti and gave him a set for his Mercedes.

Still short of seed money he turned to the equity market. He decided to go public to raise the millions he needed. It was then he learned what a neophyte was.

"The venture capitalists saw me coming and they are predators. They loved my deal and I looked like easy pickings. I learned to fight financially. I reminded them that they would be joining me and that I was not joining them." There could only be one top dog in this company and that was going to be David McCulloch.

If they thought that McCulloch did not have the heart for this adventure they did not know his history. Faint of heart is not in his nature.

McCulloch realized that he required a firm equity base of his own if he was going to maintain control of this new company. He didn't want to be just a shareholder, he wanted to be the CEO of the company otherwise he would just be along for the ride and depending on the number of shares he had, either a major or minor player in the thing that he started. Minor was not acceptable.

McCulloch was burning the midnight oil. The use of a few Valium kept him going. His telephone was a constant companion. He contacted family and friends eliciting seed money. Following that and having a solid base of his own funds he went after the venture capitalists for IPO (Initial Public Offering) money.

It is one thing to have a company on paper but it is even more encouraging for prospective investors to see an actual structure representing the company base. He built a warehouse in Niagara Falls, New York. Whereas he was/is a Canadian he could not live full time in the United States, therefore he had to drive daily from Ontario across the border into the United States.

"It was a crazy, wild, non-stop frenzy of a launch of a new, never before seen product in a foreign company."

Money, money, money. There was always a need for more money. His Ontario farm was remortgaged to raise more funding. "I'm all in." But he is moving closer to a successful trading company.

"I was always back-against-the-wall at that time. I was trying to hold on to controlling interest in my company."

McCulloch was climbing into the rarefied level of huge manufactures like the big three automobile companies and the likes of Firestone, Dunlop and Michelin tires. His money lenders would have been happy to see him fail. They could take his company over or lend him more money and thereby gain a controlling interest in his venture. And it looked as though that might happen. But McCulloch had something up his sleeve. The perception of McCulloch at that point was that he was on the brink of losing control of the company. He was broke they thought and this 'perception' could color further negotiations with prospective investors beyond that point.

Image, image, image leads to respect or downfall. You are either a hero or a dog. McCulloch chose hero. In a bold move he traded in his one last asset, his Cessna 414 twin engined airplane named Déjà vu. He didn't sell it, he traded and financed the balance.

McCulloch purchased his first business jet, a German built HFB 320 Hansa Jet, the first European built private jet with forward swept wings. This beautiful, fast looking airplane had a length of nearly 55 feet and a wingspan of just over 47 feet. It was an impressive looking airplane and no doubt would impress investors who were waiting at some airport for McCulloch to arrive. It was fast at a cruise of over 500 mph and which flew to Flight Level 380 (38,000 feet) with a passenger capacity of between 7 and 15 people depending on its configuration. McCulloch could also carry tire samples with him with a space like that.

There is no doubt that McCulloch was depending on the public's(investor's) image of a private jet as denoting wealth and with his jet it would likely dissuade any rumours that McCulloch was lacking financial stability or that he was involved in a minor project.

This would prove to be the case with one financier whom McCulloch met at a Florida airport, albeit for a different reason.

Chapter Twenty-Nine

McCulloch Rides the Fire

In April of 1989, McCulloch met with Morgan Merrill at the International Airport in Fort Lauderdale, Florida. He bought the Hansa Jet which was located in the Fort Lauderdale Airport.

"I met him (Merrill) after the deal was made on it. He had approved the deal before we went out to dinner."

Merrill was a 50 year old businessman. "Like me, he played with planes and other sinfully expensive things." Merrill owned a French fighter aircraft called the Paris Jet that was once owned by the Shaw of Iran.

"It is a very sexy airplane. I told Morgan that when I got rich I would own one. And I would make love to it."

Having this shared interest helped pave the way to a business association. The two exchanged flying and business stories. McCulloch remembers that they laughed a great deal. He told Merrill about his new venture, his million dollar deal and his plans to do an initial public offering once the company was up and running.

During McCulloch's presentation Merrill suddenly, "David, you're running out of money aren't you?"

"I already had the jet and I said of course, that's why I am buying the jet. I hate to be out of money and not looking good."

Merrill, agreeing with McCulloch's philosophy, said, "You

are doing the right thing. Don't let the bastards see you hurting." He took a small cheque book from his briefcase and wrote McCulloch a check for a quarter million dollars.

Merrill handed McCulloch the cheque. "That's for shares in your company and the French jet is yours also. Just give me another two hundred fifty thousand dollars' worth of shares when you get them, and if anyone thinks you are broke tell them to call me."

With Merrill's backing, a quarter million dollars in hand and a Paris Jet II, an asset worth that much again, McCulloch became the fair-haired boy. "I was like Rudolph The Red-Nosed Reindeer and Merrill was Santa Claus." Everyone loved him now; brokers and sharks alike.

Twin Tires & Wheels, Inc. was McCulloch's new company. Over the next hectic months McCulloch worked hard to bring the company's product to investors and the automotive industry's attention.

Promotions were organized, publicity photos were ordered. In one promotional brochure, McCulloch had the photographer take photos of beautiful, identical twin, blond models in cocktail attire; one inside an automobile and the other seated beside the blood-red Porsche 911 turbo with the twin tires prominent in the shot. He purchased a new Corvette and Mercedes 560 SL coupe, and a Mini-van to use as demo vehicles. Each automobile was suitably emblazoned with the company name and logo.

Having raised money from friends and private investors like Merrill, McCulloch did an IPO in June 1989 with the raised seed money which was valued at $1.50 per share. The IPO opened on the exchange at $1.50 which went to $2.75 the first day with subsequent stock value increases McCulloch made millions for himself and his investors.

The pilot adventurer and risk-taker was on the fast track and his life-style reflected that. He not only had the Paris Jet but he'd sold the Hansa Jet and purchased a Chinese-built, Soviet designed Mig-17 which still wore its original Chinese markings including the big red Star. In 1989 he also purchased and moved into a home on Horseshoe Bay, an elite community 30 miles northwest of Austin, Texas. The structure was 200 feet long with an 80x80 foot hangar for his two jets. His home had the added advantage of directly accessing a paved 6,000 foot runway in an airpark community. From there he commuted to Dallas where the business was located.

During an interview in May of 1991 McCulloch told Dallas Morning News reporter, Bob St. John, that he had about 9,000 flying hours. "I couldn't survive if my life was dull. Conventional things bore me."

St. John wrote that McCulloch didn't have to worry about that. He questioned McCulloch about his business life.

"In business I've been both right and wrong but I have come out on the positive side about 51 percent of the time, which is all you need."

When questioned about his private life McCulloch told the reporter, "Some of the things I've done otherwise might seem more risky than they really are. But they weren't boring."

McCulloch told the reporter the tire product would go on the market in about 30 days.

"We were on a fast track and things were either going to the Moon or bust." At this point McCulloch remembers he had tons of money, but, "I always said there are two imposters...success and failure." But this was now.

McCulloch's newly purchased Chinese Mig-17 was the result of 'strange events, culminating in an 'unusual deal' by the owner of a Learjet 23 that McCulloch was purchasing. Suddenly that sale was revoked by the seller through the airplane broker in Houston, Texas. The Learjet 23 was no longer available and the only other jet aircraft available was a Mig-17F. It was a take it or leave it deal. McCulloch's thirst for fast and dangerous decided the outcome. He took the Mig.

This version of the Mig-17F (the Chinese name was Shenyang J-5) was built under license from the Soviet Union. The jet fighter had an afterburner. For those unfamiliar with the function of an afterburner, basically raw fuel is sprayed at high pressure into the already red-hot gases of the engine's normal combustion process in it's combustion chamber/exhaust. In afterburner, the Mig-17F's engine burned 180 liters (48 U.S. gallons) of fuel per minute. To put that in perspective, McCulloch's second airplane, a Cessna Cardinal, had fuel tanks that carried about 44 US gallons which gave the plane a range of about 5.5 hours.

The Mig-17F, however, had only one seat which prevented a check pilot/instructor from going up in the airplane with a pilot who had never flown one before. To learn how to fly it you either read the manual (in Chinese) or asked someone who might have flown the thing. Barring that you used common sense and took your time. Even the instruments were in Chinese. McCulloch figured if thousands of young Chinese fighter pilots could learn to fly the Mig-17s and indeed fight in them, his years of flying experience should get him through. Still why take chances? You don't get to old age as a pilot by being stupid. One pilot axiom states, *There are old pilots and bold pilots, but there are no old, bold pilots.* But you *can* get close; and that's what makes it interesting.

To get around that one seat, McCulloch went to Reno, Nevada. There was a squadron there that had-among other foreign built aircraft-several Mig-15s which have two seats in tandem configuration. The flight controls and instruments of the Mig-15 are similar to the Mig-17's. Unlike the Mig-17F, the Mig-15 does not have afterburners and the swept wing is at less of an angle. Nonetheless he paid about $8,000.00 an hour for three hours of flight instruction, advice and caveats about flying the much hotter, higher performance, single seat Mig-17F.

McCulloch had some avionics and instruments added to the aircraft; a transponder, a DME (Distance Measuring Equipment), a transmitter and an ILS (Instrument Landing System) so that he could fly IFR.

The day arrived when he decided to take the Mig-17F up and 'wring it out'. His tanks topped off with jet-grade kerosene and a thorough walk-around completed, McCulloch suited up in his G-suit and crash helmet, climbed aboard and hooked into his oxygen system. He went through his checks and rolled along the north-south runway at Horseshoe Bay. As was required he kicked in his afterburner (AB) and began the climb, both to assure that he would not run out of runway and...well...because it just felt good.

The acceleration slammed him back into his seat as he climbed nearly vertically. "The first flight in this rocket was like your first orgasm, you don't know what happened but it felt so thrilling you want to do it again and again."

The Mig was climbing at a terrific rate of climb. " I got to 30,000 feet in 3 minutes. I am *Riding the Fire* with 20 feet of fire coming out of my ass!" McCulloch glanced at the fuel gauges. Oh, oh! Where only minutes before he was fat with fuel he was now down two thirds. "What was going on? Fuel leak?" He assessed the situation then realized what was happening. He had been so absorbed in the accelerating climb he forgot he was still using his afterburner. It was gulping fuel like it was coming out of the refueling nozzle. He switched off the ignition to the AB and returned to the runway at Horseshoe Bay.

The Mig became his business jet and his stress-reliever. He was the only businessman commuting in a Soviet designed jet. Pretty much wherever he went he drew attention. The media zoned in on this Chinese built fighter that was still sporting its

Chinese Air Force insignia; a big, red star emblazoned on the fuselage and wings.

Once he was comfortable with this jet he pushed it to the edge of its flight envelope. He took it to its service ceiling of 51,000 feet or Flight Level 510, (15,810 meters) climbing at 621 mph (1,000 kph). He burned thousands of pounds of fuel on business trips and travelling to airshows. Air force fighters are not built to be fuel efficient, at least not during the Cold War.

"On a trip to Canada I made my first contact with a writer of *fame* Don Ledger." McCulloch contacted me at my home in Nova Scotia and asked me if I'd like to have a Mig-17 do fly-bys at the airfield (Stanley Airport) where I kept my plane-a Cessna 172. I replied with, "Who the hell is this?" As the vice-president of Stanley Sport Aviation, I was the Fly-In Chairman for Stanley's Annual Labour Day weekend Fly-In. I thought McCulloch's call was a prank; perhaps one of my fellow directors pulling my leg.

I had never heard of David Donald McCulloch up until then (not realizing I'd met him 25 years earlier). In fact it was a couple of years later that I found out he was a fellow Bluenoser-a nickname attributed to the locally grown Bluenose potato also adopted by the world famous two-masted schooner, a working fishing boat, salt banker-cum International Fishing Trophy winner christened the Bluenose.

Stanley was a World War Two training airfield which in 1989 still retained its three runways, all of which were now grass strips. The confusion was cleared up when McCulloch explained that he owned a tire company in Texas and that he had seen the fly-in ad I had posted in Flying Magazine's events calendar. He invited by the Canadian Air Force to be a part of the International Airshow at nearby Canadian Forces Base, Shearwater across Halifax Harbour from Nova Scotia's capitol city of Halifax. He was going to perform at the Shearwater

International Air Show the week following our Fly-In. Beween both of these events he had taken the opportunity to visit his family in Nova Scotia where they still live.

McCulloch provided the pilots and visitors to our small airfield with a high-speed pass, kicking in his afterburner and climbing out then a dirty slow-speed fly-by (wheels down and flaps extended) all of which was a first for Stanley. He could not perform aerobatics due to our Fly-In not having a licence for same from Transport Canada.

Video of McCulloch's Mig 17 fly-bys still exist to this day.

Not only did he attract media attention at Stanley but also the following week at Shearwater. One of our Stanley members, Gary Theriault, was a Warrant Officer at CFB, Shearwater*. He asked if I'd like to go to Shearwater and see the Mig tied down there on the tarmac. Of course the answer was yes.

*From the early 1930s until the outbreak of World War Two the area CFB, Shearwater (originally Canadian Naval Air Station, Shearwater) was American owned. Whereas it was close to the water it was the water-base for the Boeing Clipper and other flying boats.

The Hansa Jet. McCulloch was going broke so he bought this jet. "Never let them see you are hurting."

The Paris Jet. Impressed with McCulloch's bold move to buy the Hansa Jet when he was going broke, 50 year old businessman Morgan Merrill wrote McCulloch a cheque for $250,000.00 and threw in the Paris Jet for another $250.000.00 for stock value in McCulloch's Twin Tire Company. The words on the nose – Argent Fou - is French for 'crazy money'.

The Twin Tires on a Mercedes with identical twin models to accent the point. The original photo on a large brochure cost $35,000.00 to shoot, rent vehicle and to pay models.

McCulloch's 5 year old daughter, Kathryn models a Twin Tired Jeep.

McCulloch with his recently purchased Mig 17

The Mig-17 with some extra painted trim. Note the dice on the Mig's tail.
A logo used to this day. Life is a gamble win 51%

After-burner on while taking off from his home air-park in Horseshoe Bay, Texas. Climbing with after-burner below. Riding the Fire (airshow)

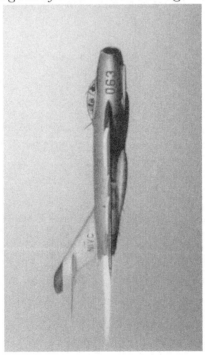

MIG fighter

By Bruce Erskine
SACKVILLE BUREAU

Flying a Vietnam War-era MIG 17 fighter jet makes driving a sports car seem slow, says Dave McCulloch.

Mr. McCulloch, a Shubenacadie native who now operates a tire and wheel company in Dallas, Tex., demonstrated what he meant Sunday afternoon during a fly-by at Halifax airport.

His 28-year-old, snub-nosed North Vietnamese fighter, which is more engine than anything else, attracted a throng of onlookers as it fueled up took off and circled the airport, trailing a stream of orange flames.

The single-seat Chinese-made jet, which can fly at 57,000 feet, did another fly-by at Stanley Airport near Windsor later in the day. It will be displayed at the upcoming Shearwater Air Show, along with Mr. McCulloch's 1958

My second contact with McCulloch as The Fly-In Chairman/VP for Stanley. McCulloch contacted me from Texas. He offered to do a fly-by at our annual Fly-In in the Mig-17. Partial clipping of Chronicle Herald story. Some videos of McCulloch's Mig flying at Shearwater and Stanley Airports back in the early 90s still exist.

Chapter Thirty

Trouble in business land.

It was a strange twist of history that I got to walk around the Mig-17F, touch it and admire this piece of Vietnam War history. I got to see McCulloch's jet, but not McCulloch himself. In fact as mentioned earlier we'd met back in 1967 (during the height of the Vietnam War) when he sold my father a cheque machine at his Esso gas station in Dartmouth.

Neither I nor McCulloch could ever have imagined he would be flying a Chinese Mig from Canadian Forces Base, Shearwater just 2.5 miles southeast of that gas station nearly a quarter of a century years later.

In the early 1990s McCulloch did a 'frenzy' of air shows and media interviews in the United States and Canada.

On September 30, 1990, McCulloch was informed that his friend and business associate; Morgan Merrill had been killed while doing stunts for the movie *Hot Shots* starring Charlie Sheen. Merrill took off from an airport in the Mojave Desert. He was flying a British trainer, a Folland Gnat T.1. Merrill made several low passes over the runway while cameras rolled. On the last low pass Merrill went into a slow roll but when the Gnat was inverted it hesitated and dove into the ground. Merrill was killed and the aircraft was totally destroyed. Whatever happened during that manoeuvre, Merrill never had a chance.

This was a blow to McCulloch who had become fast friends with Merrill. They were kindred spirits. It was Merrill who had given McCulloch a cheque for $250,000.00 when he was starting Twin Tires.

Eventually sound business practice and family considerations induced McCulloch to sell the Mig and opt for a slower, roomier Cessna Citation twin-engine jet. He would now be the CEO of a company who flew his own business jet.

'Why let some hired corporate pilot have all of the fun?'

The roomier jet would allow him to carry business people or tire samples with him or take his family along on some trips or on vacation.

Aside from having fun flying jets, McCulloch was having problems with his company.

"Developing a new patent system and being involved with Auto industry was truly over my head. Mitsubishi came along and made wheels and Yokohama made tires, but it was so small on the scale of things."

Police departments liked the twin tire. High-end vehicles such as Mercedes and Porsche used the tires because of their traction at high speed on wet pavement. But it was a select market, not the wide market McCulloch envisioned. Some of the established wheel dealers purchased the tire.

The Avanti (Studebaker) offered the twin tire on their new vehicles via purchases from Twin Tires. McCulloch had them installed on his personal vehicles with the appropriate company name stencilled on each vehicle as was his practice. "These tires were really safe. On one occasion Linda (his wife) returned from town with one side of a twin tire flat but she didn't notice any difference."

In the early 1990s the $4,000.00 cost of a set of the tires was too much for the mass car market despite the claim that a set of these tires would last three to four times longer than conventional tires. High volume sales would have lowered the cost of a set of these tires. That, however, was an up-hill investment in time; time that small companies like McCulloch's did not have.

Despite volume sales being low, Twin Tires stock trading was always active. "It was new and exciting," McCulloch recalls, "because it rubbed shoulders with high end car buffs."

Never one to remain static, McCulloch began exploring other options. "I became interested in a new venture in Austria that made plastic tires." McCulloch made a deal to sell his control in in Twin Tires. He proceeded to take on a deal that was a bigger long-shot than that taken with Twin Tires and his bold move to get the North American rights. But after a year of failed negotiations and hasty phone calls, the Austrian deal was falling through and regretfully, had to be shelved. And the sharks were circling once again. Millions of dollars to which McCulloch was entitled were being withheld. He put on the gloves and stepped into the fighting arena of big business. He began arrangements to do a hostile takeover of his own company, to get control. The purchaser had no intentions of paying McCulloch the millions owed him. It was a legal mess. It went on and on. Countless volumes of legal papers piled up; hundreds of hours in discovery meetings.

Huge lessons were learned. "It would take volumes to cover the mess in great detail." In the end, however, everyone lost. It cost McCulloch several millions to fight his case in court. By the mid-1990s it was done.

Claiming a patent infringement; another company was using the lack of sales to meet sales quota on Twin Tire's agreement with the patent holder which resulted in a substantial penalty. In fact no company was ever able to successfully make sales of the concept for low to mid-level cost automobiles. But the tire concept is still alive today with companies such as Goodyear and Michelin experimenting with the twin tire concept. The US Army has allocated a sizable amount to successful applicants to come up with a concept twin tire they could bolt on their conventionally tired combat vehicles, such as the Humvee.

Battle-torn and wiser, McCulloch returned to Canada and occupied himself with doing consulting for the Hutterites and other business interests.

His Twin Tire venture had been a learning experience with many lessons learned, principally what NOT to do. McCulloch settled into neutral to lick his wounds and consider his future. But not for long. The Mig was gone and so was the Paris Jet; each sold to purchase the Cessna Citation 501 SP. The more sedate Citation carries two crew and as many as five passengers. Its cruise speed is 411 mph with a range of 1,525 statute miles and a ceiling of 41,000 feet.

As a possible point of interest and to dispel some myths about business aircraft for those not familiar with how the company jet or prop aircraft concept works, note the following.

McCulloch has been written about in these pages as an aircraft adventurer-which indeed he was and is-but make no mistake, the planes in question were used to increase sales and or expand his business interests into areas he could not reach by automobile and often with commercial airline services. His early years in sales around the Canadian North, and the northwest, well into Alaska are a testament to this.

There is no doubt of McCulloch's love of aviation and airplanes, but his business most often comes first. He will quickly sacrifice the equity in one of his planes to put into his business; trade up or down regardless of how much he likes a particular airplane. Business is business.

Those not familiar with the concept of the 'corporate, company or private jet' ownership do not realize the time-saving and benefits of having the freedom of an airplane competitive with airline travel. To be able to leave with scarcely a moment's notice for a meeting or even the delivery of product in an emergency is extremely critical to businesses whose reputation relies on product repair or delivery of parts or technical expertise. If an electrical generator goes off-line in a major city center, the manufacturer of that equipment needs to be onsite with expertise and technical repair personnel a.s.a.p. The engineers or technical repair crew languishing in some airport, waiting for a connecting flight-often a commuter to get into smaller communities not serviced by an international airport-are just a wasted resource.

Direct to a business in need of help is one of the perks of the 'company' aircraft because it is usually much faster, particularly in today's airport security scenario where even business and first class seats endure the same time delays due to security issues and heavy airport traffic and queued up delays.

Certainly the mass travelling public should know that the 'cattle-car' passenger delivery system does not work in the high end of the business world. A two or three hour flight in a commercial jet translates into a lost day of work (8-12 hours) for smaller businesses that can't afford a light twin prop or jet aircraft but must rely on commercial airlines-usually in steerage (couch) because first or business class is just too damn expensive.

Incidentally, the most expensive business jet in the world-a Boeing 747-costs a half million dollars an hour to operate with its crew and entourage. There is an additional cost of a second 747 following behind in case the first 747 has engine or maintenance problems on trips over two hours. The user of this particular service is the President of the United States and Air Force One and Two.

President Obama's hypocritical attack on business jet use back in 2008-2009 and beyond nearly bankrupted the healthy private aircraft construction industry in the United States and Canada. Billions of sales dollars were lost and 40,000 skilled labourers were thrown out of work in the United States alone. Not a smart move for a president trying to recover an economy put in the dumper by former President George W. Bush. Small and large companies started to sell their aircraft assets to avoid the stigma painted by President Obama and embellished by the media of the *fat-ca*t CEOs using the company jet to fly off to exotic locations for the weekend. The general public swallowed this hook, line and sinker along with the usual BS promoted on the internet. Apparently it was okay for a CEO to have a $25,000,000.00 yacht or a half million dollar vehicle but not a private company airplane.

Small, private companies using small-often previously owned and therefore less expensive-twin-prop engined aircraft found them more cost effective and time saving against the regular airlines which often did not service some of the smaller communities with hospitals and manufacturing businesses that these companies served.

President Obama pandered to an ignorant electorate; even those who were highly educated but had no concept of how aviation works and its value to local communities. An ignorant public is a public that can be easily swayed when it comes time to vote.

Even now, eight years later, the stigma still exists although the industry has rebounded with sales to Middle Eastern Kings and Sheiks; movie stars and other wealthy, international, individuals with millions and billions of dollars to throw around and who could care less what the American president did. Multibillionaire, Oprah Winfrey, one of President Obama's financial supporters during his first campaign owns a $42 million custom-built Global Express XRS built by Bombardier Aerospace. "It's great to have a private jet. Anyone that tells you that having your own private jet isn't great is lying to you." Winfrey explained to reporter Robert Frank in the Wealth Report.

Back in the 1990s private jet and corporate jet ownership was not a real concern for McCulloch and other owners of business jets. It was a sign of affluence and wealth which was much admired by the public in the free world. After all he owned the aircraft he used, not the company so it was really nobody's business but his own and possibly the IRS or CRA (Canada) what he owned. The Cessna Citation, with its longer range, was his gateway to the world and a tool for him to exercise his way of doing business in the international community and the 'get it done now' philosophy and move on to the next order of business. Time was/is money.

He had purchased a Cessna Citation 501-SP, a twin engined jet. This particular model required no co-pilot to satisfy Transport Canada and the FAA's requirement for a second pilot on some twin engined jets. Whereas McCulloch was an aircraft broker (still maintained from his lean days in Toronto) he was often able to find the airplane nuggets in amongst the fool's gold. He purchased wisely and sold wisely, often upgrading into aircraft that others might not be able to afford at his 'pay-grade'. He would continue in business but at a more sedate pace.

It was during this period that McCulloch was using his Cessna Citation 501 SP to tour around Europe and drum up sales and franchise business. This was not your usual business practice, but then McCulloch was not your usual businessman. If he had to do these long junkets he in no way was going to allow some pilots up front on an airliner to have all of the fun. He would do it himself.

Having completed his business trip which ended in Cyprus he was returning from Europe and was over Greenland at Flight Level 410 (41,000 feet). He was on a flight plan that had taken him from Reykjavik airport in Iceland to Kangerlussuaq Airport on western side of Greenland. From there he would fly to Frobisher Bay airport (now Iqaluit airport) on Frobisher Bay; thence onward to Goose Bay in Labrador. He would refuel at Goose and eventually end the flight in Texas.

The loud bang and the resultant alarm bells and the flashing of lights on the panel are alarming enough but when there is nothing but the freezing cold waters of the Davis Strait below as the only possible landing option; the stress level ramps up appreciably. The right engine was no longer producing thrust and had spooled down. McCulloch told his co-pilot, George, to go into the cabin and check for fire or smoke through the windows on the right side. George checked and assured McCulloch there was no indication of fire.

The horizon ahead indicated that landfall was approaching. Even then the distance to Iqaluit was still one hundred nautical miles. And McCulloch and his co-pilot, George, were down to one engine which could fail at any moment. Could whatever had affected the starboard engine also damage the port side engine? Fuel contamination, a bad batch of lubricating oil, electrical faults; even bird ingestions; these are the questions and doubts that go through a pilot's mind when an engine fails in a multi-engine airplane.

McCulloch advised Montreal Center that he was going direct to Iqaluit. They came back with "Standby for clearance." With an engine out he wasn't going to wait around for a clearance. "I told them I was telling them, not asking." Montreal advised they had other flights. Once again he declared he was going straight in, "I have a major failure."

The Citation landed safely in Iqaluit but there were ramifications over McCulloch's declaration of a straight in approach. He received several letters from Transport Canada about the incident and accusations about his violations which is somewhat strange whereas his loss of an engine over desolate territory should have made it clear why he had to go straight in. Any lapses in Air Traffic Control decorum has to be countered by a pilot's first concern and that is flying the airplane and getting the damn thing safely on the ground. When the alarms, flashing red lights and oral warnings come at you in a cluster the pilot's first responsibility is to stay aloft and in control. Over and over in emergency situations cockpit voice recorders have shown that when the pilots are busy they have little time to carry on polite conversation with Air Traffic control. In the majority of cases they barely have time to explain what is happening before they lose communication with the ground.

When Chesley (Sully) Sullenberger was preparing to ditch his A-320 in the Hudson River his clipped responses were little capsules of time he did not have to converse. His engines were dead, he had one shot and that was to ditch. The New York TRACON is probably the busiest in the world. It's jammed with traffic, yet the controller did what he could to help and then he and other controllers cleared traffic that needed clearing.

In the end only the fact that McCulloch's airplane was registered in the United States and that he had an American flying license saved him from the proverbial death by documentation so often used by Canadian Agencies.

Once McCulloch and his co-pilot were down safely in one of the remotest regions on the planet it was discovered that the shaft on the right engine's oil pump had broken. The turbine's compressor had seized up causing a lot of damage. Another engine was flown to Iqaluit and installed. McCulloch flew the damaged engine back to the United States. When the dust had settled the cure had come in at a half million dollars. "You fly the big toys you pay the big bucks."

McCulloch's 'quiet' time could not last and did not last. It isn't in McCulloch's nature to sit around. He took the financial hit and moved on.

The Mig (back) and the Paris Jet were sold to finance the Cessna Citation below.

McCulloch's Cessna Citation 501 SP, in bright sunlight, parked in front of his home in Horseshoe Bay, Texas. Hangar is 100 feet wide. Taxi is direct to the runway.

Chapter Thirty-One

Forget the past, but not the lessons.

For McCulloch the early nineties - chiefly 1991 and 1992 - were a time for reflection, liquidation of assets; even thoughts of retirement. This involved a great deal of legal work, which is often fruitless (except for the lawyers) and tiring. He fell back on his relationship with the Hutterites, looking for opportunities there while offering his legal team to the church's assistant, Bishop, Sam Waldner. "Sam was the smartest and most honest man I'd ever met."

There was turmoil in several dozen of the Hutterite colonies who were splitting from the Central Bishop's control. Typically, religious wars are messy and never have an ideal solution. "No one really wins." McCulloch observed. "I had my lawyer from Texas and even former Canadian Prime Minister, Brian Mulroney, involved." His lawyers were working on a hopeless case involving international implications. "One lesson I learned was that lawyers are not the solution to solving complex personal issues." He caveats that with, "My daughter Kathryn, a corporate attorney in Toronto would probably disagree."

"In my next life I want to be a lawyer," McCulloch reflected, "it will add credibility to *my* B.S. and be very useful for reaching interpretations about life and business."

In any event, McCulloch found the business atmosphere he enjoyed with the Hutterites was healthy and matched his own outlook. Treat your business partners fairly and be treated fairly with them. Respect, above all, was foremost. It's a relationship he enjoys and values to this day.

The Hutterite Communities are typically comprised of about twenty-five families and are a success story in Canada and the United States. McCulloch admires their work ethic, the proud, wholesome way of life they maintain. The communities are clean and prosperous, not just for the hierarchy but for the followers as well. They are a very humble people despite the $30 billion value of the combined wealth of the communities in the Canada and US.

In 1994, McCulloch once again entered into a partnership with the Hutterites, but this time it was a mission to help with the Hutterite's effort to build a colony in the African country of Nigeria. In order to be involved and smooth over political concerns He was to be classed as a missionary.

"I know," he commented, "me a missionary? But I've got the badge to prove it."

To have a successful community required water in an area that relied on rivers and ponds (often great distances away) for their water which was and is often stagnant or inhabited by bacteria hosted by the fish and animals that live in and around them. Part of McCulloch's mission would be to seek water opportunities and distribution.

In 1994 McCulloch accompanied several leading Hutterite Ministers and the Bishop to Nigeria. They landed in Lagos on the south coast of Nigeria. "Lagos has always been a dangerous place and it was hard to survive the trip from the airport to the hotel." At the airport they were met by a Canadian Embassy official, escorted to an armoured car, surrounded by security people and driven to a hotel that was guarded by machine guns.

Shortly after they flew via commuter airline to Abak some 350 air miles southeast of Lagos. "When we arrived there the culture shock was huge." In 1994 the things western society takes for granted were few in these remote locations. Water, sewage disposal and basic human needs were few. The locals, generally known as the Annang, still maintained a strong connection to their ancestral relics of their past through traditional dances, songs, beliefs and strong convictions and temperament.

In order to give McCulloch some authority in the community he was given an official designation as a Chief with all of the privilege and clout which that title offered. "It's a very big deal in tribal Abak, but of course it was because they knew I had the bishops ear so more $$$$."

The officials from that area were not unaware of the deep pockets and amenities that could be offered by the United States via the New York Hutterites.

McCulloch went to work with a few labourers; most of them local and he supervised water installation and building construction. It is hard to believe that even in 1994 this was not considered a viable potable water option for the local population. They seemed to lack many skills we take for granted. The pilot recalls showing one man that cutting a board while it was in the center of the table was not nearly as effective as hanging one end of the board off the edge of the table and making the cut. This "trick" was met with laughter and applause when he showed them how. There are advantages to being a woodcutter's son.

In another instance they had to build shelters to get away from the Sun's heat. The walls were built and raised into place. McCulloch opted to build the roof rafters on the ground and then raise them up individually onto the tops of the walls, thereby eliminating the need for constantly climbing ladders to bring materials up and work above ground. Apparently this method had never been employed before and was met with amusement until the chore was accomplished in a much shorter time than was usual.

While McCulloch was there he helped with the construction of a small palm pressing plant which was an integral agricultural product for that region.

Just over two weeks into the projects, politics raised its eternal head. "I became aware of a rift that had occurred between the New York Hutterites and the Western Hutterites." The New York volunteer group was attempting a coup to take over the Annang colony. "I had worked with and for the New York group also and was caught in the feud." McCulloch decided he should pack it in and get the hell out of there. "I had no intention of being involved in jungle justice, or them trying to make me a fall guy." He managed to slip out undercover. He was far away from home in a country with a sketchy justice system, hot tempers, rife with corruption and seemingly little regard for human life. He knew in the long run the Canadian government would probably wash its hands of him as they have done before with others.

Unlike the United States, the Canadian government usually does not stand behind its citizens abroad and they are pretty much left to their own resources. And there is little or no protection from the Nigerian government.

McCulloch used a resource he had been relying on for nearly four decades, an airplane, a small plane that he was able to get aboard and fly-under the cover of darkness-to Lagos where he arrived early in the morning. The only white man to arrive at that time of the day. It did look suspicious, "I am too egotistical to admit that I was scared."

Fortunately he had the help of the Canadian Consul who-after he landed in Lagos gave him some limited protection and got him safely aboard a plane back to Canada.

McCulloch arrived back in Canada having once again been rewarded with no bodily harm as he was involved in a pro bono project. "All I got out of that deal was new knowledge of how those living in Africa's jungle live and think; a lesson in African politics and inter religious affairs. No good deed goes unpunished."

Chapter Thirty-Two

"When will my education end?"

The new year, 1995, offered up another possible direction for future investment. A Hutterite community in Manitoba had been dabbling in the coal-fired boiler as a heating source. They asked McCulloch if he would look at the coal fired version to see if it could be a viable business.

"I did some investigating and market research which indicated to me that coal was certainly more profitable than propane. This was 80% of the world's energy resource back then." For example, even today, 66% of the United States' electrical energy is generated using coal.

McCulloch discovered that $12,000.00 worth of coal could replace $50,000.00 worth of propane; an over 4:1 ratio in favor of coal. "We built a sample, non-working unit and did a trade show and I saw the interest."

Seeing a business opportunity and envisioning a sales strategy McCulloch sold eleven full-sized boiler units rated at two million BTUs each. "I got deposits on each unit but we did not have even one in stock or even a manufacturing plant at that point." Doctor Brand Boilers was born and is still going world-wide to this day selling millions of dollars' worth of the product. "I was unable to negotiate a royalty arrangement. I left the company on good terms but with empty pockets. When will my education ever end? There is little respect for sales people."

In 1997 McCulloch attempted a move to retirement. It was a brief interlude. He got bored and began looking into wood-burning furnaces; in particular those units that would use bio-mass fuel. An industry could and did exist where larger enterprises could use fuel developed from scrub wood and material of no other value. Private owners living in rural areas such as farmers and rural home owners with their own woodlots could benefit from this technology and perhaps offset the steady increase in fuel-oil prices.

A multimillion dollar wood burning company was created with McCulloch once again partnering with a Hutterite community.

When it came right down to it, the business pilot had no interest in running a company, in this case a bio-mass wood-burning enterprise. McCulloch sold the company early while keeping an interest in the marketing side with a royalty arrangement. This deal netted him several millions of dollars and freed him up to spend more time with his family and his growing daughter, Kathryn. "I had always regretted that I had not given my first family the attention they needed and deserved." He did not want to make that mistake again.

The world travelling pilot went into his version of seclusion which means not staying in one place for very long and keeping a low profile. McCulloch would tend to his family and play with his favorite toys; airplanes and cars. During that time one of his favorite airplanes was his Provost jet. The BAC Jet Provost was developed by the British Aircraft Corporation in 1953 and was used by the Royal Air Force – and some foreign states as well - as a trainer from 1955 to 1993. It was also configured as a more heavily armed ground attack aircraft called the Strikemaster.

McCulloch's Provost was a two seat aircraft-as they all were-which was configured side by side. "I flew that plane all over the United States and to my home in Canada a couple of times." It was a relatively docile aircraft with a cruise speed of about 400mph (644kms). It had a range of 900 miles (1,450 kms) and a service ceiling of of 36,750 feet (11,200 meters). The Provost was painted in a very attractive, blue-camouflaged design. The jet and its paint scheme drew a great deal of attention from the media wherever he travelled in the United States and in Canada as well.

During a three year period he spent time with his family in one of three homes in Calgary, Florida or Nova Scotia. He decided it would be more economical if he found a business oriented jet that could give him performance and speed. He settled on the hot-rod of the biz-jet planes, the Learjet 23.

Chapter Thirty-Three

The Aerial Hot Rod

"This mother***ker could out-climb a Lockheed F-104 Starfighter to 20 grand (20,000 feet)." Corporate Learjet pilot and J-3 owner. (I know, right?)

"The Learjet 23 killed more pilots and passengers than any other private plane for the numbers that were built." Google

"If it goes into a Mach 'tuck' it will dive and tear itself to pieces."

"I want one!" David Donald McCulloch.

In 2005 McCulloch acquired an airplane he had been interested in for some time. The Learjet 23 was one of the first private jets to arrive on the private executive aircraft market with a maiden flight on October 7, 1963. It was introduced to the public on October 13, 1964. 104 were built by the end of its run in 1966. The chief purchasers were private buyers however, a smaller number were sold to various military concerns. Frank Sinatra was the purchaser of a Learjet 23. Unlike McCulloch, he did not fly his plane.

Actually, referring to the Learjet 23 as a hot-rod (taking an old 1930 or 40s automobile, chopping the roof down and dropping in an engine with 10 times more horsepower) would be misleading. Comparing the Learjet 23 to other business production airplanes is like comparing NASCAR racing cars to the family Honda Civic parked in your driveway.

The Learjet 23's designer, William Powell (Bill) Lear, based his design on that of a Swiss designer Hans-Luzius Studer who had a doctorate in engineering. Lear purchased the company, the rights to the design which was meant to be a fighter/trainer for the Swiss Air Force.

Bill Lear had the ability to think-outside-the-box. In the mid to late 1920s it was deemed impossible to fit a radio into an automobile. Seriously, the radios of the day were in some cases the size of a juke-box. As a collector-for parts- (from my paperboy deliveries days) of old radios as an electronic nerd, one customer gave me a Westinghouse 'compact' radio built in 1933. Its case was mahogany; measured 30 inches long by 14x14 inches and weighed about 35 pounds. No wonder it was thought impossible to mount one of these most modern of radios in the dash of the family car.

Bill Lear thought it was possible to miniaturize the radio. Despite the scoffing of the industry in the late 1920s Lear proceeded to do just that. He had smaller induction coils designed and built, tubes reduced in size, transformers and capacitors reduced and produced a radio head that could fit in the dash with the power supply nested in the trunk. The company was eventually called Motorola.

In the 1930s Motorola went on to invent sophisticated auto-pilot equipment, improvements and radio direction finding equipment that greatly enhanced pilot and passenger safety.

Lear reasoned in 1961 that the same principle he relied on for the car radio could be applied to jet-powered private airplanes; a viable jet aircraft that a private pilot-with some instruction-could fly. It took him a couple of years and a million dollars-a mere pittance compared to the fees incurred in the modern era-to complete the plan.

The much touted fact that the prototype crashed ignored the fact that this was not the fault of the plane but the pilot. An FAA inspector was flying the airplane on take-off and had the spoilers up which robbed the wings of lift. The Learjet just could not get airborne. The insurance pay-off allowed Lear to complete the plane and get it on the market. The line produced 104 Learjet 23s before that model was discontinued in 1966 and moved on to the Learjet 24.

There are many reasons why the Learjet 23 and the other models in the line were so appealing. From the 23 onward the jet had and still has sex appeal. There is something about the shape of the Learjet that draws pilots in. The fact that the first Learjet could be dangerous just added to its allure. After all, highly manoeuvrable, fast, small jets were the territory of the air force. They should be a little dangerous.

The Learjet 23 was powered by two General Electric CJ610-4 turbojets, each producing 2,850 lbs of thrust. The CJ610-4 is the civilian version of the General Electric J-85 military jet engine that is equipped with afterburners. The J-85 was a very popular engine and still is to some degree. It powers the F-5 fighter and the T-38 Tallon trainer. The famous North American F-86 Saber Jet (the American version, not the Canadair Version) was powered by this engine. It is notable that the Learjet 23 could out-climb the F-86 to 40,000 feet. In fact the Learjet 23 had a service ceiling of 45,000 feet (13,750 meters) which enabled it to cruise well above airline traffic. The Learjet 23 is a fuel guzzler at sea level.

The Lear's sexy appearence, speed and maneuverability had gripped McCulloch for years. In 2005 he had the opportunity to purchase one of the 9 planes still flying. Some 30 Learjet 23s had been destroyed in accidents by 1998 while others were acquired by museums such as the Smithsonian in Washington, DC. The rest were either in military hands or had been taken out of service.

McCulloch purchased Learjet 23 (SN-84) built in 1965. He now owned one of the hottest biz-jets in service. All he had to do was to get his endorsement (rating) to fly it. Since he had already flown five different jets including a Mig-17 and a Hansa Jet (which was powered by the same engines as the Lear 23) this should be a walk in the park. But once endorsed, he could <u>not</u> fly it without a co-pilot who was qualified for that position, albeit not to the degree that McCulloch was about to experience.

In 2007 McCulloch took a two week course at Sim Com International, a flight training school in Orlando, Florida. "The course was a real ballbreaker. Most of the other trainees were young guys looking at the right seat of an airliner. Many were military types getting primers for the air force. So here I am, a 65 year old Indiana Jones looking to qualify on my Learjet and paying $15,000.00 for the privilege." It was either that or McCulloch would have a very expensive conversation piece sitting in a hangar in Florida.

"The simulators were amazing," McCulloch recalls, "they were very realistic. You look through the "windows" and see a layout of the airport you are taking off from. The taxiways and runways were complete with other aircraft taxiing, etcetera."

In 2007 it was a safe way to get an introduction to the flight characteristics of the Learjet 23 while not burning hundreds of pounds of fuel in the process. The '23 burns about 400 pounds of fuel per hour just taxiing so their owners used only one engine to do so. At FL 450 it would burn about 700pph in cruise, per engine. That translates into 200 US gallons of jet fuel per hour.

"Ground school was hard for me but easy for the younger jet gurus. The training was tough. I had a good co-pilot, another old guy. We had a plan."

For example he told McCulloch, "When you see my hand move toward, say the gear, call gear down." When McCulloch called gear down only then would his co-pilot do it. The instructor stressed that he must call it out.

"I've watched body language all my life (females) but not that of male pilots."

The flight test was no picnic. And it was carried out in a Learjet 35. McCulloch had to fly from Miami to Atlanta, stop there, then with a full load fly to JFK in New York. He had to circle approach and ended up with a missed approach on the first try. The overcast was at 800 feet with a 1.5 mile visibility but the minimums at JFK were 700 feet so he had only a 100 foot margin to work with. He nailed the second approach. He then flew direct back to Miami International Airport.

Despite the fact that the whole flight was in a simulator it was still nerve racking. The simulator still acted like a Learjet, was just as fussy and with narrow margins for error-or none at all-at high Mach numbers.

Many a pilot has emerged from the simulator stressed and dripping sweat from the tests they were put through, they are that real.

The jet is a slippery airplane with little drag. Despite its smaller-than-an-airliner size (it is still faster than many airliners) it still stalls out at 140 mph with the gear and the flaps down.

His two week training successfully completed, McCulloch did his actual air work in his own jet with Richard Romero, an FAA inspector in order to complete his qualification.

McCulloch was now free to fly one of the most exciting private aircraft on the planet. It is the one plane that he has kept for over ten years. His recent fleet also included an Aerostar Super 700 which can accommodate seven passengers, a Piper Seneca and a Piper Dakota 235.

But the Learjet 23 will remain one of his favorites and on the wish list for many other pilots who enjoy the adrenalin rush of the first private jet's accelerating takeoffs and climb outs.

McCulloch's life was different now. He was moving into newer territories.

The Cessna Citation SP 501 gave way to this jet, a BAC Jet Provost. It was developed by the British Aircraft Corporation in 1953 and was used by the Royal Air Force - and some foreign states as well - as a trainer from 1955 to 1993. A military fighter version was called the Strike Master. In this photo, McCulloch taxis for takeoff at Pine Shadows Airpark in North Fort Meyers, Florida. But then this sexy biz-jet came along (below).

The Learjet 23 lands at Pine Shadows, North Fort Meyers, Florida.

McCulloch sits on the left wing of his beautiful Learjet 23.

McCulloch (left) the author and Dr. Joe Campbell, McCulloch's close friend and the co-pilot of the Learjet behind us. On the tarmac at Hanover airport in Ontario during a COPA convention in 2013.

Chapter Thirty-Four
Losses and Gains

The years 2006 and 2007 were periods of good living. Royalties were rolling in from bio-mass sales. Sales were exceeding production. If one tracks company sales the royalties can be assumed to be accurate. So with that in mind and "free" time on his hands, McCulloch had to do something about that free time. He took trips to Europe, principally Germany, and then to China.

McCulloch sees industry overseas exploding, particularly in China while North America is slipping behind the rest of the world in general; two nations in denial.

North America, he finds, is all about politics; "…no-action-governments which has become a haven for self-serving, vision-less wimps."

It is seldom that governments are actually elected with talented people suitable to the task of governing. Rather they rely on the expertise of the legions of suits that profess to have the knowledge and the bureaucracy that has been in place for decades; a system that is always uncomfortable with change. Systemic stagnation is the nature of newly elected governments. In opposition one party will rail against the incumbent government. They will make changes when they are in power.

Often they do so once elected but have found that their outsider position had little knowledge of the problem. They are now forced to make the changes anyway and once made they will never admit they were wrong, that they made a mistake. That would imply weakness and an inability to foresee the consequences of their actions. No matter who gets hurt, who loses jobs, what business goes under as a result there is only one deciding factor. Will this lose us votes if we admit we made a mistake? Better to move on and rely on the voter's ability to forget.

For his own company's part, McCulloch found that, "When things are going along smoothly, idle brains stray." He is no longer at the helm and now receives royalties while the caretakers got comfortable with regular sales and the status quo.

By the year 2010 the company's 66,000 square foot factory is suddenly idle. It is decision making time. Royalties are stopped. McCulloch stays on until his former partners are back in the game and get things under control. "But my passion for the heating industry is gone. Timing is everything."

I'm free. No revenge; look for a new venture.

McCulloch decided to give up the full time working habit. A settlement was made with his former company. "The best place to hit your business enemies is in their pocketbooks." He is pissed off but he falls back on his belief; "Forgive your enemies, but never forget." He quit working, full stop and then another blow. In 2011 McCulloch's wife of 35 years leveled a broadside. Linda McCulloch had decided she did not want to be married anymore. She left McCulloch in October of that year. One of McCulloch's life philosophies is live your own life, "I always did."

He didn't fight it. An agreement was hammered out, by May of 2012. "We liquidated. She got the liquid and I had me and my toys."

The divorce was made final in December of that year.

With the marriage trust gone he discovered there is no middle ground. The marriage was over. He was 73 years old-not far from 74-and single.

"Seventy-four years of age is not a good time to re-boot your life. I've always faced fear, head-on. I awake each day with fear my constant companion. It is the closest we ever get to visit our ancestors. I go to sleep every night a winner I won another day."

Enter the scribe.

McCulloch resigned himself to bachelorhood. His daughter, Kathryn, living in Toronto and at that point had been articling (interning with a law firm) and anticipating being soon accepted to the bar society in Ontario.

Whereas our biographical principal figures he is now too old to chase romance, he slides back into the next exciting new thing; finding a new business to start. He's been retired for about a year. It's not for him.

I'm the scribe, McCulloch's ghost. We hooked up in February of 2012 but even then while going through his divorce he was travelling around North America and Europe looking into possible business ventures. Document shredding,, waste recycling, wind power, Diesel outboard motors, biodegradable plates and cups made from hay and even a perpetual energy system in Germany. None of them appealed to McCulloch, particularly the perpetual energy system which he considered BS.

He explained much of this and his business history to me over a few luncheon meetings. He wondered about me doing his biography and if I agreed, how we should proceed. The idea was that we would do his biography and then have a few books printed off and he would pass them out to his family.

I agreed to the project and we made great strides early on then bogged down when McCulloch picked up the scent of a new business idea. From then on it was gathering information via emails and the occasional meeting (over lunch) and notes passed to me before he was off again to the United States, Europe, Africa and points west of Nova Scotia in Canada. It was hard to nail the man down sometimes.

To shut me up on one occasion he flew me down to North Fort Myers, Florida where he hangars the Learjet. He, his co-pilot Dr. Joe Campbell and I flew to Hanover, Ontario so McCulloch could honour his commitment to Canadian Owner's and Pilots Association (COPA) to offer up a ride in the jet to a lucky ticket holder. This was the second time he'd done this. The cost of fuel far exceeded the money taken in on ticket sales by COPA.

In any event it gave me a week to question Dave on many points about his businesses and a chance to see first-hand his philosophy about business and his dedication to flying.

A year had passed and McCulloch found himself minding the void left resulting from his divorce. He wasn't looking for a permanent relationship, and certainly not marriage but female companionship was becoming more of a need than he had imagined. Despite this he still resisted the need of a companion. This contradiction of emotions resided in the back of his mind for some months. He was travelling constantly and was on occasion, a bit cranky. McCulloch, in my estimation, always seemed to be pleasant, not bubbling over happy, but in good humour for the most part, but on a couple of occasions when we met he seemed dour; he looked thinner and impatient.

McCulloch had discussed this with friends and business associates one of whom had a friend who knew of a business woman. She was described to him as a widow, an adventurous woman and like McCulloch she was a serial traveller who's business required her to fly a great deal. McCulloch had made a few phone calls to this woman. The opportunity arose to meet her in Fort Lauderdale, Florida. Her name was Margaret

Lipworth. She was about McCulloch's age. She dealt in the Fine Arts and moved in the art world, was very successful and well known in those circles.

Margaret had lost her husband in October of 2011. She frequently flew to New York, London, Paris and Rome.

McCulloch flew to Fort Myers, Florida. Margaret recalled that, "David took the trouble to drive across from Fort Myers, on the West coast to Fort Lauderdale on the East coast to meet me. We had a very easy, delightful dinner out, and discovered our mutual attraction for 'adventure'."

McCulloch added, "I would try to be charming and attractive."

Both of them enjoyed their first meeting and shortly after met again.

Margaret had to leave for another commitment in South Africa, the country of her birth. She keeps a time share in Cape Town which she enjoys for five weeks spanning January and February of each year. "Much to my joy and amazement David arrived for a 4 day visit. I knew then, this man was no ordinary man, and anything predictable was out the window."

"She made the mistake of inviting me to come to South Africa and see her." The next day McCulloch booked an airline seat to Cape Town.

McCulloch joined Margaret on a Safari in the neighbouring countries of Botswana and Namibia. This was the type of safari where tourists would encounter and see African animals but not hunt them. Their relationship was on.

Back in the United States the relationship continued. Whereas McCulloch's home in North Fort Myers had been sold during his divorce, he stayed over at Margaret's home on several occasions. "I had my own bedroom." He was quick to add.

As already mentioned, McCulloch, who had been semi-retired for a few years, was missing the challenge of developing a business. And of course he needed to fly. And of course he liked combining the two. He wanted to develop another company, a big one with capitalization, more or less, of $200,000,000.00. "It was like looking for a needle in the proverbial haystack. At seventy-four years of age business didn't need me, I needed business; a business to support my north side of a half million dollar a year lifestyle."

Having already explored several business avenues McCulloch's attention is drawn to the food industry. He notes that food is always a business magnet. There are thousands of success stories in the supply-of-food business. Once his interest had been noted by others he found himself surrounded by those who professed to know everything about the food business.

There are people in his life that have lent normalcy to McCulloch's hectic lifestyle. One of those people is his daughter Kathryn. Back in Nova Scotia with her father on occasion, McCulloch encouraged her to get her pilot's license. She achieved both her Private Pilot's License and her Law Degree in the same year. "She flew from Halifax to Calgary in our Piper Dakota with me in the right seat." Kathryn did all of the flying. A distance of over 2,300 miles.

McCulloch still had a lot of friends in Calgary; Leo Kelly, his accountant for 35 years, Dave Yates himself a businessman of 40 years and Rick Boiselle who was his co-pilot on his first plane trip to Europe.

On occasion McCulloch had mentioned doing another long-range trip involving his daughter and in 2013 he used his latest airplane acquisition, a twin engined Piper 601-P Aerostar to do just that.

He and Margaret had continued their relationship. "David and I continued dating, and after a while I discovered his aviation world." McCulloch invited her along on the trip. She accepted. She did not realize the depth of McCulloch's involvement in aviation until she flew to Nova Scotia and stayed at McCulloch's home in Valley a small community just east of Truro. Her stay was an eye-opener.

Margaret discovered McCulloch's history and his devotion to flying. "Only after I visited his Nova Scotia home and ransacked his videos, did I fully appreciate his truly amazing aviation adventures and his modesty at being embarrassed by my respect...looking at all the extraordinary planes he owned and flew, and the newspaper clippings, all of which he never mentioned. I found his modesty one of the most endearing attributes he has." The trip was "...an amazing adventure whetting my appetite for more."

McCulloch flew Kathryn and Margaret from Canada to Europe via Greenland and Iceland, Scotland to London. "It's still a great trip and one most pilots only dream about."

Live your dreams, face your fears, ride the fire.

Additional Photos

This twin (graphic image) is being painted to do short hops for the pie company. Modified Aerostar 700. Logo will be painted on the nose. Dr. Joe Campbell (left) and McCulloch lean on the nose of Campbell's

Cessna 336. There is a 2ⁿᵈ engine behind the cabin. Campbell also owns a Beech Baron twin and at the time of photo a Cessna 150. As McCulloch's Learjet co-pilot he has probably flown with McCulloch more than any other. Joe is one of the nicest people I've ever met. Author (Florida 2013)

McCulloch's plastic jet fleet. These models represent the jet powered aircraft he's owned. The Learjet (fore-front) is still in his hangar in Florida. From top left; the Hansa Jet, top right, the Provost Jet, middle left Cessna Citation, Paris Jet ,middle, and Mig-17.

Dave McCulloch in his happy place; the left seat of any airplane. This photo taken in his Learjet 23.

Dave McCulloch and daughter Kathryn in Hanover, Ontario 2013.

Chapter Thirty-Five

From the ground up.

As 2013 came to a close McCulloch was disappointed that he still had no firm deal to work with although he did come close. He nearly purchased a bakery chain but changed his mind. He had gone that route before, piggy backing on someone else's idea, someone else's dream, someone else's previous decisions. This time he decided to start from scratch.

At this juncture he had no plan, no product; only the desire to build his own $200 million dollar plus project from the ground up. Pilots work from the ground up.

McCulloch began what became six months of research into the food industry and baked goods in particular. It soon became obvious to him that good tasting, pure, clean food was a thing of the past.

By this time he had settled on pies as the food he would build upon. Some of his friends would ask, why pies? Pies are common enough on super market shelves they would say.

McCulloch would counter with the argument that coffee was common enough too. Every restaurant has coffee on its menu as do most fast food outlets including McDonalds. But then there are dedicated coffee outlets all over the world such a Starbuck's, Tim Hortons, Dunkin Donuts not to mention smaller speciality coffee outlets; and they make tens of billions of dollars each year for a product the ordinary person can make at home for very little. Yet they will lay out five bucks at Starbucks for one cup of coffee.

Why do people lay out big bucks for the same product they can make at home? McCulloch reasoned that people want an experience, not just another mundane cup of coffee. It was and is McCulloch's mission to do that with certain types of pies, mouth-watering berry pies made the way they should be. Pies that should not be laced with additives that enhance colour, taste and appearance; substituting ingredients that bulk the product up with cheaper additives, that can make the product last for months with chemicals that kill bacteria and that the buyer ingests as well.

One beautiful flying day McCulloch flew Margaret to a country airport that was next to a wild blueberry field. They strolled over to the field and McCulloch picked some wild blueberries for Margaret. It was when he saw her reaction to the taste of these delicious berries that the proverbial light bulb went off in his head. When he returned home he called his sisters, Joanne and Alice, asking them to make some pies the way our mother made them. And as they say, the rest is history.

McCulloch was impressed by the fact that from the very beginning his pie idea was exciting to others. Many contacts and acquaintances of his said, "...if you do a deal, count me in." Before he had a name on a business plan numerous cheques had arrived in his mailbox." Excitement is contagious. "We picked a name, iPies, the corporate name. On July 14, 2014 we dug the foundation for the 20,000 square foot bakery in South Dakota."

Now he had to find the ovens and the machinery to put together the thousands of pies that would be required each week. They would be marketed as ***berrybestbrand.com***

The 20,000 square foot BerryBestBrand pie bakery being built in South Dakota by the Hutterites (2014)

The inside of the bakery. Nearly ready to receive machinery for baking and processing (2014)

Chapter Thirty-Six

"Up for adventure and game for anything."
~Margaret Lipworth about David McCulloch~

McCulloch was beginning a new chapter in his life that continues to this day as he builds his newest business. A company seeking a $200,000,000.00 evaluation doesn't take off over night. In the two years following the building of the bakery in South Dakota McCulloch travelled tens of thousands of miles in commercial airliners and his personal aircraft - 81 flights on airliners in 2015 alone and another dozen in his own planes. This was necessary in order to purchase the proper equipment, set up the infrastructure such as distribution depots, hire people to run them as well as seek out and find those entrepreneurial spirits like himself who could run the business for him once it is operational.

He interlaced his business trips with visits and trips with Margaret. "We for now will have to juggle business with 'pleasure'." she remarked, "Not a hardship for us as we are growing younger and younger." She seems to have captured McCulloch's spirit.

In the summer of 2016 they have a trip planned to Spain from Nova Scotia in McCulloch's Aerostar. Margaret is an adventurous spirit and has already taken private pilot instruction and looks forward to an adventure together with the man she finds humble, modest, sweet and full of energy. "He's kind, caring, supportive, funny, clever, hard working. The best pilot ever. He keeps me safe." She has described him as a loving family man, passionate and cute looking.

This is not the end, but only the beginning.

Printed by Amazon Italia Logistica S.r.l.
Torrazza Piemonte (TO), Italy

10313525R00182